Escaping The Arroyo

A True Crime Novel

Joyce Nance

ISBN: 0985621214
ISBN-13: 978-0-9856212-1-6

LIKE ON FACEBOOK:
FACEBOOK.COM/ESCAPINGTHEARROYO

FOLLOW JOYCE NANCE ON TWITTER:
@ESCAPETHEARROYO

BLOG: ESCAPINGTHEARROYO.BLOGSPOT.COM

AUTHOR WEBSITE: JOYCENANCE.COM

COVER DESIGN BY MARGARET L. BRIGGS

EDITING BY MARGARET L. BRIGGS

AUTHOR PHOTO BY C. J. JOHNSON

FORMATTING BY JASON G. ANDERSON

TABLE OF CONTENTS

ACKNOWLEDGMENTS

Many thanks to the many people who helped make this book a reality.

A thousand thank-yous to Margaret Briggs, my editor and mentor extraordinaire, and to my family for putting up with my reclusiveness during the monumental amount of hours that it took to write this book. I want to thank Kathy Ostermiller for giving the book a final proofread, Steve Shoup for advising me on 1981 Albuquerque history, Alexandra Swanberg for her excellent input as my Beta reader and Todd Heisey and the Bernalillo County District Attorney's Office for their help and kindness regarding this case. I want thank the volunteers at the Albuquerque Community Writing Center who encouraged me as a writer when I really didn't think I could call myself one. I want to give a big thank you to James Tuttle, whom I was honored to meet in 2011. Lastly, I give thanks for Colene Bush, without whose bravery and sheer will to live, I would not/could not have written this book.

PREFACE

This book is based on a true crime that occurred in Albuquerque, New Mexico, on April 5th and April 6th 1981. There are many versions of the how, when, where, what and why the crime occurred. This book, except for the Guzman's interview in Part II and the trial transcripts in Part III is based on my version of what happened. I have logged in thousands of hours of research and conducted hundreds of hours of interviews regarding this crime. Although this story is based on fact, some of the details of some of the scenes are what I imagined happened.

The actual names of the principals of this story are used. Sub characters that did not testify at public trial are for the most part identified by either first names only or pseudonyms.

Note: The original transcripts for the District Court trial were accidentally destroyed many years ago and only the trial audio cassettes remain. I spent several months transcribing verbatim those audio cassettes so that I might have the details of the trial for this book.

DEDICATION

This book is dedicated to Julie Ann Jackson and Colene Bush

PART I

THE CRIME

CHAPTER 1

TIJERAS CANYON 1981

Walter and Bob weren't exactly sure *what* they were seeing as they drove on Interstate 40 just east of Albuquerque, New Mexico, early that Monday morning. They had already driven for eight straight hours, trying to make it back to Amarillo in time for their physics class at West Texas A&M later on in the day. They knew they should have left Phoenix earlier, but Walter had wanted to stay and take his girlfriend out to a late lunch, and it was his car.

Bob was driving now - it was his turn. The word tired was inadequate for how he felt. Exhausted was closer, but that wasn't it either. With blurry eyes, he drove onward. Out of the corner of his eye, on the highway median, he caught a glimpse of something that jarred him wide awake.

"Walter . . . do you see what I see?" Bob asked.

"See what?" Walter replied.

"Something's on the side of the road . . . over there," Bob said, motioning with his finger.

"I do see something," Walter said, looking hard out the window.

At first, Bob said that it looked like some kind of dead animal, but then Walter said he thought he saw it moving, and as they slowed down to take a look, their hearts almost stopped. Peering through the bug-spattered windshield, their eyes got as big as Texas. A partially nude girl lay sprawled on the blacktop. She lifted a couple of bloody fingers in a slight wave of her right hand, and then dropped them on the dirty pavement where she lay. Her left hand clutched her neck and blood was everywhere.

Bob screeched the car to a halt and both young men jumped out.

"Holy fuck," Bob said.

"What happened to you?" Walter asked. The girl mumbled a couple of words that he didn't understand, her eyes barely open.

"Are you alright?" Bob asked in the only voice he could summon - a whisper.

"Pain . . . need hospital," she groaned. Dried blood caked her face.

"Don't worry," Walter assured her. "We'll get you help."

"Cold . . . need to get up," she said and lifted her bloody arm.

"No, no . . . *no.*" Walter gasped in horror and guided her back to the "lying down" position. His complexion turning almost as pale as hers. "You need to stay down . . . we'll get you help . . . you gotta stay down." He took a deep breath.

"Did you get hit by a car?"

Head shake, no.

"Do you know who did this to you?"

Vertical nod, yes.

The girl's eyes shut. "Oh, jeez," Walter said and looked upward for guidance. None came. He gulped air and shined his flashlight slowly over her body. His own breathing shortened as the flashlight beam flickered on her neck. It had been slashed more than once. Blood oozed from her cheek, arms and chest. To keep from fainting, he looked away.

"She's still breathing . . . barely . . . just barely. But what do we do? What do we do?" Bob asked Walter.

"Well, number one, we have to get something on her. It's freezing!" Walter said.

The girl wore only hospital scrub pants and no top on at all, and at 2 AM Walter knew it was no more than 25 degrees in that canyon. He raced to the trunk of his '74 Plymouth Duster, yanked out his newly purchased goose-down sleeping bag and ran back to the girl.

He gently laid it over the girl to warm her up - to cover her up. Kneeling next to her, his long dark hair blowing in the canyon breeze, he held her bleeding hands in his. He did not want her to feel alone, whether she was conscious or not, whether she lived or not - that remained unknown. But he could hold her hands, damn it. His grandfather had been driven off the road by a drunk driver a few years back and died in his car alone. This greatly upset Walter and his family and it was his personal quest to sure make this girl, whoever she was, feel his presence as she lay bleeding, perhaps to death, on the side of the highway.

"We're in over our heads on this one, Bob. Wave someone down. Get someone to stop," Walter said and tucked the sleeping bag tighter around the girl. "We've got to get her help – fast."

"Will do," said Bob.

Cars and trucks sped by Bob's wildly gesturing arms, not stopping.

"Take off your jacket and use that," Walter yelled to Bob. Bob did as he was told and flapped his jacket at the oncoming traffic.

The car lights zoomed by like space ships heading to the mother planet. They still did not stop.

"Bob, come over here and stay with this girl," Walter shouted above the car noise.

Walter ripped off his white t-shirt, leaned dangerously into oncoming traffic and frantically waved the shirt.

Finally, a semi-tractor trailer rumbled to a stop. Walter ran to its open window.

"We need help, mister."

"What's up, son?" the leather-faced trucker asked. The lines on his forehead deepened as he looked past the wild-eyed young man and saw a blood-covered girl crumpled on the ground. She couldn't have been more than 18 years old, the same age as his daughter.

"Don't know," Walter said. "We pulled over 10 minutes ago and found her. Don't know how she got here. She needs help . . . bad."

Without further discussion, the trucker grabbed his CB radio and pressed the "talk" button.

"Mayday, Mayday. This is Red Rider. Mayday . . . I have an emergency on I-40 East . . . anyone copy?" The trucker said with as much control in his voice as he could muster.

"Emergency, emergency . . . anyone copy?" Shouting, "Anyone?"

"I copy Red Rider . . . this is the Colonel. What's your twenty?"

"Colonel . . . I'm on 40 East, about three miles east of exit 170 . . . south side . . . on the median . . . female, maybe 18 years old . . . needs emergency . . . cut up bad . . . stabbed . . . throat slit . . . hardly breathing . . . maybe almost dead . . . lotta blood. Needs medical. ASAP."

"Three miles east of exit 170 on I-40, south side, is that correct?

"10-4 . . . on the median. Big Van Lines rig and a green Plymouth coupe stacked up in the middle."

"That's a roger. Calling 911 right now . . . (garbled)."

"Come again?"

"Ambulance is on the way."

"OK, thanks . . . clear."

"Good luck . . . clear."

***

FAR NORTHEAST HEIGHTS, ALBUQUERQUE

"This is 911. What's your emergency?"

"Ma'am, this is Colonel Whitman. I'm relaying a call I'm getting from a trucker out on I-40. He's sending a Mayday on his CB right now. He says there's a girl down on the side of the highway. She's injured, stabbed maybe . . . close to dead maybe. He didn't know anything about how she got there."

The retired Air Force colonel sat hunched over his beloved radio equipment located in the at-home command center he had built in his Far Northeast Heights adobe. Mainly through mail order, he had assembled a state of the art "base" setup in the back of his garage. He had all of the latest gear, which he constantly reassessed through avid reading and frequent discussions with his like-minded buddies. His main unit, the Viper 153SX along with a LoStatic D401 lollipop mic and a three tube amplifier, was his pride and joy. He had installed a 75-foot tower that had required a variance in zoning and a bunch of money, but it was worth it. He could receive calls from all over Bernalillo County and then some. His wife thought he was crazy. *Well, it came in handy tonight, didn't it? So who's crazy now?* the Colonel thought.

"Okay, sir, where is she at? What's her location?"

"They're on I-40 eastbound, south side . . . about three miles east of Carnuel exit 170, he said . . . a trucker's there with her." The Colonel had all kinds of maps attached to the walls of his radio room. He had already found what he thought was the exact location of the emergency on his East Mountain topographic map and had stuck a big red pin in the spot.

"Okay, I need to verify that location... I-40 . . . three miles east of exit 170?"

"Yes, ma'am. On the median."

"Okay, stay on the phone with me. She's stabbed?"

"Ma'am, I'm not at the location, but he said it looked like she was stabbed, throat slit maybe."

"Is she responsive?"

"I don't know, ma'am. Didn't sound like it."

"Hold please."

"Yes, ma'am."

"The ambulance is on it its way. You can hang up now, sir."

"Thank you ma'am. Please tell them to hurry."

✳✳✳

TIJERAS CANYON

That he was on this run through Tijeras Canyon at all was a fluke. Red had planned for months to take his wife to the Beach Tree Inn in Florida City, located right off the turnpike only minutes from Everglades National Park. That's what the brochure said.

But there had been an upheaval at Van Lines Inc., where he worked, regarding seniority benefits. Ten drivers just flat out quit and went to work at Jet Stream Trucking Company in the next county over, without giving notice. So because Red was "management", a low level supervisor really, he was told that he had to fill in on one of the runs for the upcoming weekend. That's how he ended up driving from Missouri to California that particular Sunday

6

night. He was supposed to have been on the beach holding a beer and getting sunburn, but instead he was just outside of Albuquerque pulling an all-nighter - and not the good kind. He wasn't mad really, but his wife was. When he took off two days earlier, he did not know why in the great scheme of things he had to get stuck doing this run.

But Red would say later, in his all-knowing way, that it must have been providence that he *was* making that run, on that day, in that place and at that time.

That's what was going through Red's mind as he sat inside his Van Lines truck after broadcasting the mayday call on his CB. A few moments earlier, without thinking much about it, he had responded to a young man on the highway signaling for help. The kid told him her throat had been slit. She sure wasn't moving. For all he knew, she might be dead.

***

911 DISPATCH

"Calling all units in or near Tijeras canyon…female critically injured… I-40… three miles east of exit 170….multiple stab wounds… possible throat slashing."

"10-4. This is unit 1185 . . . we are leaving base now . . . ETA 10 minutes."

***

TIJERAS, NEW MEXICO

New Mexico State Police Officer Juan Chavez, fiddling with the sight on his rifle, jumped when the police radio lying on the floor crackled his name.

"We have a 27-9," the 911 dispatcher said, "Female bleeding . . . suspicious circumstances . . . approximately 18 years old . . . located on Interstate 40 south side . . . Tijeras Canyon . . . three miles east of mile marker 175 . . . paramedics en-route."

"I'll get there as quick as I can," Chavez said.

After kissing his sleeping wife goodbye, he slid into his chilly squad car, lit it up and sped towards the canyon.

***

Barreling down the road at 95 miles per hour, the Albuquerque Ambulance driver easily spotted the big rig up ahead. A thoughtful somebody had illuminated the highway with road flares. Braking to a stop, the ambulance driver surveyed the scene before getting out. He saw three men and a lumpy green sleeping bag. One of the guys, the one with long hair, sat Indian style next to the sleeping bag and held a pale, bloody hand in his.

David jumped out of the driver's side door and his partner, Richard, flew out the back, yanking a gurney behind him. David got to the victim first. Disregarding the nearby men, he peeled back the sleeping bag and saw a shirtless woman with a multiple stab wounds. She was ghost white and covered in blood.

"Oh, my God. What do I do first?" Richard asked rhetorically, reaching the girl a micro-second after his partner. Quickly he began pushing pads against her wounds.

"What happened to her?" Richard shouted to the men huddled nearby. As he began assessing the girl, he lobbed questions at them. "Who is she? What's her name? How'd she get here?"

Walter, now kneeling next to the girl, told him in a quiet voice that he and his buddy had found her this way, except for the sleeping bag, when they pulled over about 20 minutes earlier. He told the paramedic that she'd said she did *not* get hit by a car, but he had no idea what had happened to her. Walter told the paramedics that when he and his friend first got there, the girl had also told them she was cold and in pain but after that she only moaned.

As the medics assessed her, the girl continued moaning, her eyes open ever so slightly. Walter mentioned to the paramedic that the girl's scrub pants had the words "Presbyterian Hospital" stamped on the waist band. "She might work there," he said. Beyond that they knew nothing.

Trying to find a pulse on the victim, Richard put one hand on her neck and the other on her wrist. He felt a weak flutter in the neck. His partner pulled the stretcher alongside her and checked for spine and back injuries. They placed her on the gurney, strapped her in and scooted her into the ambulance.

***

Officer Juan Chavez got out of his squad car with one hand holding a flashlight and the other resting on his service revolver. After a quick survey, besides the rescue vehicles, the officer noted in his report, a semi-trailer truck and a Plymouth Duster were parked on the interstate median. A Bernalillo County District 10 Rescue unit was there along with three "citizens". One of the District 10 personnel advised Chavez that the victim was already inside the ambulance.

Officer Chavez immediately went to the ambulance side-door and attempted to speak to the girl. "Ma'am?" he asked. "Who did this to you?" But she only groaned.

"She's can't talk. She's lost too much blood . . . we've got to get her to the hospital right away," the paramedic said and slammed the side door shut.

In a screaming second, the ambulance accelerated and was gone. David had just bet his partner that he could make it downtown in 15 minutes. He would end up doing even better than that, which was good, because the trauma team at Presbyterian Hospital would need every second it could get.

Officer Chavez returned to the group of men and asked for their IDs. The truck driver, Red, stepped forward and handed the officer his driver's license. "Glad to see you, Officer," Red said. No, Red told the cop, he didn't know what had happened, nor did he know who the girl was. Chavez asked Red if he had seen anyone else in the area since he had been on the scene. Red said that beside the people present he hadn't seen anybody else.

"I was driving my rig to California," Red said, "I was supposed to be in Florida with my wife this weekend but I had to work. These boys here flagged me down." Somberly Red told the cop his suspicions that it seemed like someone had tried to kill this girl. Officer Chavez repeated the same questions to each of the men one by one, interviewing them separately. The young man with the long hair looked close to tears.

Officer Chavez showed no emotion as he ran his flashlight over Red's ID and then the others. He had been trained to restrain his feelings in situations like this. It was up to him, as the professional, to maintain the calm. Inside, though, he felt sick. He had a daughter too, and he had told himself long ago that if anyone ever harmed or tried to harm his daughter, he would make sure that person was brought to justice.

Back in his cruiser, he radioed in the witnesses' names to the dispatcher to check for priors and warrants. They came up clean.

After taking all three men's names, phone numbers and statements, Juan Chavez told them that he would contact them soon.

***

INSIDE AMBULANCE, INTERSTATE 40

"Jesus Christ, she's been stabbed a million times." Richard shouted to David over the shrieking siren.

Accelerating toward Presbyterian Hospital, David shouted back, "I know, I know . . . how the hell is she still alive?"

"I have no idea," Richard replied softly. A paramedic for Albuquerque Ambulance since becoming certified in New Mexico four years earlier, Richard had seen all kinds of horrific accident victims: car crashes, shootings, explosions and tons of stabbings, but nothing like this. The neck slashings alone were unbelievable. He tried not to get emotionally involved but this was barbaric. What the heck happened to her?

At the scene, David had cut off the girl's blood-drenched scrubs in order to better determine the extent of her injuries. Later, he described these injuries in his report as a slashed throat, a laceration on the left cheek, a laceration to the right shoulder, a three to four inch laceration to the right bicep, a laceration to the upper back, lacerations on the back of her left hand, the left thumb was split down the middle, a stab wound to the right and left side of her abdomen, three to four stab wounds to the left upper chest and one stab wound to the right upper chest.

Richard put another blanket on the girl and glanced over to ensure her IV was flowing properly. Even though her hands were a mess, he had to attend to the gashes on her neck, chest and stomach first. He did what he could and then he essentially had to hang on until they got to the hospital – like she did.

He kept talking to her, hoping that she might wake up – regain consciousness. "Hold on, girl. You'll be okay," he said, as a parent might comfort a child. "Just a little bit longer and you'll be at the hospital," he told her.

The girl only moaned. Richard continued chattering. "Hang in there, girl. We're almost there. Those doctors know what they're doing. They'll fix you up."

As he talked and treated her, one eye, then the other, cracked open on the girl, causing him to drop his clipboard. He saw her tracking him through the slits in her eyes.

"Hello," he said. No response, but her eyes still tracked him. "David," he called out, barely able to contain his excitement. "She's opened her eyes."

"What's that?" David yelling loudly but eyes straight ahead on the road. "Is she awake?"

"Yeah, she's awake."

"Find out who she is. Who did this to her?"

Richard nodded and turned back to the girl. "What's your name?" he asked.

No response.

"Do you know your name, girl?"

No response.

"OK then . . . where do you live?"

Long pause. "Stanford," she murmured.

"Do you know who did this to you?"

A slight nod and a mouthing of the word yes.

"Who? Who did this to you?"

No answer. She closed her eyes. Stone-faced, Richard called out to David, "Faster, man . . . she's not awake anymore . . . you gotta get there . . . faster."

The paramedic looked at the young girl's colorless face and hoped she made it to the hospital alive. *How did she get like this*, he kept wondering. She looked too healthy to be a druggie or a hooker. How did she get herself practically thrown into the face of oncoming traffic? What was she doing on Interstate 40 with no vehicle nearby? No one lived in that area. It didn't make any sense. She must have been stabbed somewhere else and dumped out of a car - like the trucker said - but who would do that? What kind of person could have so brutally attacked her? And why? He hoped that she would live to tell them.

CHAPTER 2

For February, it was pretty warm, about 65 degrees in the tiny kitchen, a little warmer yet in the sun, where the scratched-up wooden table and chairs stood. Drab and dirty, the room smelled of stale grease and cigarettes. Only the sunshine and the peeling wallpaper, with its bright, giant sunflowers, made any attempt to alter the dreariness.

Having little kids made it hard to keep the house clean and drinking beer until three in the morning made the word "housework" sound like the word "headache". Plates were stacked chest high in the sink and piles of clothes, rivaling peaks in the Appalachian Mountains, erupted from the floor.

Lack of ambition aside, Linda had cooked up a pot of beans the night before and was elated upon waking, to discover that breakfast had already been made.

She sat at the table with her sister, whom everyone called "Auntie", elbows propped, sopping up cold beans with stale tortillas, loudly discussing the dilemma of the day - younger brother had landed in jail again and needed bail money. Linda thought she might be able to sell an old washer and dryer sitting in the garage and her sister had a gold necklace she felt was worth something. With pencil in hand, the two short, roundish women calculated the value of their treasures.

"I think I can get a $100 for both of them," Linda said, "and I got about $50 in my purse –."

"*What?*" Linda screamed, breaking the conversation with her sister and glaring at her two year old son, Michael. The toddler had just sauntered into the room, with a sick little smirk on his face and a very bad smell. "What the hell are you doing?" she asked disgustedly. He just stared at her.

"God damn it, you little turd," Linda said, kicking the bottom of his feet. "You're two years old already and you don't even know how to go potty in the toilet? What's wrong with you? I don't want to keep cleaning up your shit," she said and popped him on the back of the head with the heel of her hand. "Learn how to use the damn bathroom."

Standing in the middle of the kitchen with a very full diaper and nothing else on, he screamed, then screeched, then threw himself onto the ground. He was an extremely large child for his age, weighing over fifty pounds and already as tall as his mother's waist.

"You like pooping in your pants so much, go ahead . . . keep 'em on," she said and kicked him again.

After the second kick, the boy stood up, picked up a full bowl of beans from the counter and heaved it at her. Missing his mark but achieving his goal, beans and broken glass exploded upward from the floor, thoroughly splattering his mother's legs.

Covered in muck from the waist down and furious, Linda pushed a fistful of beans into the side of her son's face. As she pulled her hand back, he bit it, sinking his baby teeth deep into her flesh. She shrieked and then reached for a nearby broom. The aunt watching from the table, rose up, grabbed Michael from behind and carried him outside.

"That boy's no good," Linda yelled.

"You got that right," Auntie replied.

***

DENVER, COLORADO MAY 11, 1970

The paste tasted as yummy as ever but art class was over. The bell rang and the whole 3rd grade class/mob got up as one and positioned their sticky, stale-milk selves, up against the wall. Julie, the "line leader", was wedged between her classmates and the door. "Go," said Miss Fisher and they escaped to recess. It was warm enough now to play outside.

There was so much to do, too: hopscotch, tether-ball, patty-cake, like that, but Julie loved the swings. Quickly settling into her familiar leather seat, she arched her back and kicked up her legs as high as they would go. In a matter of seconds, she was flying high and feeling great. In her mind, she was almost to Jupiter. She vaguely heard her friends below, but her eyes were closed and the sun felt great. Back and forth she flew, loving the moment, being above it all.

The ending recess bell eventually rang and slowly she came back to earth. Pausing for the second it took her to "ground" herself, she quickly ran over to join the class/mob as they trudged back to the classroom.

Miss Fisher, returning from a smoke in the teachers' lounge, was a tiny bit late, but the kids didn't mind. That just put off the inevitable a little bit longer.

It was time for the students to recite their poems. The other kids weren't very excited about the prospect but Julie was. She stood up and faced the class.

"*The Wish*," Julie began in a clear voice . . .

If I could make a wish right now
And sit atop a faery's brow
The wish would not be grand at all
More like a chanting white dove's call

Oh I would love to really fly
Or have a genie dropping by
My wish lies not on distant star
But right nearby, no never far

The only wish I wish right now
Is falling light from heaven's bough
Wealth nor fame mean naught to me
Just home and safe I ought to be

***

TIJERAS, NEW MEXICO   JULY 28, 1971

"Wo-oah," Colene said and swung her little legs off her horse, Patch, surveying the scene with a squint. It was a baking hot day, so she walked the mare over to the water trough and let her drink her fill. She then rubbed even more water on the horse's head to make sure she was completely cooled down. Patch, three-quarter Quarter horse and one quarter pony, was the best darn horse she ever had and, as she told her mom, she "took excellent good care of her."

Even though Colene was only ten years old, she felt the need to get a job in order to have extra money to help with expenses. When the Deckers suggested to her mother that they would pay Colene fifty cents an hour to clean out their horse stalls, she took it! It was a dirty job but as long as the horses kept eating, it was a steady job. That summer, for the better part of four hours every Saturday morning, she shoveled horse poop into the back of the Decker's rusty white pickup truck, took the short ride away from the stables with Mrs. Decker driving and shoveled it back out onto one of the many side yards of the 80-acre property.

Every Saturday afternoon, when she rode Patch home, she smiled a little smile, because she was now two dollars richer and that was something to brag about to her little brother and sister.

***

MORIARTY, NEW MEXICO MAY 22, 1973

Seated in the front of the gym, the school band tuned up their instruments as the Moriarty High School graduating seniors and their parents streamed in. The band was to begin the ceremonies. PTA president Maud Humphrey, her glasses down to the end of her nose, quieted the crowd with a shush as she motioned for the lights to be dimmed. The band played *Also Sprach Zarathustra* by Richard Strauss, AKA the theme from 2001 A Space Odyssey, with the rousing kettle drums and emotive horns working perfectly to both heat up and inspire the crowd. The school principal stepped to the microphone and spoke of the graduates' promising futures and presented various awards. The majority of the honors went to the same group of over-achievers who seem to monopolize every graduating class. Next, the football coach spoke and he promised that next year's team would turn it around. "But never forget," he said. "This year's team has a lot to be proud of."

A few more uninteresting speakers monologued their way on and off the stage, accompanied by the requisite applause, and it was time for the band to play again.

Colene, although only in the eighth grade, sat in the second chair of the flute section. She wasn't really that crazy about the flute, but it made her mom happy. The band leader waved his hands, pointed, and a tear jerking rendition of "A Bridge over Troubled Water" began. The parents sat with their hands in their laps and smiled while the students whispered amongst themselves. Finally, it was time for the main speaker and the principal, moving with authority, regained control of the microphone.

"Ladies and gentleman," the principal said, "Please join me in welcoming tonight's keynote speaker, former Moriarty High School student and current assistant to Governor Bruce King . . . Mr. Toney Anaya."

***

ROSWELL, NEW MEXICO JUNE 12, 1978

The American Legion sponsors it. The top females from their respective high schools go to it. It's super political. Not what you know, but who you know . . . like that. This year 285 "citizens" showed up at the New Mexico Military Institute in Roswell for it. The "citizens" had to wear yellow beanies wherever they went. Dorky, but that's Girls State.

Mrs. Melvin Hatcher, the director, scheduled something for every minute of every day. 7AM Wake up to inspirational poem, 8AM March to the mess hall for breakfast, 9-3 Classes all day . . . blah, blah, blah. It's an honor to get invited. Prepares the weaker sex for higher power. Like becoming a senator or a congressperson. You never know, it could happen. Mainly useful for getting away from home in the summer. Something else to put on the resume. Learn something new. You never know, it could happen.

3:30 PM Chorus practice. All citizens had to sing. As chorus practice began, the girls had to chirp a couple of notes for Mrs. Charles O'Connor to determine which "voice" they sang in. Colene did not consider herself a singer but Mrs. O'Connor called her an alto. Colene didn't understand, if the purpose of Girls State was to empower females, why were all the women using their husband's first names and not their own? Quirky! Anyway, all the top Girls State songs were in the "Songs of Friendship" book. Mostly patriotic, "This Land is Your Land," stuff like that. The Girls State chorus mainly sang off-key. It didn't matter though, because senators and congresspersons don't need to be good singers. The sopranos sounded slightly better than the other "voices". Colene's future University of New Mexico buddy, Julie, was a soprano. Colene would meet a lot of neat new friends at Girls State that summer but she would not meet Julie for another year and half.

**

JAL GYMNASIUM, JAL, NM   MARCH 2, 1979

She didn't know it yet, but this would be Colene's last game as a senior. The Moriarty High School Pintos faced the Jal High School Panthers for the Regional AA Girls' Basketball elimination game. Even though she participated in volleyball and track, basketball was her main sport - playing varsity all four years. She love, love, loved playing basketball.

Colene, wearing Moriarty's white and green uniform, road #23, started at the shooting guard position. At 5'6", and a lean 127 pounds, she didn't really have the size to dominate on the court, but she made up for it through hard work and grit. Using a hoop attached to the family's barn door, she practiced every evening before dinner and twice a day on the weekends. Her dribbling and ball handling skills improved dramatically as a result of being forced to use a rocky dirt yard as her athletic facility. She discovered that, if you can control the ball on a moonscape, the gym floor is a piece of cake. Her shooting abilities became highly proficient as well, based on her own winning formula of the 3 F's: form, focus and follow-through.

Jal's gymnasium bleachers sagged under the weight of the overflow capacity. The Moriarty parents were there, of course, but the bulk of the gym was filled with as many of the 2,000 locals as could squeeze in. High school basketball in Jal was a religious experience.

Colene was among the starting five and the tip off went to the Jal, who scored on their first possession. As the game squeaked along, it developed a back and forth rhythm, trading points, neither team able to generate much momentum. Then, in the fourth quarter, with seven minutes remaining, the Jal Panthers suddenly took a thirteen point lead. A sloppy couple of turnovers, combined with a few wicked fast breaks and . . . boom . . . the Panthers were ahead by six buckets and a free throw. The Pinto players hung their heads in frustration.

The Moriarty coach called a time out and the team crowded around.

"Ladies," he said. "Did we drive all the way out to this God-forsaken town just to lose this game to this God-forsaken team? Do you want to give up and let them have it? Do you want to quit? No? Okay, then play like you want it. Get out there and make something happen . . . *now*. This is it, ladies. Crunch time. Tired isn't in our vocabulary. Don't embarrass me. Don't embarrass yourselves. You have to dig down deep and give them everything you've got and then some. Control the ball, ladies. We need some points. Let's get a break."

"PINTOS!" the team screamed and the starting five jogged back out onto the floor.

The intensity of the game picked up dramatically. Individual Pinto players became almost unrecognizable as they blurred across the court and began recording bucket after bucket.

The Jal game plan had been to pass the ball in to their six-foot center and then let her score, but as the clocked ticked downward, the Panthers were unable to fight off the Pinto's ferocious press. After scoring on two succeeding possessions, things were looking up for Moriarty. In fact, they were making it look easy.

The ball was bounce-passed into to the boyishly agile Colene who dazzle-dribbled right, spun left, then drove straight up the middle. At the last second, she dished it off to Annette, who leaned into the glass and scored. In order to contain Colene, Jal began to double, and then triple team her. But it was too late to stop her now. Even as the game's insanity swirled around her, Colene's mind slowed down. She saw what needed to be done and did it.

As the fast and furious pace continued, both teams tired. That is, except for Colene. The "Burning Bush", as she was called, raced back and forth, working both sides of the court, as if on fire. The endless "suicides" she had run in practice now made her stamina almost superhuman. Her coach had preached, "Go a little bit farther than you think you can go. Push yourself. Do a little bit more than you think you can do." Colene took those words to heart . . . at practice and now in this game. For the team's sake, she was pushing herself a little bit further than she thought she could go.

It was the Panthers' ball again. They got it to about half court, when Colene picked it off, scored and was fouled. The Pintos lined up for the extra point and whoosh, she nailed it. The game was tied.

Time out Panthers. The Jal coach stomped his feet, tore out what was left of his hair and let loose a spew of profanity. The girls stood silent. Meanwhile on the Pinto bench the atmosphere was tense but optimistic.

Back on the court, the Pintos immediately scored another basket and free throw and with 16 unanswered points, they went ahead by three.

The Panthers took another time out. Gesticulating and red-faced, both coaches made their final speeches and the players trotted back to the floor. The teams could only match baskets as time was running out. Finally, with only 12 seconds remaining, the score 61-58 Pintos, Moriarty forward/center Jeana set her feet and established position against the hard-driving Panther point guard, who sped fatefully toward the Jal basket. Stampeding over young Jeana, the playmaker knocked her to the ground and scored. A whistle shrieked and a foul was called, but it was against Moriarty. Screaming chaos erupted from both sides of the stands, with the Pinto fans furious and the Panther fans delirious. Amid a cacophonous uproar, the Panther point guard sunk the extra point as time expired.

The Jal coach would later tell the Moriarty coach that they were hometown-ed on that particular call, but the basket stood and at the end of regulation, the score was tied 61-61.

In overtime, the Jal Panthers prevailed, with a 69-67 final score.

Colene took it personally. She felt she let the team down. If only she had played a little bit harder, done something a little bit better, her team might have won the game.

As it was, Colene ended up with nine assists, seven rebounds and 23 points accounting for over one third of Moriarty's total score.

***

South Valley, Albuquerque   June 12, 1979

Charley liked to fish. His favorite spot was below the foot bridge just south of Rio Bravo Blvd. He got up early every Tuesday morning, walked the three blocks from his house, past the drainage canal, down the slope to the Rio Grande and set up his folding chair and cooler. It relaxed him to sit and fish by himself near the big river. He could sit for hours and never get bored. Watching the river and the sky fascinated him.

If he could catch enough fish, he would be able to feed his family for a couple of days. He had recently lost his regular job as an iron worker and still had four hungry mouths to feed. Last week he caught six large cutthroat trout and was hoping for more today. If he didn't catch anything, then he would go to the gym and work out, which was his second favorite thing to do. Charley was a big guy with even bigger muscles. His large size allowed him to move around with confidence in the rough neighborhood where he lived.

An hour had passed since he sat down to fish, but still he had no bites. Charley reeled in his line, peered at the empty hook and pulled out a jar of night-crawlers from his cooler. He poked a couple of squiggly ones on his hook, threw the line back in and resumed the fishing position: slouched back in his chair with his hat pulled rakishly over the eyes. He was half asleep when a loud snap jolted him upright. It came from the back side of the bridge.

Charley looked behind him and in horror saw a teenage male, hanging by the neck, about a foot off the ground from the bridge. The teenager's arms and legs flailed as he dangled. No other people were in the vicinity.

Suddenly, the kid reached up with both hands and tried to escape from the noose. First, he tried taking the belt off, and then he tried pulling his head out and when neither of those worked, he mouthed the word "Help." Color drained from his face and his eyes started to bulge. He appeared to pass out. Charley couldn't believe what he was seeing.

"What the heck are you doing, man? You can't do that," Charley yelled.

Charley rushed back to his gear, grabbed his big fishing knife and ran the twenty yards over to where the boy hung. The kid's head drooped and his eyes rolled back into his head. Charley didn't know if he was already too late, but with a mighty slash of his knife, he cut the young man down. Even though Charley attempted to cradle the boy as he descended, he fell anyway, with a thud. The big man stood over the fallen teenager, trying to remember what one was supposed to do in these types of situations. Not having any better ideas, he reached down and put his thumb and forefinger on the kid's neck to see if he could find a pulse. He felt a weak throbbing, so he knelt beside the boy and waited. Time passed slowly, there was no quick way for him to telephone for help and he didn't want to leave the boy alone. Finally, the kid opened his eyes and blinked into the bright sun.

"You okay, Bud? Charley asked.

"Yeah," the boy said blankly.

"Were you trying to die?"

"No . . . yeah, but I changed my mind." Anger now in his voice.

"Why did you do that, man? Did you break up with your girlfriend or something?"

"No. I don't know. I hear voices. I tried to do it at my house but my mom got mad and told me to do it somewhere else. She doesn't understand. I hear voices, sometimes," the teenager said again, sitting up and rubbing his back where it had hit the ground.

"Your mom told you what?

The boy frowned but did not answer.

"What kind of voices?" Charley persisted.

The kid glared at him. "I don't know. Voices. God maybe. I don't know who it is, but the voices tell me to do stuff," he said. "The voices told me I don't belong on this earth."

"You need to talk to a shrink, man."

"I did. He said I was angry."

"Yeah, I see that. Okay, whatever. We gotta get you some help, man. Can you walk? We need to call somebody . . . like the ambulance. What's your name?"

"Mike . . . I mean Miguel . . . yeah . . . Miguel," he said, standing up slowly. "Don't call a ambulance. My mom'll kick my ass if she finds out. Call my cousin. My cousin'll come and pick me up."

"Okay, it's your deal, man," Charley said and held out his hand. "What kinda problems you got that's this bad?"

"My mom hates me . . . she takes my money and then kicks me out of the house. When I'm at home, she beats me up."

"Why don't you just move out, man?"

"I can't . . . I don't have money."

Charley shook his head.

***

Santa Clara Dormitory, UNM   August 22, 1979

All Colene brought was three boxes of personal items and a bean bag chair. Her mom, grandma and younger siblings escorted her up the three flights of stairs to her new home. After depositing her stuff and chatting for a while, her family drove back to Tijeras, leaving Colene alone in her dorm room.

The room was small, about 10X12 with two single beds, two desks and a vanity with no drawers. Colene had looked forward to this day for a long time, maybe all of her life. Now that it had finally arrived, she had butterflies in her stomach. A shy country girl from the East Mountains, she had every intention of spending all her time on her studies, but she also knew that a whole new world, with all of its imperfections, beckoned her.

Sitting on her bed in a dreamlike state, she could see the football field from her window. This was a Lobo team that knew how to win, bare knuckle brawlers and not afraid to show it. Watching them practice would provide daily entertainment.

Right now though, she couldn't decide what to do first: unpack or explore. Shortly, the decision would be made for her.

"Knock, knock," she heard someone say from the other side of her still open door.

"Howdy, neighbor," a short, blond teenage girl said. She moved toward Colene with an extended hand, "Hi, I'm Julie," she said. "I live next door at 318."

"Hi . . . Colene. Nice to meet you." Colene liked her new neighbor instantly.

"Nice to meet you, too. Just got here today from Farmington. How 'bout you?" Julie said, settling down on Colene's chair

"East Mountains," Colene replied.

"Do you know anybody here? Anyone from high school or anything?" Julie asked.

"Probably. Don't know who all is here yet."

"Yeah, me neither, but I've already gotten the mini-tour from Lori, and good news, the cafeteria is right out the back door. Wanna to go get some coffee and check out the campus?"

"Sure," Colene said with a resigned smile. She could unpack later and besides, maybe she had just met a great new friend.

***

NORTHEAST HEIGHTS, ALBUQUERQUE   FEBRUARY 4, 1981

The warehouse stood abandoned, except for the cats, just off Tramway Boulevard. It had once been a self-storage center, but the owner had defaulted. Overrun with weeds, trash and the reek of cat pee, locals steered clear. Sometimes, the city would it board up, but a guy could tear it down easy enough if he needed a private place. It was righteous, really. No nosy neighbors and all the little rooms inside were a bonus.

Mike and his girlfriend Monica were excited about the party, plus Mike knew that Paul would be there. Paul worked as a waiter at the same restaurant where Mike washed dishes. Paul was Anglo, but cool. Other waiters didn't like Mike so much, but Paul had his back.

Paul had a second job as an auto body guy down at the Collision Repair Center during the day. Mike loved doing auto body work. The sanding, the grinding and the unending quest to make the rough metal perfectly smooth, was man's work. Way better than washing dishes, which wasn't. He would ask Paul about a job tonight.

Mike and Monica and Monica's cousin, Felix, got there late. They were ready to party and get drunk. It didn't matter to Mike, or anyone else, what the drinking age was. That was a technicality for someone else to worry about. Monica, seven months pregnant, probably shouldn't be drinking at all, but they had come to have fun and "right now" was all that mattered. Mike immediately made his way to the big punch bowl in the back.

"What's in this?" Mike asked a tall guy in an embroidered western shirt.

"I don't know, man, but it'll knock you on your ass – guaranteed. I was here last month and it fucked me up. Fast. It's bitchin'," he said.

"Cool," Mike said, trying to sound white.

People were dancing, the music was loud, and for a while it seemed like a great place to be. Mike slouched alone against the wall, watching the sweaty bodies sway. Monica had deserted him, but that was alright. He noticed that people there were mostly white – redneck types. Only two others were Latinos. Mike started to feel edgy and out of place. *Time for more punch,* he thought.

On the way back to his spot, Mike bumped into a girl and spilled his drink. The girl, a white chick with long blond hair, lots of makeup and a very short skirt, frowned. Embarrassed, Mike stared at her for a long couple of seconds.

"Sorry," he said at last.

"That's okay," she said. "Do you have a light?" Pushing a Kool 100 between her pouty red lips.

"Yeah," he said and leaned in, touching his body to hers. He lit the end of her cigarette with one flick, hoping to impress her. Instead, she inhaled deeply and then blew the smoke in his face. Mike smiled, thinking she was flirting with him.

"Don't touch me, vato," the girl said with a sneer and stepped away. "My boyfriend's over there," pointing to a short, wide guy with a thin blonde mustache and a cowboy hat.

"Axel, get over here and take care of this Mexican," she yelled.

Mike slapped her face. "Why you coming on to me like that bitch, if you don't want it?" he said. The girl staggered sideways and a crowd appeared.

The girl's boyfriend pushed through the crowd and ran up to Mike. Mike towered over him by a good 10 inches.

"What the fuck you think you're doing, Jose?" Axel demanded, craning his neck to make eye contact.

"The bitch made fun of me," Mike said, striding outside.

"Don't walk away from me fuckhead and don't slap my lady like that," Axel said, following him outside.

Mike, staring at Axel, saw a short, chunky, girly-looking white guy, who was sweating a lot.

"I'm going to have to bust your face, Taco-breath." Axel said, his hand balling into a fist.

Mike seethed.

"I said, I'm going to have to bust your face, asshole Mexican. You deaf, too?" Axel's arm drew back to strike.

Mike grabbed the oncoming fist with his right and cracked Axel squarely in the nose with his left. Axel crumpled to the pavement, blood dribbling from his left nostril. He tried getting back on his feet, but before he could,

Mike slugged him again, this time in the stomach. Air whooshed from Axel's mouth like a deflated balloon. Not pausing, Mike wordlessly squeezed his long arms around Axel's short neck and held him in a headlock until he folded to the ground. No one tried to help. Everyone except Axel knew this guy was not to be messed with.

Meanwhile, Monica waddled over, daring the other girls to rumble. It was mostly talk, but even at seven months pregnant, Monica scared them.

"Get back, babe, I'll take care of 'em," Mike said. "That baby means a lot to me."

Just then Axel got up and popped Mike when he wasn't looking. It was a roundhouse to the jaw and Mike fell back, almost to the ground. Mike rubbed the blood from his face, picked Axel up and bashed his head against the brick warehouse. Blood poured from Axel's head.

"Put him down, you fucker," Axel's girlfriend said. Mike ignored her. Another girl hit Mike in the back with a brick, yelling at him to stop. Mike ignored her too and continued slamming Axel against the wall.

An older woman standing nearby screamed for Mike to be taken down.

"Kick him in the nuts," the older lady said. "Someone get a gun and shoot this dirty Mexican."

This sent Monica into a tizzy and she rushed over to the pack of girls. A face-off ensued.

Mike, seeing Monica in danger, tossed Axel to the ground like an empty beer can. "Monica . . . don't," he said. "I'll take care of you and the baby."

Someone in the crowd finally scooped Axel up and took him away. Mike glared at the crowd, daring anyone to make a move or speak. No one did.

Eventually, Mike grabbed Monica, yanked her into the car and started it. Cousin Felix was already inside.

As Mike tried to pull away, the blond girl jumped onto the hood and pounded on the windshield, screaming at him.

"Stop. You God damn son-of-a-bitch, pussy Mexican. You tried to kill my boyfriend and now you run away. Somebody call the cops."

Sticking his head out the window, Mike yelled," Get the fuck off the windshield, or I'll break your damn neck." He put the car in reverse and gunned the engine.

The girl finally rolled off and he squealed away. Mike knew that he really would have broken that girl's neck, because like he always said, "That baby meant a lot to me and it still does."

***

CORNELL AVENUE & CENTRAL, UNM AREA   MARCH 10, 1981 3PM

She kind of hated walking down Cornell because of the group of guys that hung out in front of the pool hall. Despicable sorts. Guys that had to prove their manhood by humiliating women. But she needed to get to class quickly and Cornell was the shortest distance between two points. Those jerks shouldn't be dictating which streets she walked on.

As she neared the pool hall, it appeared to be all clear, but right before she got there, a huddle of slimy guys oozed out the door. Julie decided she would just put her head down and walk fast. With her notebook pressed tight against her chest and moving at almost a trot, they full-force let her have it as she walked by, with whistles, animal sounds and lewd remarks. One of the men, and she didn't know which, bore his eyes into her with such intensity that she felt a crawling sensation on her skin for the rest of the day.

***

SANTA CLARA DORMS UNM   MARCH 15, 1981

It was a little bit dark outside but she recognized him right away. It was that Mike Castro, the one that was always trying to hook up with her old dorm mates, the very attractive Bellamy sisters. Colene didn't live in the dorms anymore, but because men weren't allowed in, he wanted her to go in and fetch his dates for him. Colene paused and looked him over.

"Hey, you look like you've lost some weight, mister," Colene said.

"Yeah," he replied, standing up a little straighter. "I just got into the Albuquerque Police Academy. I'm gonna be a cop."

"Wow," Colene said. "That's great. What do you have to do to get in? I've always wanted to do something like that . . . either go into the military or be a cop or something."

"Yeah, you'd be great, but they're making people have two years of college now before they'll take you. You're only a sophomore right?"

"Yeah, okay," Colene said dejectedly. "I guess I'll check it out later then. I really like going to college and all . . . but I'd love to be a cop."

***

CENTRAL AVENUE, FAIRGROUNDS AREA   MARCH 17, 1981

Gwen had already put in a long day waiting tables at the Sundowner Motel at Central and Laguayra Drive. Having just worked a double, she looked forward to some quality downtime at home.

Downtrodden eyes, crooked smiles and bad complexions were all that sat at the front bar that evening. As strange as the men looked, they were all regulars and harmless enough. The customers varied little from night to night. Occasionally the stray geek tourist would stop by because of the tiny bit of fame this particular Route 66 motel had gained back in the '70's. It had been a "base camp" for Bill Gates and Paul Allen, the Microsoft guys who developed the computer language BASIC while throwing back shots of whiskey at the Sundowner.

Tonight, someone had come into the bar that didn't belong there, but Gwen hadn't noticed. If she had noticed, her skin might have prickled and her heart might have raced. A young man with predator eyes and a clenched jaw tracked her every move as he pretended to sip beer in a darkened booth. But a different girl waited that section, so the man never crossed Gwen's radar. When her shift was over, Gwen punched her time-card and grabbed her purse. As she walked out the back door, the man wordlessly slid out of his seat.

Changing from pumps to tennis shoes, she started the engine of her VW bug and headed east on Central, listening to KRST, the new country-western station in town. As she approached the intersection of Central and Wyoming, she noticed a brown pickup truck behind her. But big deal . . . there were lots of people out driving that night and they were all in a rush, so this was probably just one more asshole in a hurry. In fact, she lost sight of the truck pretty quickly and you know what they say . . . out of sight, out of mind.

She took a left at Wyoming and drove north towards the VW dealership where she had purchased her car two years earlier. Looking in her rear-view mirror, she thought she saw the same truck again at the corner of Wyoming and Lomas. This time it appeared to be tailgating her. As she made the turns necessary to reach her street, Sellers Road, the truck was still behind her. She was puzzled. But once again the truck disappeared from view. She shrugged it off. The truck was most likely going to the same apartment complex where she lived. Lots of people lived in that complex.

Too tired to much care, Gwen pulled into her parking lot. She noticed an El Camino parked in Mr. Gamboa's space – the slot directly behind hers. *Hmmm?* She thought. *That's strange . . . Mr. Gamboa doesn't own a vehicle.* But no one was in the truck, so? So what. Maybe Mr. Gamboa had a guest?

She sat in her dark green VW for three or four minutes like she usually did, to center herself, before she got out of her car. She was thinking more about the meatloaf leftovers in her refrigerator than her surroundings. Getting out, she turned to lock her car door, and as she reached for the handle, a very tall teenager with a baseball cap worn backward stepped out from a darkened patch of nearby bushes and approached her. Gwen's heart pounded and her eyes widened.

"Hi," he said, in what would be described later as an average tone of voice. "Do you know if the Jeffersons live here?"

"No," Gwen replied, not wanting to engage in conversation with him at all. "There's no Jeffersons here." *He's just a kid,* she thought . . . *just a kid . . . but. . .* She turned nervously back towards her car - to the task of locking her door. Her key-hand shook.

"Don't scream," she heard the man whisper a moment later as her skin felt the burn of his breath. He grabbed her arms from behind and then, almost immediately, she felt something cold, metallic and sharp shoved against her throat. "Don't even make a sound lady, or I'll fucking kill you where you're standing." His vice-like grip squeezing her so tightly she could barely breathe. Her mind went gray with fear. She knew she had to snap out of it or die.

"Oh, my God," she gasped. "What do you want?"

"I told you, lady . . . don't make a damn sound," he said angrily, "Get over by that car." He pushed her hard toward his pickup truck. Her mind raced. *I need to stop this guy now,* she thought. She desperately wished she had her .38 revolver that she kept in her apartment. But she didn't.

The man savagely forced her against the side of his truck and then temporarily released his grip. But the sharp metal object, which she now realized was a screwdriver, was still at her throat. He yanked open the truck door and ordered her in. She hesitated.

Grabbing a large amount of her dark brown hair in his right hand, he jerked her head back and dragged her halfway onto the passenger seat. Pain echoed in her skull. It felt like a patch of her scalp was about to be torn out. She struggled, letting out a muffled scream as he tried to wrench her by the hair even further into the front seat of his truck. Gwen noticed that the man was panting and shaking. She wondered if it was fear she smelled and not just his sweaty perversion.

"Let me go," she cried out in desperation. "I'll do whatever you want. Do you need money? . . . I have money. I have 60 bucks in my purse . . . you can have it." She pushed her head as hard as she could against his hand lest she be completely swallowed up by his truck.

"No. I don't need your damn money, lady. Get in the fucking truck. I just want to talk to you. That's all."

Fighting against his strong grip, Gwen turned her head towards him and said as fearlessly as she could, "You're making a big mistake, Mister. My son is a captain in the police force and if you do anything to me, he will hound you til the day you die."

The man froze and stared at her with flickering black eyes. Time stood still while he contemplated this new information. Gwen kept her eyes locked onto his. Eventually, his grip slackened and he released her hair. He stepped backward, away from her, but the screwdriver remained in his hand. A few more slow moments of silence transpired as he weighed his options, then he said, "Sorry, sorry, lady. I didn't mean nothing. I just was lookin' for someone to talk to." Gwen tried to maneuver away from him but he grabbed her hair again, fearing she would flee.

"I'm sorry . . . I just don't have any friends," he lied, his large face looming inches from hers. "I don't wanna scare you."

"Look," Gwen said. "I'll talk to you. If I can help you, I will . . . but I need to go upstairs to bed. I worked too many hours and right now . . . well, right now; I've got to get some sleep. I can give you my number and you can come back." She wanted him gone.

The man's face became agitated and his eyes blazed. "You don't want to talk to me neither," he shouted. "You're just like everybody else. You don't care about me." He snatched her arm again.

"Okay, okay. If you want to talk – let's talk. We can talk right here, right now," she said, sensing he was about to turn violent again.

"Don't tell me you don't live here," he said unprompted. "Don't tell me that you don't live at the top of these stairs." He began prodding her up the steps.

A new wave of fear exploded inside of Gwen's chest. Somehow he knew which apartment was hers. "Listen," she implored, "You're going to have to let go of my arms so I can open my door." He continued gripping her tightly until they reached the top of the stairs and then let her go.

"Sorry I hurt you, lady," he said, entering her apartment. "I won't touch you no more."

Inside, he asked her for a Coke. She told him that she didn't keep carbonated drinks. She asked him if he would like some water instead and he said that would be alright. He stood in her living room, as out of place as a cigar store Indian in a china shop, shaking and drinking his water. He asked her for a cigarette and she gave him one. She noticed him glance at the end table where a photograph of her son in his APD uniform stood. He said nothing.

"What's your name?" she asked him.

He stopped shaking and smiled in relief. He sensed that she was going to let him off the hook. He told her that his name was Toney. She told him there were places in town that he could call for help, professionals that would talk to him. He told her that he worked in an auto body shop and that he was from California. She told him that he was a nice looking young man and should have no trouble making friends. He said that he didn't understand why he had no friends either and he was sorry for scaring her but it was time for him to go. She wrote down her name and phone number on a piece of paper and told him that the next time he needed to talk, to please call her and not go friend-hunting with big screwdrivers. He laughed self-consciously and said that he would for sure call her. Mike drove away and never contacted her again. Gwen called the police as soon as he left and reported the entire incident.

CHAPTER 3

The alarm went off precisely at 6:30 AM, like it did every weekday morning. It was a school day and she knew that when she finally got up, she would spend the rest of the morning in class. After class, she would change into her running clothes, go for her afternoon jog down Central and then reward herself with a cup of coffee and a cinnamon roll at the Frontier Restaurant. But for now, she rolled over and hit the snooze button. Due to her low-economic status, her couch doubled as her bed, and today it felt extra cozy as she grabbed a little extra sleep.

She didn't *want* to wake up. She was having a grade-A dream/nightmare. It didn't make sense, but then most dreams don't. She found herself on a train in Germany, heading east to Berlin. Her fellow travelers wore dark heavy coats and their eyes were filled with fear and loathing.

In the narrow dining car, she sat with perfect posture. Across the car, an obese man gorged on antelope-foot stew. Bits of foot and oil dribbled down his jelly-fat jowls as he ate. A soldier wearing a green jumpsuit slid into her booth and seated himself at her table. His eyes were as dark as Cuba and the twisted scar on his nose as mysterious as Egypt. The soldier placed a brown paper package in front of her. It was addressed to X. While staring at the package, she noticed fresh blood oozing from its creases. A scream unfolded in her throat but was not articulated. The train belched to a stop.

Riii-iing. "Dammit," she said and struck the alarm down again.

The blue-suited conductor appeared at her table. No longer a man but a nicely dressed circus bear, his paw reached for her elbow. She fled, knowing full well that Satan often disguised himself as a circus bear. As she ran, she discovered that every door she exited returned to the dining car. The bear appeared to be running out of patience. She ran out the door again and this time found herself on a beach in Florida. The sand slowed her speed. Looking over her shoulder, she saw the soldier with the bloody package in his hand, gaining on her.

Riii-iing. She sat bolt upright in the bed, realizing that her scary trip to Europe might have caused her to oversleep.

"Oh, oh," she said, blinking awake. With a quick look at the clock, she knew she had to hustle in order to make it to her 8 AM Drawing II class. She liked this class and most of her other classes. She loved learning. As a sophomore she had aspirations: possibly to obtain a Masters in Architecture (to please her dad) or maybe even go to medical school (to please her mom). The sky was the limit - but that was later, right now, Colene loved to draw. She had been drawing since a young age, mostly horses, and she did it well. She could, with a plain piece of paper and a pencil, create a finished picture that was so astonishingly detailed; it more resembled a photograph than a drawing. Her eyes were like an expensive camera, her hands an artisan's exquisite tools.

"Shit," said Colene "I'm going to be late." Padding the five steps from her bed to her bathroom, she jumped into the shower and quickly rinsed off. To appease her sense of breakfast duty, she gulped down a cup of cold instant coffee and then picked up her satchel, flung it over her shoulder and flew out the door. With only ten minutes until class, she sprinted. As she ran, she thought of her dream and wondered what it meant. She had never even been to Europe or ridden a train, except the one in Chama, but that wasn't this. Probably means nothing, she thought, and pushed it out of her mind.

Not in the least bit winded, she slid into her classroom with five minutes to spare.

"Good morning, Colene," Ms. Williams, the art teacher said with a smile.

"Good morning," Colene said and settled into her seat.

***

Duck Pond, UNM Campus March 26, 1981

Her blond hair pulled back into a tight ponytail, Julie sat on the university grass with a diet cola in one hand and a book, *The Stranger*, by Albert Camus, in the other. It was too cold to be outside but James had just gotten his new dragon kite in the air, so knowing it would be awhile; she put the hood up on her blue down jacket and settled in. As she half-watched her boyfriend jet around like a joyous ten year old, a soon-due history paper as well as what to have for dinner tonight ticked in her head.

Who should I write about? She thought. Thomas Jefferson? Boring. William Tecumseh Sherman? Asshole. Lasagna? Mmmmm lasagna. Spinach lasagna. Healthy. I like it.

James wove through the splotches of people sitting on the open lawn near the campus duck pond. Once, he came within inches of tromping a momma duck and her ducklings who had unwisely ventured onto land.

Eleanor Roosevelt, maybe? Maybe. But maybe someone slightly more quirky like . . . ah . . . like Mary Todd Lincoln. Julie remembered her from high school history. She'd be a good one. Oh, yeah and a big salad. With bell peppers and pine nuts. And I'll make my own dressing too, the balsamic vinegar kind. Like James likes.

Sun glinting off her wire-rim glasses, Julie's roundish face grimaced as she thought of poor old Mary Todd Lincoln, who was put in a nut house by her last living son, Robert. Supposedly because she was excessively paranoid about family members dying (who could blame her?) and spent large amounts of time with her psychic, but . . . so? President Lincoln had been into psychics too and no one had committed him. Robert obviously wasn't that great a son. So what if his mom was slightly eccentric? So what if she worried about him? She was his mom and she loved him.

Julie shook her head as she thought about Robert Lincoln. She had been taught to respect her parents. Just last weekend, she visited her dad in Farmington, and spent most of that time working at his bakery so that he could have a couple of days off. He had scrimped and saved all his life to get his kids through college and she wanted to help him out anyway she could.

James, finally done flying his kite, jogged over to Julie and lifted her up off the ground. He caught her by surprise and after a moment of disorientation, she smiled her big Julie smile and away they went, looking for their next adventure.

***

CENTRAL AVENUE, UNM AREA   MARCH 26, 1981

After her sprint to class earlier in the morning, Colene thought she might be able to back off on her afternoon run, but what the heck, it's good for you, right? So, putting on her running shoes, she loped out the front door, her long strides moving her quickly down the neighborhood, whizzing by the afternoon's losers and snoozers. Some were awake enough to nod hello. She nodded back, jogged down to Central and headed west.

Central Avenue, old Route 66, ran through the heart of the University of New Mexico's commercial district, where all the cool shops and restaurants were located. Playing a game with herself, Colene raced the cars as she ran down Central and for the first 10 yards, she won every time.

"*Oh look*," thought Colene, *There's my buddy, Alyesha from basketball intermurals, I'd better say hi.*

"Hey, Alyesha . . . whatsya doing?" Colene sing-songed as she pulled to a running-in-place stop at Yale and Central.

"Not much. Are you trying to get a leg-up on me, running around town like that?" Alyesha asked with a smile.

"Oh, no. We all know you're the queen of Rock, Show and Go. I'm just trying to get some exercise, that's all," Colene replied.

"I see. Well, have fun. See you on the court." She gave Colene a soft high five and walked off in the opposite direction.

Colene strode onward. She felt absolutely great. Her intention was to run hard on Central, even harder on Girard, turn around at the golf course and jog back. Naturally, the return trip would include a stop at the Frontier Restaurant. *Mm-mm,* she thought. *Coffee and a roll, such a delicious treat for only $1.25.*

But after the promised stop at the Frontier, her day took a decided turn for the worse. Running by the Vickers Gas Station, at Columbia and Central, her left foot landed awkwardly on the curb and folded unnaturally downward. She bent over reflexively from the pain, but after a couple of deep breaths, she gathered herself and hobbled back home.

***

MONICA'S APARTMENT, CENTRAL & TRAMWAY   MARCH 27, 1981

"Why do you keep arguing against me?" he screamed in a red heat that she had seen before. "You fucking slut," each word enunciated separately and venomously. She barely had time to flinch before she saw his hard brown fist rocketing out of his dark denim shirt. The blow slammed her unprotected face, snapping her head back like a milk bottle in an arcade game.

"Why you with that guy?" he grilled.

No answer - only sobbing. He smacked her again. Harder. The pain of the impact correlating with the volume of the punch. No crying this time, she bit her lip in defiance.

"I told you, if I ever catch you with another guy, I'm gonna kill you," he yelled. "You think this guy's better'n me?"

"I *told* you," she gasped, "I wasn't doing nothing. I felt dizzy . . . I thought I was going to pass out . . . I just sat in my girlfriend's brother's car for a minute . . . that's all." Her brown eyes red, inky mascara streaming down her battered face.

"Liar. Cheating liar. Slut. Whore," he screamed, his eyes pitch black. "Liar," he screamed again and unleashed a raging flurry of hard slaps, pummeling her until a light purple covered her head and upper body.

Her hands doing a poor job of protecting herself, reached out in a stop signal. "Michael, no more," she whimpered, "Stop. Stop hitting me . . . you're gonna hurt the baby."

He froze.

31

"No, no, no," he cried out at last. He had forgotten that she was eight months pregnant. "Oh, God. Oh, my God. No. I can't hurt my baby. What am I doing?" His body shook and twisted, almost to the point of seizure. He held his breath, then turned rigid, then blue, followed by a return of fanatical fist flailing.

Only this time, he was pummeling himself. Monica screamed. He paid no attention to her. Walking over to the full length mirror that hung on the living room wall, he looked at himself for half a beat and then hurled his head forward into it - shattering the glass it into a zillion pieces. He continued smashing himself until his forehead was a sparkly crimson, ultimately collapsing cross-legged on the floor, with his now achromatic eyes, askew.

***

UNM CAMPUS   MARCH 27, 1981

Colene sat on a bench outside of the UNM student union thinking about her walk home.

"What's up, Colene?" Julie asked as she ambled toward her friend.

"I messed up my foot yesterday. I don't think I can make it home."

"Let me see?" Julie said, easing herself into a deep squat and touching the swollen foot. "It looks terrible. Have you been to the doctor yet?"

"I don't have money. Remember?"

"Let's go to Student Health, there's a doctor there and it's free."

"I guess I should."

"I'll walk you over."

Gripping Colene's elbow, Julie helped her hobble the block and half over to the UNM Student Health Services and led her into the waiting room. She didn't have to wait long.

"You probably have a stress fracture, young lady," Dr. Roybal told her after looking at the x-ray. "Nothing's showing up on the picture yet, but since there is swelling, it's likely. Normally, it takes a while to show up on the x-ray. Let's wrap it up and get you some crutches. You need to stay off the foot altogether for a couple of weeks."

***

CENTRAL AVENUE, UNM AREA   MARCH 29, 1981

Once Mike got off work, he had one thing on his mind and it sure wasn't Monica. One, maybe two weeks ago, he had seen a girl that he wanted. He'd seen her near Central . . . by UNM. A white girl. A young, blond-haired, blue-eyed white girl. He really wanted to see her again, so he drove by the college as often as he could. No luck yet, but he was determined. He thought he knew this girl. In his mind, he did. She was either the same white girl that had jumped on his back at the cowboy party, or her twin. He was still mad about that night. Furious really.

He wanted to get back at all of those bitches. He had tracked down the old lady a couple of weeks ago, at least it sure looked like her, but that had gotten kind of screwed up. Mike had no way of knowing that her son was a cop. But this girl was too young to have a cop son. He had promised himself that he would keep looking. He wanted her.

***

JAMES AND JULIE'S HOUSE, GARFIELD AVENUE, UNM AREA   MARCH 30, 1981

It was better to watch the news at James and Julie's house, the simple reason being, they had the better TV. Sure it was only a 15" and had occasional reception problems but it was color and thus trumped Colene's 9" black and white by a mile. The only drawback, and it was a pretty funky drawback, was that you could not get a picture unless you dropped the car keys just right onto the coffee table. That's right, the coffee table turned on the TV. James said it sounded like a bad date. No one in the room could explain why it worked or even how they had discovered it, they just knew that it did.

Colene hibble-hobbled the two blocks over to James and Julie's house on her newly acquired crutches to watch the evening news with them. The President of the United States had been shot earlier in the day and she felt drawn in by the seriousness of it. James was the first to try to get the TV going. Plink, plonk, plunk. James dropped his key ring three times. He could not hit the mysterious yet important mark.

"Let me give it a try," Colene said and reached high over the coffee table with the keys, waved her other arm in a magical motion and then dropped them. Ping! The TV came on. James applauded and Julie brought in a plate of nachos and some iced tea. They all settled in front of the now working TV.

Walter Cronkite described what had happened that day in Washington D.C. A man named John Hinckley shot President Ronald Reagan with a .22 steel blue revolver as Reagan walked from his hotel to his waiting car. Hinckley had gotten off six shots in three seconds but missed the president with all six shots. However, he had wounded Reagan's press secretary James Brady, D.C. cop Tom Delahanty and secret service agent Tim McCarthy with direct hits. He had also wounded the president with the sixth and final bullet when it ricocheted off the limousine and went through Reagan's armpit and into his left lung. The shooting was made all the more deadly because Hinckley had used exploding bullets, Devastators they were called. The doctor treating James Brady was pretty sure the bullet that had lodged in

Brady's brain had exploded. It was widely reported that John Hinckley shot the president in an effort to impress actress Jody Foster.

"What a nut," Julie said and they all agreed. The trio continued to watch the news unfold for several hours, into the evening, until James finally drove Colene home.

***

CENTRAL AVENUE, UNM AREA   MARCH 30, 1981

Driving up and down Central in front of UNM, Mike vaguely wondered if he looked suspicious to the people on the street. He decided he did not. After all, this part of town was *his* stomping grounds, too. The pool hall that he regularly frequented just happened to be located behind the Frontier, which was across from UNM. So what?

Mike loved playing pool with the boys. Not that he was any good at it, but sometimes he just had to get away. Matter of fact, it was coming out of the pool hall that he first saw that girl. He was walking out, not really thinking about anything, and bam, there she was, walking, almost running really, towards him. His buddies had made some crude remarks but he didn't think that she noticed him in particular. That was fine. He wasn't ready to make his move anyways. He was of the opinion that she lived somewhere nearby. Very nearby. Probably a student.

No one was aware of his interest in this girl. Not his friends and especially not his old lady. More importantly, no one would ever know - if he did it right. He wouldn't mess it up like last time. Luckily, no one had found out about the old lady . . . except Monica . . . and she didn't believe him.

But this girl, she was pretty and . . . he was sure she was the same one from the party . . . when he finally found her, he would show her what a man he was. Sure he hated all Anglo bitches, but this one . . . she would respect him . . . he would teach her to respect him.

***

UNM CAMPUS   APRIL 3, 1981

Julie cleaned her desk and neatened her area. *A clean desk is a happy desk,* she thought. For some reason Mr. Halley didn't give her enough to do, so she was always scrounging additional work from her co-workers. Might as well stay busy, have to be here anyways, she always said. Although not much of a party girl, she was happily anticipating the upcoming weekend. Knowing she would probably be studying most of the time, she had firm plans to go out to dinner with her fiancé, James, and high hopes that her sisters would be able to join them as well. She worked so hard during the week that she had to schedule in some fun. She also hoped to squeeze in some time to see her good buddy, Colene.

Doing mostly clerical tasks, Julie worked on campus about twelve hours a week at the Student Housing Services. It was fine with her that it wasn't too complicated; she was already going to school full time and didn't need any extra thinking. When she finished up her schooling, that's when she would be able to use her brain and get paid for it. But that would take a while. Her major was biology, and she planned to go to medical school after graduating from UNM. Right now, she was only looking to make a little extra money to pay for books and personal items.

Mr. Halley, her supervisor, was pleased with her as an employee. She was a hard worker, didn't complain and the other people in the office liked her. She completed all assignments immediately and correctly. He wished all of his student-workers could be like her, but they weren't. They were mainly self-absorbed and lazy, which was typical. But she wasn't typical, she was dedicated, and Mr. Halley really appreciated that about her. He remembered the time she came in on the weekend with a fever of 101 and helped him finish an important grant project, when no one else would. He bought her a box of chocolates to show his appreciation. It was the least he could do. He would have been sunk without her.

"Have a great weekend Mr. Halley," Julie called out and flashed her big smile.

"You too, Julie . . . I'll see you on Tuesday," Mr. Halley said, returning her smile and lifting his hand in a wave.

***

VASSAR DRIVE, UNM AREA APRIL 4, 1981

James and Julie walked into Danbi's Pizza and looked around the crowded, noisy restaurant. It was kind of smoky but they could stand it. A few steps in, Julie let go of James' hand and ran over to her two sisters who stood in the corner talking. She put one arm around each of their shoulders. They smiled and hugged her back. The sisters' dates nodded hello as they stood off to either side.

"Did you guys order yet?" Julie asked.

"No, nut-ball, we were waiting for you," her sister said with a playful smile.

"Well, I'm starving, so let's eat. I don't want to waste away," Julie said.

Her sisters laughed.

When the pizzas finally arrived, they ate like bears and played goofy drinking games. One game involved trying to down a glass of beer before James finished whistling the song, "Dancing Queen".

After a few more beers, they all got into it. Julie wasn't drinking but she thought maybe she had a contact high from all the spilled beer and was feeling goofy right along with them. They stayed until closing. Julie and James could not remember having so much fun. On the walk home, the young couple discussed their glorious future together.

CHAPTER 4

"I sure hope these little black pills work," Julie said, pulling the bottle out of the paper bag. "Keep me from falling asleep in class."

"Just so they don't keep you awake all night . . . or keep me awake, because you can't sleep," James said.

Julie rolled her eyes. "I'll be all right. The pharmacist says they're like a half a cup of coffee. It's only over-the-counter, so I'm sure it's fine."

"I just don't want the over-the-counter to put you over the top," James said.

***

It was a beautiful spring day, a little bit cooler than usual maybe, but not bad. Colene had to study for an upcoming biology test but she didn't want to miss out on her sun time, so she sat on her front porch with her left leg propped on a milk crate, her crutches leaning nearby.

The usual cast of Stanford Street characters blew by as Colene studied. She had to read Chapter 7, *Genes -The Basic Unit of Heredity*, in her biology book. The reading was pretty dry. Occasional street diversions helped.

Joggers, strolling little old ladies and tons of dog walkers rambled by. There were a few "special" people that happened by as well. Like Derrick, the guy who wore only a Speedo brief, no matter the weather. Derrick sauntered by first, his chest hairs pointing straight out in the early spring chill. He was followed by Helen, the opera singing jogger, who today performed a boisterous aria from La Boheme - and in fine form, Colene noted. Then there was Leo, an oversized biker-type with massive amounts of body hair, muscles and tattoos, walking his teacup poodle, Missy, whom he referred to as his wife. The distractions on the street just made the day more pleasant and the sun felt great. Time flew by despite the boring homework.

After three hours though, Colene grew weary and thought seriously of making it an early bedtime. Between fried eyes and having to constantly use those damn crutches, she was toast. She went inside, boiled water for the Top Ramen that would be her dinner, grabbed her sketch book and collapsed on the couch.

While the Ramen cooked, she reviewed the drawing she had been working on for weeks. It was a self-portrait and was proving a tough task to get just right. She looked in the mirror, then she looked at a photo of herself and then she looked at the drawing. All three were so very different. She guessed that was okay. The mirror is what you are, the photo is what you were and the drawing is anything you want it to be. Maybe with a few tweaks, the drawing would more closely resemble the final product she had in mind. Colene became immersed in the tweaking. A little darkening here, a little erasing there, a little slurping of the Top Ramen and it was all starting to come together. When the phone rang a couple of hours later, she almost didn't answer, but at the very last minute picked up.

"Hello," she said.

"Hi . . . Hi, Julie."

"Yeah, I'm good."

"Nothing, just drawing . . . I'm drawing me . . . don't know why."

"You can see it when I'm done."

"No, I don't wanna go out tonight . . . too tired."

"No, really."

"Really, really!"

"Okay . . . alright, alright, okay . . . I will . . . for a little while . . . but just cause you want to . . . but my foot's killing me. I guess I can make it that couple blocks to the Frontier . . . in an hour or so? Okay, I'll be ready. Ready as I can be."

***

TINGLEY COLISEUM, NEW MEXICO STATE FAIRGROUNDS   APRIL 5, 1981 7:30 PM

James and his brother drove together that evening to Tingley Coliseum to attend the Rush concert. James paid the $2 for parking and went inside the auditorium.

But then . . . something didn't feel right. James told his brother that he couldn't to go to the concert after all. His brother wanted to know why and James didn't know why. He told his brother that he couldn't explain it but he did *not* want to go the concert. His brother reminded him that they had been looking forward to seeing this group for months and that Rush always put on a good show. He suggested that perhaps James take a few minutes and think it over. Maybe it was something he ate and maybe if he waited awhile, he would feel better. James said okay, he would wait. They sat down on the linoleum floor of the giant anteroom at Tingley Coliseum and played backgammon. While James processed his feelings, the concert went on without him.

***

MONTGOMERY AND LOUISIANA, NE HEIGHTS   APRIL 5, 1981 9:30 PM

Mike had worked all day and most of the evening and it hadn't really been that great for him. He had gotten into trouble about some missing money. Normally, he worked in the kitchen washing dishes but one of the bus boys hadn't shown up, so when it got really busy at dinnertime the boss had yelled "Hey, Mike. Go clean off those tables up front."

Mike didn't like people yelling at him but he took his hands out of the warm soapy water, dried them off and headed for the front of the restaurant, mouth turned down. He cleared the dinner plates and trudged back to the unending supply of dirty dishes.

Mike did not like the customers at this restaurant. Comme Chez Vous was a French restaurant located in the far North East Heights and catered to a high-end crowd. The customers were mostly white people who sometimes called him racist names. He thought that they thought they were better than him. Occasionally, when he was in the dining area, he would hear things like, "Hey Pepe, get me some more coffee." Or like tonight when that fat bitch screamed, "Hey you, Paco, come here and clean up this broken glass."

"My name is Michael," he said, his face flushed with rage.

"I don't care what your name is boy, I need this glass picked up now or it's going to cut my kid," the angry woman yelled.

Mike turned and walked away without cleaning up the glass. These Anglos did not treat him as if he were human.

"Well, maybe I'm not human," Mike said.

He had taken a lot of trash talk from the customers that night, so when the boss confronted him at the end of his shift, he didn't know if he would be able to restrain himself or not.

"Mike, can you come into my office before you leave?" the boss asked.

"Sure," Mike said.

"There's missing tip money from a table that you bussed tonight, Mike. Do you have it?" the boss asked. "You're not allowed to touch the money. You know that, right? Mike?"

Mike ground his teeth and crossed his arms in front of his chest. "No," he said defiantly. "I didn't take no money. Why you asking me? Ask Eric . . . he was bussing too."

"Mike, Eric was on break then, you know that . . . and the waiter saw his customer put $10 on table 5. Any ideas what happened to it?"

"*No*," Mike said firmly.

"Okay," the boss said. "But if it happens again, you'll have a new problem."

Darkness spread over Mike's face like a time-lapse sunset. He glared menacingly at his boss. At last, he put on his jacket and stomped out of the office. As he crossed through the kitchen, he saw a small restaurant knife glimmering like a bright jewel on the butcher block table. Mike's brain told him that such a knife could come in handy, so up his sleeve it went. With an unlit cigarette clamped in his teeth, he did not look back as he hit the parking lot.

***

COLENE'S APARTMENT STANFORD STREET, UNM AREA   APRIL 5, 1981 8:30 PM

Her apartment was big enough for her and that was about it. Colene could barely afford the rent, but it was so very convenient - close to school and just two blocks from Central Avenue in an area called Nob Hill. The Albuquerque Nob Hill, not to be confused in any way with the swanky San Francisco version of the same name, was comprised mainly of students, with a fair amount of life-long residents as well. Although not considered a wealthy neighborhood, this Nob Hill was about as swanky as the Duke City got back in 1981.

Colene's front porch was a mess. She had recently re-potted her geraniums, and hadn't gotten around to cleaning it up yet. When Julie arrived, she had to step over piles of dirt in order to reach the doorbell.

After a couple of rings, Colene answered the door wearing a UNM sweatshirt.

"Come on in," Colene said, "How's it going? Sorry about the dirt . . . the maid comes in tomorrow." Julie wheeled her 10-speed into the house.

"Ha, ha, yeah right, I forgot how rich you are," Julie replied sarcastically. "Have you been studying much?"

"Yeah, all afternoon . . . genetics. I'm using that book you lent me. My brain's fried."

"Well, then a coffee break is a perfect idea. I'm glad I thought of it."

"Yeah, that's cool . . . but I don't want to use my crutches to walk over to the Frontier."

"Why not?"

"I am just so sick of them and I'm getting a rash under my arms. I want to try to walk down without them. Can I lean on you if I need to?"

"Of course, I'll help you. Are you sure you don't want me to bring the crutches in case you need them later?"

"No, no . . . it's only a block and half. I'll make it."

"Okay. If you say so. Are you ready to go?"

"Yeah, let me grab my jacket."

Colene locked her front door and she and Julie began the slow walk to the Frontier Restaurant. This was Colene's first time out without crutches, so she kind of hopped at first, then found a spot on her heel that didn't hurt too much and shuffle-stepped the rest of the way. They were in no rush. It was pretty dark on Stanford but there were a few other students walking around. The women didn't think much about their safety. As they walked, Julie talked.

Still buzzing from her date with James the previous night, Julie told Colene about the great time she had at Danbi's. She told her how she met up with her sisters and that they had stayed until closing playing a fun, dumb game. She asked Colene to go with them next time. Colene said she would.

A play had just let out at UNM's Popejoy Hall and Central Avenue was flooded with people. When the girls turned the corner onto the main street, it was so crowded they had to thread themselves through the crowd. They ducked into the Frontier Restaurant and waited in line to order. Established in 1971, the Frontier, at that time, was actually two store fronts pieced together into one coffee shop. Located directly across the street from the University of New Mexico, it had always been a hangout for students. Colene and Julie sat down in a window booth in the first section.

"People Watching 101" at the Frontier was practically a required course at UNM. Looking out the window, they saw loitering students who obviously didn't want to go back to their claustrophobic dorm rooms and, of course, they saw plenty of street people. A couple of them were checking out the food recycling bin, also known as the garbage can, in front of the restaurant. Ee-ew, some guy scooped up a half-eaten burger right in front of them. They were glad they had not ordered a burger. Julie noted that it still had its pickle attached. Ee-ew.

"Number 17," the PA system said.

Julie jumped up to retrieve their order. They were having the usual - coffee and a cinnamon bun. Cheap yet delicious. Julie was the talkative one tonight. Colene, book weary, just listened. Julie had a story and/or opinion on just about every person and subject she had ever encountered.

***

LINDA'S HOUSE DON GABAL, NW ALBUQUERQUE   APRIL 5, 1981 9:45PM

Mike headed south to I-25, then curled around the Big I and drove west on I-40. Exiting at Rio Grande Boulevard, he drove the few short blocks to his Mom's house, parked but did not immediately get out. His uncle had given him a case of Coors the day before and Mike had told his mom he would bring her by a six pack after work, but it didn't look like anyone was home. Maybe she had gone out somewhere with Willie, the guy she was currently sleeping with. Or maybe they were already in bed or down the street at the bar?

After smoking a cigarette, Mike got out of his car, grabbed a couple of beers and sat down on the front porch. He was thirsty and the beer tasted good. His mind started to slow down and he felt in control again. But then he thought about work. His boss had pissed him off, yelled at him, embarrassed him. But no, that wasn't it. It was the customers, those motherfucking Anglo customers that he hated. His rage meter began to elevate again.

Oh, and that ugly white bitch ordering me around like that. That's fucked up. He drank a second beer and his composure returned, reminding himself that he was "the man." It didn't matter what his mom, his girlfriend or any other dumb bitch said. He was in charge. He was the man.

The beer began to smooth Mike out. As he said later, he was able to get a little bit a shit off his mind, but he still wanted to see his mom. Opening the trunk of his car, he pulled out a six pack and despite the fact that the house was dark, he went in. Once inside, he heard sounds, TV sounds. He followed the noise to find the people.

"What's going on?" Mike asked Willie, sprawled on the bed next to his sleeping mom, Linda.

Willie said nothing. His eyes were half-mast as he watched the flickering images of men wrestling on TV. Empty beer cans surrounded the bed.

"Is she crashed?" Mike asked, pointing at his mom.

Willie nodded and patted the bed, motioning for Mike to sit down.

"Um, Willie," Mike said, pushing aside some takeout bags, "I brought you guys over some Coors."

"Far out," Willie said. "We need more beer. We almost out."

"Yeah," Mike said quietly and hung his head.

"Wassamatter wid you, Mike?" Willie slurred.

"I'm tired, Willie."

"What you say? Tired a what?"

"I'm tired a people fucking with me," Mike said.

"What you mean by that?"

"I'm fucking tired, Willie. Nobody'll give me credit . . . or not much credit, when I do shit for them."

"Mike, just hang on in there, man. People might won't care about you, but we do. Wass happening? Tell me."

"No, I'll be okay," Mike said, setting his jaw with determination. "I gotta go home . . . see my old lady."

"I got ya, Mike," Willie winked. "Come by tommorra, kay?" Willie held out his fist for Mike to tap. Mike tapped him weakly and walked out.

***

FRONTIER RESTAURANT, UNM AREA   APRIL 5, 1981 10 PM

Julie told Colene a story about a guy she knew from Farmington named Allen. He went to UNM and he was in a few of her classes. What a pothead he was. Stoned from the time he got up to the time he got off. She had known him since the fifth grade when his nickname was Stinky, Stinky Rogers. Not because he smelled bad or even because his last name was Rogers but because that's what everybody called him. He got the Rogers because he wore cardigan sweaters all the time like Mr. Rogers and he got the Stinky because his Hungarian mother sent him to school with stinky leftover dinners. Julie said it was the day he brown-bagged in the paprika catfish that got him messed up. The catfish smelled bad - flat out stunk, even his teacher held her nose. So, for the remainder of elementary school, he was stuck with Stinky.

Colene laughed and asked Julie, since she had the two good feet, if she wouldn't mind getting them another round of coffee. "No problem," Julie said and took their two cups to the coffee refill station. Refills were free at the student-friendly Frontier.

Turning serious, Julie told Colene that her grandmother had died recently. She would miss her, she said, but she felt at peace with her passing. The two had been very close when Julie was younger, spending most of their summers together in Texas. Colene saw the sadness in her friend's face and could tell, despite what she said; she was affected by her grandmother's passing. She put her arm around her buddy and gave her a hug.

"Graveyards are very tranquil, you know," Julie said in mid hug. Colene pulled back, trying not to look too weirded out. "No, I mean it," Julie continued. "I go all the time. I go to the one right behind my house . . . The Fairview." Colene gave her a baffled look and Julie explained what she meant. She told her that she went there to study when she really needed to focus. That it helped clear her head.

"I know it sounds crazy . . . but the green grass and the big trees are calming to me and it's so quiet there," she said with an otherworldly look on her face. Okay, Colene thought, that makes some sense, but then Julie got freakier still.

"Sometimes I can feel their presence," she said.

"Whose presence?" Colene asked.

"The dead people." Julie smiled and continued. "Sometimes, if I listen closely, I can hear them talking. It's not scary or anything . . . it's transcendental. It's like I'm visiting eternity." She looked at Colene for her reaction. Colene was perplexed. Julie invited Colene to go with her next time and Colene replied that she would think about it, but it didn't seem likely. Julie nodded and told her that if she changed her mind, she would gladly take her there.

***

JAMES AND JULIE'S HOUSE, GARFIELD AVENUE, UNM AREA   APRIL 5, 1981 10:30 PM

Having blown off the concert, James returned home early. Only the hallway light was on when he walked in. Julie must already be in bed, he thought. He hung his jacket on the hook and whispered loudly, "Hi, honey, I'm home," and walked towards the bedroom. His head did an involuntary jerk as he came to a stop in the doorway. Despite the fact that the room was dark, he could plainly see that no one was there.

"Where are you?" James said and walked the entirety of the small house - no Julie. He did not think she was playing a game, but again he said, "Where are you?" Her bike? Where was her bike? He looked on the back porch where she kept it. Gone. He looked on the refrigerator for a note. They always left each other notes about their whereabouts and/or affirming their unending love for the other, on the refrigerator. There was still one on there from last week. "Hi honey," it read, "Went to library. Back at 6, Love you – Julie." He read the note a few times and it made him feel both better and worse. There was no new note. This wasn't like her.

Then he remembered that he wasn't supposed to be home yet. She probably went out with one of her friends and would be back shortly. He sat down by the front door and opened a book.

***

CENTRAL AVENUE, UNM AREA   APRIL 5, 1981 10:45 PM

He *should* go home . . . he knew that . . . but he wanted to cruise first. A twisted little thought was stuck in his twisted little brain. The thought throbbed like an erection. He wanted to look for that girl again.

While driving away from his mom's house, his mind spun. He thought about all the Anglo chicks that had riled him recently - they were starting to blend together. He needed to get his hands on one of them . . . soon.

Dirty Mexican. Nobody called him a dirty Mexican and got away with it. At the restaurant, where he worked, he had been very close to exploding. That fat white bitch, with her nose up in the air, had all but said it, when she rudely called him Paco. And then there was that old lady at the party and, and . . . He had to shake himself in order to focus while he drove. He was getting madder and madder. He realized that he needed to get rid of his negative "anger" vibes and channel them into more productive "vengeance" vibes.

Turning east on Central, with renewed purpose, he drove the six and half miles to his ultimate destination, the University of New Mexico. He slowed down upon reaching the outskirts of campus.

He was afraid he might not recognize her if he drove too fast. It was cold out, freezing really, and everyone had extra clothing. It was hard to tell who was who. But arrogantly, maybe even presciently, he told himself that he would see her soon.

He was already a little bit excited as he rolled his window down and looked hard at the students and student wannabes walking the sidewalks in the UNM area. Youthful chatter from the street drifted into his car, but he tuned it out, he had to focus. He wanted so badly to find her tonight. Anyone that knew him could tell you that he did not like waiting but he was on a mission. So many big groups of people. *Was she among them?* He slowed to a crawl at the four block stretch in front of the university. He wanted to be meticulous. He cruised east, turned around, cruised west and repeated. Nothing. He was close to giving up when ... out of the corner of his eye . . . through the well-lit window of a restaurant . . .

'Mmmm, there she is," he said out loud. "And she has a friend with her . . . even better." He saw them sitting in a booth, inside the Frontier. He quickly found a parking spot on Central, right in front of the restaurant, and turned off his engine. He would wait.

***

Frontier Restaurant, UNM Area   April 5, 1981 11:05 PM

As Colene continued to sip her cold coffee she said, "You know what, Julie? I've got to get home and get some sleep. I have class tomorrow morning at 8 and so do you."

"Okay. I know, let's go," Julie said. "But I could stay here all night talking to you."

"I know," said Colene. "But I'm exhausted . . . we'll do it again soon."

"Okay, yeah, let's do that," Julie said.

As they got up from the table, Julie bussed their plates and Colene grabbed a Daily Lobo. They headed out the front door.

CHAPTER 5

He watched with unblinking eyes as the two girls left the Frontier. The one he wanted wore a blue down jacket and glasses. He liked the glasses. *Must be smart*, he thought. Normally, the smarter chicks didn't care for him, but this time it didn't matter.

He saw that the other one limping badly. *She won't cause any trouble*, he decided. *Something's wrong with her.* The one with the glasses did all of the talking. Neither one of them paid any attention to him as he leered at them from his parked car.

***

Because of Colene's limping gait, the girls made their way home slowly. Julie didn't mind the plodding pace at all . . . it just gave her more time to chat.

"I don't know how I will get that ten-page history paper done by next Friday," Julie said, beginning a new monologue. "That darn teacher gives too much homework. I've already been to the library three times and I only have five pages done so far. I guess I'll just have to be creative and stretch it out to ten."

"This paper is supposed to be about inventions from the 19th century," she continued. "Did you know a guy named Humphry Davy invented the first electric light? I didn't either. It wasn't Thomas Edison like everyone thinks . . . he just improved it. It was this other guy who no one even knows a thing about. What a drag to do something that monumental and still never have been heard of. I wonder if I will ever be famous. Ha, ha."

"Ha, ha," Colene said, otherwise only nodding and making encouraging sounds as her friend rambled on. Julie *was* exceptionally talkative tonight, Colene thought, but that was fine, that's just Julie.

As they made their way back to Colene's apartment there were plenty of other people out walking on Central; regardless that it was both cold and late. Just to the north of where Colene and Julie walked was the front entrance to the University of New Mexico campus. In general, UNM students, including Colene and Julie, felt safe walking in the vicinity of their school. Neither one of them spent any time worrying about possible dangers as they walked home that night.

***

STANFORD STREET, UNM AREA   APRIL 6, 1981 11:18 PM

The girls turned south onto Stanford Street, the street where Colene lived. They were about a block away from Colene's house when a tall Spanish-looking man in a dark heavy coat walked toward them on the sidewalk.

"Hi," he mumbled, causing Colene and Julie's stomachs to ball up. Neither girl stopped nor looked directly at the man as he walked by. Colene wet her lips and kept hobbling, perhaps at a slightly faster pace. Julie moved quicker, too.

Abruptly, the man flipped direction. From behind and with blinding speed, he grabbed the two young women tightly around their necks. Towering above them by more than a foot, he had one woman in each arm and the blade of his knife at Julie's throat. Julie's color ashened and her eyes filled with tears. The evening had changed in an instant, from a pleasant night out with her friend, to her worst nightmare.

"Just keep walking, ladies," the man said with a slight Spanish accent. "Keep quiet and don't scream. Do what I say and no one will get hurt. "The stone-cold knife persuaded the blind-sided girls into silence.

"I'm just lookin' for someone to talk to," he said in a low voice. "I don't want anything from you, ladies. Okay? I'm just lonely. Everything's gonna to be okay. Just do what I say." The three of them walked as one, north on Stanford, while he maintained his double choke-hold, occasionally switching the knife back and forth between the girl's throats as an incentive for cooperation.

Colene never imagined a scenario like this. She had no training on how to act or react. Her first instinct was to struggle - to try to get away. She jerked herself free, but he grabbed her again, pushing the blade into her face, pricking her cheek with its tip - twice. If there had been any question as to whether or not the man would use his knife, that had been answered.

"Stop fighting me, bitch," he said as two thin streams of blood appeared on Colene's face.

"Slow down, Buddy," Colene said, wiping the blood away. She was mad, not only because she was being forced down the street by some goon but her injured foot could not keep his pace. She wished she had taken her crutches with her; they might have made a good weapon. But it was too late to think about that now.

"My name's not Buddy," the man replied venomously and squeezed his arms tighter yet around the girls' necks.

"What is your name then? You have to have a name." He did not answer.

Both Colene and Julie looked hard at the darkened houses as they passed by each one. No one putting their cat out, no one pulling into their driveways, no one at all.

He herded them unchallenged down the deserted street, ultimately walking them over to his waiting Ford convertible. He opened the driver's side door and forced Julie inside.

Colene again tried to get away, but again, at the last second, the man grabbed her and curled her back into his body with his large arm. Colene attempted to wrestle with the man to get his attention away from Julie. If she could free her friend, she thought, maybe she could get away too.

"Run Julie," Colene shouted, continuing to struggle with the man. "Open your door. Get out. Go. Run away."

Julie lifted her right hand towards the passenger-side door, but after a long look, her hand dropped back into her lap. She stared directly ahead.

"Go," Colene yelled again.

"Get in the car and shut the fuck up," the man said hatefully. He did *not* look concerned about any escaping via the passenger-side door. That possibility had been eliminated earlier with a few turns of the screwdriver.

Finally, Colene saw what Julie saw - the passenger door had been tampered with. The door handle, the window crank and the panel itself had been removed. There was no way to get out that side of the car.

Once inside, the man did not start his car. He sat behind the wheel, frowning.

"Can either one a you drive?" he asked at last.

Julie opened her mouth but was silenced by Colene's sharp elbow.

"Nope, we can't," Colene said.

"We're taking a ride, ladies," the man announced flatly. "I'm sorry, I'm really sorry. Don't worry, don't panic. I'm just looking for some nice girls to talk to."

Colene was in pain. He had already slashed her face, what else would he do? She wanted to make a break for it. She wanted out of the car, but the knife wedged under his leg told her she needed to wait.

***

JAMES AND JULIE'S HOUSE, GARFIELD AVENUE, UNM AREA   APRIL 5, 1981 11:20 PM

"Think," James told himself. "Think." Logically speaking, what were the possible reasons why Julie might not be home? There had been no fight and even if there had been, she still would have left a note. Nope, this wasn't like her.

She must have gone to someone else's house. Colene's maybe? He remembered that she said she might. Looking at the phone numbers taped to the kitchen wall, he dialed Colene's number. Ten rings, maybe twenty - nothing. Exhaling, he tried to calm himself. Maybe they were sleeping. Maybe Colene unplugged her phone. Maybe the phone was out of order. James didn't know what to do, so he decided to get some sleep and look for her at first light if she wasn't back. Which she would be.

***

CENTRAL AVENUE, OLD ROUTE 66   APRIL 5, 1981 11:40 PM

Trapped inside the stranger's car, Colene knew she had a job to do. She knew she needed to start memorizing details . . . for when they got away. The police would need a description, so she studied him. Hispanic, young, close to her own age, short dark hair, mud brown eyes and a head that hung forward as if it were too heavy for its own neck. Big lips on a big mouth that hung open like a big hole. So tall that his head pushed into the roof of the car. He did not seem like a college student.

Shifting into first gear, the man took a left on Cornell. He told the girls that he didn't have any friends . . . and that he was scared. He repeated that he wouldn't hurt them and he told them to just relax. "I just want somebody to talk to and if you guys want to call the police or whatever, you can," he said. At no point, were there any opportunities to call the police.

As he drove, the man peered out both windows, with one eye glued to the rear view mirror. Occasionally, he would flip his head around and stare behind him. He told the girls he thought he was being followed. After making a quick cut down an alley, he seemed to relax, perhaps believing he had given his pursuers the shake. He lit a cigarette and blew a couple of smoke rings.

How can we get out of this? Colene thought and then remembered some training she had received at the Agora Crisis Center. They taught students how to deal with people in distress. "Keep them talking," Colene remembered the Agora Center staff members instructing. "Find out what interests them, what they like . . . just keep them talking."

"Why are you so lonely?" Colene asked, trying to implement her training. "Why don't you have any friends?"

"I don't know," he replied. "Nobody likes me. Nobody wants to be my friend." He made a left turn onto Coal and began traveling east.

"What's your names, ladies?" he asked. The question blew an icy chill into Colene's stomach. Julie looked uneasy as well. "It" was trying to find out personal information. Names were normally reserved for people you liked.

"Julie," Julie rasped and then looked ill.

"Pat," Colene said in almost a spit, and at the same time thought, *fuck you, weirdo, I'm not telling you my real name.*

Looking him in the eye, Colene asked, "What's your name, Mister?"

The man pushed his lips into almost to a cartoon pucker. "Raymond," he said and then sucked them back into his mouth. "My name is Raymond," he repeated.

"You seem kinda scared, Raymond. What do you want?" Colene asked.

"Nothing," he replied with a hint of anger in his voice. "I'm just looking for someone to talk to. I don't have friends. I can't trust nobody." It was dark inside the car, the only light coming from the faint blue glow of the radio, which was silent. "I'm sorry I have to do this ladies, I really am," he said. As he spoke, Colene detected alcohol on his breath, but he did not seem drunk.

"I can't believe you don't have any friends, someone must be your friend." Colene said, sounding more like a counselor than a kidnap victim.

"No, I don't. Even the bums at the bars don't like me," he said. "I don't know why no one likes me."

The man told the girls that he enjoyed doing auto body work but right now he worked in a restaurant, "just to make some extra money." He said that he had just moved to town three weeks ago from New York City and he didn't know hardly anyone in Albuquerque. He told them that he had grown up in El Paso and his parents still lived there.

***

The man looked at Julie and asked her where she was from and mechanically she replied "Farmington."

Julie had spoken little thus far, only speaking when spoken to. Her mind was elsewhere. She was thinking about other things. She thought about her parents and her siblings. She thought about her husband-to-be, James, how he was probably home by now, and how worried he must be. She didn't want him to be upset. She thought about how much she loved them all. She knew she had done nothing wrong but felt bad for the amount of pain it would most likely cause everyone when they found out. She knew she needed to get a grip. Her heart was beating way too fast. She knew she needed to think about escaping, but that didn't seem possible unless she could calm down. Then out of nowhere, her third grade poem floated into her head. The last line of it anyway. *Just home and safe I ought to be.* That's right, she thought. *Just home and safe I ought to be.* It saddened her but comforted her a little too. It also comforted her to have Colene's hand to hold onto.

***

Meanwhile, Colene continued to study the kidnapper. His face was oval, his eyebrows bushy and his teeth enormous, like horse teeth. He had a big white scar over the bridge of his nose and he wore a light colored T-shirt. She could see a cheap gold watch pinching his right wrist and even though it was dark, she noted that his car was black and white with a round hood ornament.

"Why don't you have any friends?" Colene asked the man. He didn't know, he said. As they drove onward, the street they traveled on, Coal, name-changed into Zuni. He reminded her that he was new in town and he hadn't had a chance to meet many people yet.

"Hey," he said suddenly. "I don't know these streets. I'm lost."

"We don't know them either," the previously silent Julie said, surprising both Colene and the kidnapper. Their heads turned in unison toward her. "I think we're coming up on Highland High," she said. They stared at her, waiting for more words but none came. Julie resumed staring straight ahead, her hand squeezing Colene's knee even tighter.

Why is he doing this? Colene thought. *What is in his little mind? I'm really scared and he has Julie close to terror. I've got to keep him talking. That's our best chance. What else can I do?* They were at Zuni and Wyoming now, getting further and further away from the UNM campus.

"Where are we driving to?" Colene asked.

"I don't know, we're just driving," he said.

"Maybe we could stop at Sambos or something, get some directions, have some coffee and talk," Colene offered.

"No," he said. "I can't do that, can I? Someone might see us there together and I can't have that." He continued driving east.

It was at this point that Colene started to get nervous. Really nervous. Not because she didn't think they were in terrible trouble before, but because she knew that the street they were on, Zuni, was about to merge into Central and they were starting to "run out of town." They were about to leave Albuquerque.

She informed him that Zuni was about to end and he needed to turn around. He didn't acknowledge this information and when they got to the intersection of Zuni and Central, he drove on. They drove past a string of dumpy neon-lit motels, squat cinder block auto repair shops and finally the open-all-night Allsups Convenience Store. Each passing business knocking a rung off the ladder of hope for Colene and Julie.

As they neared the edge of town, the kidnapper turned philosophical. "Do you believe in God?" he asked the girls. They both replied that they did. He said that he personally knew God, loved him and that God was his friend.

"Yes, God is our friend," Julie said. As the discussion turned to God, Colene thought that it seemed to settle Julie a bit. "You are right, God is your friend," Julie told him in a strong steady voice.

"Mister," Colene interrupted, "We're almost to Tramway, you need to turn around, this is the end of town."

***

You dumb, stupid cunt, he thought. *I know where I am. I live two blocks away. Christ, I can fucking see my house from here. I know where I am and I know where I'm going. Man, I wish this dumb bitch would shut the fuck up.* His eyes flashed and his breathing increased as he drove past the point where he lived, but he said nothing. Without pausing, he proceeded onto the Tramway on-ramp.

"You know you're getting on the freeway?" Colene said, shifting in her seat.

"Oh, not really, I'm just driving," he lied. "It doesn't really matter where I drive." And just like that, they were on Interstate 40, going east at 65 miles per hour. "The freeway is beautiful," he proclaimed. "The freeway is like God . . . it never stops." The girls looked at each in disbelieving horror. Colene and Julie both knew that by getting on the freeway they had just entered a new level of danger. Once they left town, the idea of him "just wanting to talk to them" faded as fast as the twinkling lights of Albuquerque.

CHAPTER 6

Not slowing down at all, the man pulled off the freeway at the Carnuel exit. He stopped at the stop sign and then inexplicably turned right onto Old Route 66, heading back into Albuquerque. After driving about a quarter of a mile west, he slammed on his brakes and made an abrupt U-turn heading east again, away from Albuquerque. Colene's heart leapt and then sunk again at this rapid succession of events. For an instant, she thought that he had come to his senses and she and Julie had been saved from the unpopulated abyss of Tijeras Canyon. But that was not to be.

The three unlikely night-travelers drove in virtual silence on Old Highway 66. He was going faster now, maybe even speeding. Street lights became few and far between and as the canyon darkened, the atmosphere inside the car turned black as well. The night ride became hideously surrealistic, like some B-grade science fiction movie turned into some D-grade horror movie. Approaching objects whizzed by, distorting into eerie bending lights. Cars, traffic signs and structures grew grotesquely large as they loomed ahead, pulsating briefly with an unworldly glow and then entirely swallowed up by the dark, as if they had never existed at all.

Colene had no concept of time. Her hand gripped her friend's hand which was gripping her knee. She prayed this maniac would turn around yet again, drive back to town and let them go. But he did not. They drove over the over-pass, through the entirety of Carnuel, with its tumble-down houses, corrugated tin roofs and trashy double-wides teetering on condemnation. She recognized the taxidermy place as they sped by and she knew they were fast approaching the notorious Dead-man's Curve. After that, there was nothing. Nothing but unlit, desolate straight-away, heading even further east, even deeper into the isolated bowels of Old Route 66.

"Is this your car?" Colene asked, breaking the trance.

"Yeah," he answered.

"When did you get it?"

"This week."

"Did you do the body work?"

"I haven't had time . . . but the seats are new," he said with a slight smile. Colene looked at the seats and saw only shabby brown vinyl seat covers. "They look nice," she replied. "Did you get them when you were in New York?"

"What?" he replied, flustered. "New York? No."

Then Colene saw it. Actually they all saw it . . . the bright headlights of another vehicle looming large in the rear view mirror. The other car was actually so close that its lights lit up the interior of the convertible. The kidnapper appeared nervous . . . very nervous.

"I don't like this," he said. "Someone's following us." He pulled off Old 66 and onto a dirt side road.

"No one's following us," Colene whispered. He said nothing, turning off the engine and the lights. They sat in silence until the other car drove past and then let out a sigh of relief. The girls did not.

***

TIJERAS CANYON   *APRIL 6, 1981 12:08 AM*

Recovered but still shaken, he started his car and backed quickly down the frontage road. So quickly, it seemed he might go off the road

"Hey, Mister. Watch out. You're going to go off the edge," Colene said.

"Shut up," he said bitterly and jerked the car into first gear. "And stop staring at me. I don't like nobody staring at me." He turned onto the first dirt path and guided it straight down, with his car coming to rest among piles of rocks. They were in a rock quarry in an arroyo.

The girl next to him, Colene, kept asking him questions . . . and staring at him. She pissed him off. He was in no mood for conversation. It didn't matter what he said before - about wanting to talk. He certainly did not want to talk now. The girls eyed him apprehensively, waiting for his next move. They watched as he squeezed the steering wheel and grunted. Finally, he pulled the knife from under his leg and frowned.

"Okay, ladies," he said somberly, "The fun's over."

Colene and Julie looked at each other.

"Strip," he told Julie. "Take off your clothes." He pressed the flat of his knife onto her neck. She hesitated. "Take 'em off. Now," he said angrily. Still, she hesitated. "Take. Your. Fucking clothes off. NOW! Before I put this fucking knife in your friend's gut." He pushed the tip of his knife against Colene's chest, just below her heart.

Julie then took off her clothes. "Faster!" He switched hands and held the knife in front of her face. "Throw 'em in the back seat."

"Now *you* . . . strip." Redirecting his knife towards Colene. "I don't want no talk. *No* more talk. *Strip!*"

"What for?" Colene asked.

"Shut up," he said and poked the blade towards her. "You're pissing me off. Strip, I said."

"I won't," Colene said.

"I really don't like you. You're a smart ass. Go 'head. Try something." He moved the knife toward Julie.

"Okay, okay, leave her alone," Colene said, slowly pulling her sweatshirt over her head.

"Do what I said or one a you is gonna get hurt. Hurry the fuck up," he yelled.

The man was secretly relieved that they were buying into the "playing one against the other" game. He would remember to always get two girls at a time in the future. It actually made it easier.

He opened his door. "Get out," he said to Colene and pulled her out. Julie stayed inside.

"You come with me," he said and locked Colene's arm behind her while he held the knife to her back. Herding her to the rear of the car, he opened the trunk.

"Get in," he said.

"What for?" she asked.

"I said . . . get in."

"No."

"I don't just have this knife you know," he said, "I have a gun."

"Let me see it," Colene said.

"I don't like you. Get in the fucking trunk."

"It's too small . . . I won't fit," she informed him.

"Sure you will." And he shoved her towards the open trunk. "I'll *make* you fit. Get the fuck in."

As she continued to hesitate, his patience waned. He grabbed her arms and shoved her in like a big bag of laundry and then slammed the trunk door. She was right though, she didn't fit. The door hit her in the backside as it came down. She cried out. The locking mechanism punctured her back, gashing her above the hip. He paid no attention to her screams and shoved her in again, pushing harder this time. Colene searching for something, anything, to block the seal of the door when it came down, found a box and quickly slid it in the path of the closing door. But it didn't work. The force of the slam disintegrated the box. She was trapped.

Inside the trunk, in complete darkness, all hope of escaping gone, she had to keep herself from panicking - especially after she heard the key turn in the lock and him walk away.

***

JAMES AND JULIE'S HOUSE, GARFIELD AVENUE, UNM AREA   APRIL 6, 1981 12:15 AM

James, tired of trying to sleep, got up and called Colene again. No answer. He'd already called everyone else on the list, despite the late hour. A few had seen Colene or Julie earlier that afternoon but not together and nothing after 5 PM. He called Colene's parents. No, they had not heard from her today. Her mom said that she had called the day before, but nothing sounded amiss. She hadn't mentioned that she was taking any trips.

James finally decided to call the police. He wanted to report Julie missing. He wanted help. The Albuquerque Police Department gave him the standard response: the person had to be missing for 24 hours before they got involved. In his mind, James needed an answer sooner than that. This was not like Julie at all and he had a bad feeling.

***

TIJERAS CANYON   APRIL 6, 1981 12:23 AM

At a little over 6'5", he was tall, especially compared to Julie, who stood only 5'3". It wasn't difficult for him to overpower any woman, let alone one so much smaller than himself. He had been taller than almost everyone else for as long as he could remember. In the 4th grade, he was already 6'2" and his classmates made fun of him. It was only a schoolyard chiding, nothing more. They called him the Jolly Green Giant, things like that, and the girls giggled at him. He did not like girls giggling at him.

But tonight, everything was different. He had a hard-on from the time he stopped his car on Central. He was proud of himself so far. He had seen something he wanted and he took initiative and went out and got it. These white girls were too small and too weak to fight off the large and powerful man that he was. He would dominate them. They would not dare giggle at him. Sure he was scared, but that just made it more exciting. He would pull it off.

"Lay back," he whispered to Julie with the knife held inches from her face. "Just relax . . . just take it. I won't hurt you."

"Don't," she said. But there was no stopping him now. She inhaled his rank odor and numbly thought of other things. *Let it be quick*, she thought and it was. He couldn't hold back. It was over in less than a minute.

"Is that it?" she asked.

"Yeah," he said flatly. "Get out of the car," Stained and out of breath, he slid out the driver's side and pulled her with him.

"Let's take a walk," he said.

***

Car Trunk, Tijeras Canyon   April 6, 1981 12:25 AM

To say that being locked in the trunk of a car is scary and beyond comprehension, is not only stating the obvious, it's an understatement.

Stay calm . . . stay calm, Colene thought, forcing herself to breathe normally. Hearing him turn the key in the trunk had caused a medium sized panic attack. She knew she *had* to stay calm or she would have no chance at all.

She thought back to when she was a kid, to the games she had played. She remembered hiding from her brother and sister in a crazy country-style version of hide and seek. Wedging herself in a tiny slot beneath the horse feed bin, in a barn that was dark, tight and smelly, she had hid. Similar in conception, but a couple of light years different in perception. Hiding from your siblings: fun. Imprisoned in a trunk by some nut-job criminal: fucked.

Some good news though . . . the car was a "beater"; therefore, it was not air tight and she had plenty of oxygen to breath. Still, she had to force herself not to hyperventilate. The physical and psychological brutality she had endured so far, came close to overwhelming her. Inside the trunk, it was cramped and pitch-black and beyond that her back hurt tremendously from the trunk door hitting it.

Time passed without definition, she wasn't sure how long she had been in the trunk. Five minutes? Maybe even a half an hour. She couldn't tell. She worried about her friend and hoped that Julie would somehow find a way to get away. She wished hard for a miracle but had no concept as to how that might occur.

Right now, wishing was not helping, and furthermore, she couldn't possibly help her friend while trapped in this claustrophobic, coffin-like trunk. Forced to curl up fetal-position style, she lay against empty beer cans, gross half-eaten food and greasy motor oil containers.

She thought she heard Julie's voice, but she couldn't make out the words. Her heart pounded. Colene, attempting to fight off the fear of freaking out, tried controlling her breathing and thinking calming thoughts. Like about her family and her future - she had to force herself to believe she had a future. She knew she had to keep it together in case, somehow, someway, an opportunity presented itself to get away.

Then . . . and it was faint . . . she heard a door squeak open, followed by the sounds of footsteps walking away from the car.

Instinctively, Colene knew this would be her only chance to escape and she knew she had to act fast, even as she grimly assessed that no matter what she did, she had very little chance of success.

***

TIJERAS CANYON   APRIL 6, 1981 12:30 AM

In the lightless arroyo, the kidnapper forced Julie up a small hill. "At least, let my friend go," she said. He laughed but said nothing. His hand imbedded between her shoulder blades, he prodded her onward.

Naked and freezing, her teeth clattered involuntarily. He guided her roughly towards a large cedar tree and panted as he walked, not from exhaustion or anxiety, but from excitement. He couldn't wait.

"I'm cold," Julie said, hugging herself to stay warm.

"You won't be cold for long, babe," he said. "Now, shut the fuck up and keep walking."

She thought about kicking him somewhere hard, but he stayed behind her, so she never got the chance.

When they reached the tree at the top of the hill, he stopped and let her go. "Sorry babe," he said with a slight frown. "But I can't have no witnesses." and pulled the sharp knife with its four inch blade from his back pocket. Julie took off running. He laughed again. She didn't know where she was going but she ran as hard as she could. Quickly the man, the one that had already assaulted her, caught her. Grabbing her long hair, he yanked her back towards him. The knife, poised above his head, its cruel destiny already written, began its descent. Coming from behind, the blade traveled the short journey en route to its target - her heart. At the last second, she saw the knife curving towards her and tried to block it. He swatted her arm away like an annoying mosquito and sunk the blade deep inside her chest. She screamed once, more of an ear piercing punctuation mark than a verb and then crumpled to the ground. He reached down and calmly removed his knife from her body. Without wiping it off, he stuck it back in his back pocket.

A red puddle formed next to Julie's fallen body, her formerly expressive face . . . blank. Her future, once ripe with promise and endless dreams, erased. Caused by a teenage monster, who this night called himself Raymond, stealing the tomorrow of an innocent girl to appease his racist, woman hating need for power. But he wasn't done.

***

His sick mind churned. She looked dead, but he needed to be rock-solid certain. Flat on the ground next to her, grabbing both sides of her head, he pushed her down hard – face first into the ground. The plan was . . . if she tried to breathe, her lungs would fill with dirt. He knew this because a buddy of his had once casually mentioned to him how he had finished off a neighbor's annoying cat this way. The kidnapper, now killer, held Julie's head until it was still . . . dead still and then got up, lit a cigarette and strolled back to his car for the other one. *It's almost like sex*, he thought. *I'm ready to go again.*

***

CAR TRUNK, TIJERAS CANYON   APRIL 5, 1981 12:32 AM

Slowly and methodically she touched every square inch of his smelly, despicable trunk. Having no previous experience with trunk insides, she did not precisely know what she was looking for. She knew she had found something promising when she felt some loose canvas at the very back, behind the spare tire. The car was empty now. Julie and the kidnapper had left to parts unknown. *Gotta get out.* Colene thought. *Gotta escape. Gotta find Julie.*

Colene's hands moved quickly to shred the canvas and then she punched an opening big enough to squeeze her body out. Climbing through the newly created hole, she found herself in the backseat of the car . . . alone. The drivers' side door was open. After allowing herself a deep breath of clean air, she spied her clothes. She put on her pants and scanned for the return of Julie and/or the kidnapper. She was about to slip on one of her shoes, when she saw something and her body tightened. She saw a lit cigarette, its glow swinging back and forth in the distance. It was him. The ember swung leisurely at first and then it stilled.

***

The man stopped and puffed his cigarette as he puzzled out the movements inside his car. Belatedly, he realized that the girl in the trunk was getting away.

"Hey, what the fuck are you doing?" he called out and ran towards her.

***

She jumped over the front seat, leapt out the open door and sprinted into the night. Despite the fact that her foot was broken, she had to put that out of her mind and run like it wasn't. She knew she had to break away - run fast, like when she anchored her high school relay team, but faster. This time she was running for her life. Her goal was Old 66. Hoping to put some distance between herself and the knife wielding maniac, she zigzagged through the quarry. She ran and ran but sadly, the busted foot *was* slowing her down. She was the injured rabbit and he the bloodthirsty coyote.

Unfortunately, the stress fracture, combined with the darkness, lack of terrain knowledge and good old fashioned bad luck, got her laid out prone. A pile of rocks she didn't see tripped her up and propelled her downward onto her belly. He was on her like wrong on right.

***

For a few stressful seconds, after she first took off, the man wondered if she *might* get away. She had actually outdistanced him by a good thirty yards. Panic crept in his chest when he realized that he could no longer see her. *Don't worry,* he told himself, *I'm the man, I'll catch her.* No doubt about it, he was the man. The big creepy man with the very sharp knife.

But before he could catch her, he had to run. Lucky for him, he thought, he'd put on his tennies and not his oversized clunky boots, like he sometimes wore to work. Pumping his long legs to cut her lead, he realized that he was not the athlete that his prey was. In the close to pitch darkness conditions, he had trouble maintaining sight contact. But he got a break. "Oof," he heard, followed by a loud thunking sound. Tracking the noise, he found her, panting softly, out of breath and splayed face down on a pile of rocks.

With his large body looming over hers, he didn't waste a second, and slammed his knife into her upper back, deep into her ribs. She rolled left as he buried his blade inside her. The rolling caused the knife to both miss her vital organs and to slip out of his hand. He wildly tried to grab back the knife. "Fuck," he screamed and Colene got up and started to run again, the knife sticking straight out of her back as she fled.

Twenty yards was about all she got this time before he tackled her to the ground. He wanted his weapon back. Holding her down with his left hand, he pulled the black handle with his right, but it wouldn't come out. It was stuck.

She howled and kicked as he continued to waggle and yank. He told himself he needed to slow down and use two hands. As soon as his hands were off Colene's body, however, she rolled away and got up. Frazzled, he pulled her back down, but like a big angry cat that refuses to be held, she broke his grasp. He grabbed her again, grappling with her and pulling at his knife at the same time. Ultimately, the knife made the decision. It broke in two, part in the hand of the attacker and part in the back of Colene. The attacker retained control of the larger part, but his satisfaction was short lived. At the moment the blade snapped, perpetual motion caused the man to fall away from Colene and she was up and running again. But once more he caught her and threw her roughly to the ground.

"God damn it already, bitch," he said. "You don't get it, do you?" In a rage he reached down and slit her throat. Her face imploded with pain. He paused momentarily, watching the blood first spurt out, then bubble up and finally dribble back down her neck like spilled paint, but he did not stop. He raised his knife again, this time aiming for her belly. Reflexively, her arm went up to obstruct the blade, but that did not help her. The sharp knife sliced through her hand and into her gut. Lots of blood and bad noises followed. First, she moaned a hideous moan and then the sick hissing sound of air escaping from her stomach could be heard.

But she would not stop. She got back up, and again tried to get away, and again he seized her. "Son of a bitch, lady," he said in a deep growl and shoved the knife in her back a second time. Pulling down with great force, he slashed a deep, foot long gash on her backside. This time, she seemed to stay down, so he grabbed her head and pushed her face savagely into the dirt, trying to smother her. *This worked with the other one*, he thought, *I'll do it again*. Not this time. Colene still had too much fight left in her and she twisted away again. He paused to regroup.

***

Lying on the ground, fighting the monster, Colene didn't have much time to consider the pain that shot through her body. She was in survival mode. Occasionally, the question "why" would flicker in her mind but she couldn't dwell on it. The man's continuous assault gave her little allowance to react let alone think.

Finally, when he stopped for a minute, even though he still stood over her, Colene was able to gather herself and struggle to her knees.

"What do you want from me?" she asked, hands clenched together, choking back tears. "What did I do to you?"

He said nothing, so she asked again. "What do you want from me?"

"You know what I want," he answered bitterly. "All my problems are because of you Anglos," and he reached out and stabbed her again, once in each shoulder. No longer able to run and certainly unable to get up, her only defense was to deflect the incoming blade with her hands, but for that she paid a big price. He virtually cut off part of her right hand.

***

The man did have to admit that this lady had game. *But so do I*, he thought. *So do I*. With renewed confidence, he calmly walked over to where she lay and slit her throat again. This time from ear to ear.

***

MONICA'S APARTMENT, CENTRAL & TRAMWAY   APRIL 5, 1981 12 MIDNIGHT

Where was he? Drinking with that fucker Bobby again? Don't come home then. He was such an asshole, when he got drunk. And a horny one. At almost full term pregnant, she was definitely *not* in the mood.

But, where the fuck was he? Didn't he remember he was supposed to bring her something to eat? Thank God she went to Lotta Burger with her mom after shopping for baby clothes this afternoon. But she was still hungry. Did he want her to starve or something? Dammit. He said that he'd get her some of that fancy restaurant food from work. He should have called. Was he out screwing some whore because she was too fat and he didn't want her anymore?

Where was he? He should have been home by now. He was three hours late, goddammit. The baby had been kicking the hell out of her all day and she wanted him with her. He tells everyone how much that baby means to him, but he hardly comes home. Sometimes he acts like he doesn't give a damn about the baby. He sure doesn't give a damn about me.

Did he decide to stay overnight at his mom's house? Monica could maybe call Mike's mom and see if he was there, but his mom could be pretty bitchy. So, no to that. Probably just best to go to sleep and find him in the morning. After all, he'd stayed out all night plenty of times before and hadn't called. Why stress out about it now? That was just Mike. He did what he wanted.

***

TIJERAS CANYON   APRIL 6, 1981 12:45 AM

After slitting her throat a second time, followed by a couple of angry kicks to the gut, he flipped her over and thrust his blade deep into the backside of her neck and sliced across.

Covered in sweat, dirt and blood, he stood up and said, "Lady, you're gonna stay laid down, if I gotta cut off your whole fuckin' head off," and then hammered his knife into her upper body savagely and relentlessly. Towering over her, he narrowed his eyes and saw that she could barely move.

Her eyes locked onto his as she tilted her head upwards and begged, "Please . . . please, God . . . you've done enough . . . let me die in peace." The words, a spell breaker, caused him to stagger backwards.

Why is she not dead? he thought. She should be dead. It was starting to piss him off. He decided he needed to ramp up his efforts. Wiping his bloody hands on his pants, he went back at her, slashing her throat yet again and stabbing her repeatedly with a ferocity that matched his animosity.

Finally, finally . . . she stopped moving.

***

She was dying, she knew that. Even though her mind told her she could still fight back, her body said no.

So somewhere amidst the fierce stabbing, Colene made a split second decision, opting to switch tactics and commanding herself to not move a muscle. She remembered another game from her childhood. She had done it way back when . . . to scare her little brother and sister. They had bought it then and he would buy it now. She played dead.

***

Shaking badly, he leaned on his car door and wiped his forehead. Had he done enough? She was motionless. He was sure that he had. Maybe he should just get the hell out of there. He wanted to leave immediately but he had to be prudent, so he went back and took one last look.

He stood for a long time over her blood soaked body looking for any movement. He kicked her hard three, maybe twelve times. Then he stabbed her a couple more times in the chest, just to be double-dog certain. She did not respond or move. *She's dead,* he thought. *Really dead.*

In the end he had enjoyed the fight. It had been so fucking bitchin' every time she got up and tried to run away and then whack - Mike the Macho Man would stab her yet again. *Wham, slam, shank you ma'am,* he thought with great satisfaction. He got hard just thinking about it. Dumb white chick, asking all those dumb white chick questions. Poke, poke, poke. Why did she keep poking at him with her dumb-ass questions? It wasn't his fault, making him so damn nervous. Why the fuck did she keep staring at him? He told her not to. Dumb white bitch. He had planned on killing her anyways, but why the fuck did she have to give him so damn many reasons?

At first, he was surprised when she didn't stay down and die, but then he found he enjoyed the challenge. Sure he had a knife and a huge weight advantage but she had made such great sport of it. So when she finally, finally, did just lay there, he knew it was game over. Besides it was getting late and he needed to get home to his old lady.

As he walked over to his car, he instinctively took a quick look around. It was all good. No one was there. No one alive anyways. His work here was done. He looked at his clothes and saw that he was saturated in blood. Her blood. That reminded him again of what a winner he was and he smiled. His wife would be impressed with what he had done for her. With foresight, he had parked his car facing outwards, toward the highway. He jumped in, turned the engine over and sped away.

Driving back to Albuquerque, he felt himself coming down, down from a few minutes ago when he had felt so great, so alive. He had felt like fucking Superman. His brain had been as engorged as his penis but now they were both shriveling back down to the walnut size that they normally were. That was okay, he couldn't be fucking Superman all the time. He still had to work and take care of his lady, not to mention his baby, which technically could be born any minute now.

He tried to process what had just happened. He realized he might have gotten himself into one his little messes again. Killing two girls - if word got out that it was him, that might bite him in the ass. What if someone did find out? God had told him to do it, right? Or was it the devil? He would try both angles and see which one worked best. If that somehow became necessary.

Someone might find out? That was stressful, but who was going to know anyway? Dead people don't talk. He made a mental note to not get himself into this type of fix again. If God could just do him one last favor and get him out of this, he promised to not kill anyone anymore . . . even if he felt like it. It seemed like a fair deal, one God most likely would agree to. He started to feel a tiny bit better. He knew he would have to tell his wife, but she would understand . . . or at least she wouldn't tell anybody.

***

BOTTOM OF THE ARROYO, TIJERAS CANYON APRIL 6, 1981 1:05 AM

She waited until she heard him drive away before she dared even open her eyes. When she finally did, her assessment of the situation was grim. It was coal black outside, the new moon having phased in a couple of days earlier, so she could not see even three feet in front of her. Her brain was cloudy, she had no shirt on and the temperature continued to drop. And she could not recall her name. *What's my name?* She thought. *It starts with a . . . mmm . . . I don't remember.* She felt so incredibly light headed. Then she remembered . . . not her name but her number . . . her high school basketball number. In fact, she remembered both of her numbers: 22 was her at-home number and 23 was her away number. She decided she was away.

Realizing she was probably in the process of bleeding to death, she understood that she had to get help immediately or die. The problem, of course, was how to mobilize herself. Somehow, she had to command herself into the reality of having the physical where-with-all to move, to get going. Her first attempt to stand was a failure - she got about half way up when her knees buckled, causing her to crumple in slow motion back to the ground.

"Have to live," she said. "Have to get help." Everything was fuzzy and getting fuzzier. *Don't want to die . . . too young to die,* ran through her head. "Have to live," she said again. "Can't let my parents down. Not going to die at the bottom of an arroyo. Let's go 23." She got on her hands and knees and made the only forward movement her body would allow . . . she crawled.

As she crawled, she also had to focus on her breathing. Not because of excitement or nerves but because there was a gaping hole in her neck. Her

64

wind pipe had been so savagely cut that she could no longer take in air through her nose. She had to breathe through her neck.

Up ahead, there was a light . . . she saw it. She even knew what it was. It was the Land Grant Building. She thought there might be people there, despite the late hour. But she couldn't quite judge the building's proximity from where she lay. She crawled toward the light, counting numbers as she crept, to stay conscious, to stay coherent.

"One, two, three, four . . . one, four, three . . . no, no, no." When the numbers got out of sequence she stopped moving, regrouped and counted again.

With considerable disappointment, she realized the Land Grant Building was too far. (It turned out to be about a half a mile away.) She further realized that she had to change her objective in order to survive. She decided to make Old Highway 66 her destination of salvation instead. But first she had to crawl from the arroyo that currently entrapped her, up a cactus-infested, seemingly sheer-face mountainside, to get to that highway. This particular embankment was about 70 feet high with a 60 degree slope. In her normal state, that climb might have been a formidable but manageable feat. However, the ligaments in her left hand had been lacerated; her right bicep cut, her throat slashed and she had already lost so much blood she could not stand up. Calling it an impossible goal was an oversimplification.

Fearing that time was her enemy, she closed her eyes, prayed to a God that she had never met, and initiated her ascent. As she edged up the mountainside on her hands and knees, she found that her traction was close to non-existent. The ridge was mostly sand and gravel, strewn with garbage and covered with prickly shrubs. Her strategy was simple: grab onto the closest available bush and/or tiny tree and pull her body up as quickly as she could to the top of the embankment - to Old 66. At best, she was able to inch up bit by bit and at worst the shrubbery gave way and she slid back down, erasing the painful progress she had just made. In addition to the multiple life-threatening gashes and slashes she had received, she also had twelve or thirteen relatively-speaking less severe defensive stab wounds on her arms and hands. Creeping on top of the underbrush had only made bad matters worse.

But giving up was not an option. With one hand stuck up inside her throat to stop the bleeding and the other grabbing at shrubs, she scratched her way to the top and to what was then her ultimate goal: reaching Old 66. *Hallelujah*, she thought. *I've made it to the road. Someone will help me. I'll be saved.*

She lay on the side of Old 66, ready to wave down the first oncoming vehicle. After waiting what seemed like a long time she finally saw a pair of headlights coming her way.

But her mind flashed terror and her heart raced anew. It was *him* - the man with the knife. She was sure of it. He was coming back to finish her off. She recognized the vehicle - a black and white convertible. At first, the car slowed down and it seemed as if it were about to pull over to where she cowered. Her heart and stomach flipped in renewed panic, but the car drove away. Relief. About a half a block down the road, however, the convertible made a U-turn and returned to the area where she crouched. The car drove by v-e-r-y slowly, even slower than the first time. She knew it was him. Her heart pounded . . . she thought it might explode . . . but the convertible did not stop, it drove on by.

Gathering herself, she crawled back onto the edge of Old 66 and began her wait again. This time no one came. Her heart sank.

"Gotta do it," she sighed. "Gotta do it." What she meant was, she had to climb a second 70-foot embankment, with the same 60 degree slope, to get herself up to Interstate 40 where she knew there were people - lots of people. It was the third largest Interstate in the U.S., by God, running from Barstow, California to Wilmington, North Carolina. *Someone has to find me if I can get up there.*

She looked up to the top of the embankment. It might as well have been the top of Mt Everest, as far away as it seemed.

"Gotta do it," she whispered with little conviction. "Gotta stay alive."

By this time, her hands and legs were cut up and bruised from the rough brush and her limbs were going numb from the cold. But she had to disregard all of that and hit the restart button. She had to get up that embankment.

She reached for a small oak and started the long climb upward. After getting about two-thirds of the way up, she gripped a shrub, a chamisa, but it had no substance. The shrub's root came free and she slid downward. Grabbing wildly for anything within reach, a branch, a rock, anything to block her descent, she continued sliding. She couldn't stop herself and slid all the way down, back to the bottom of the embankment. As she lay there panting in the bits of broken glass and discarded wrappers, she heard the hideous howling of a nearby pack of coyotes. That didn't help. The hopelessness of the situation was starting to overpower her, she wanted to cry but she didn't have the energy.

"Okay, okay," she said, gathering herself. Her head said, "I can do this," but her heart began to have doubts. She wondered if she *was* going to die. *Would* she be able to get to the top of this damn embankment and then find someone to help her in time? It seemed like an unlikely scenario at this point. For the first time, her own funeral flashed into her mind. She saw herself looking up from her casket while friends and family filed by with grief-stricken faces.

Too young to die, she thought. *I'm only 20 years old. Can't disappoint my parents. Gotta go again.* And with a shake of her head, she forced those black thoughts away. Gritting her teeth, she took a breath and crawled five paces farther east. Judging this potential path somewhat more do-able, she reached for a solid shrub to pull herself up and began again.

"Can't give up . . . don't want to die . . . gotta get to the top," she chanted to herself every 30 seconds or so. She could not let herself think of the things that had happened to her that night, nor could she allow herself to think of possible failure. Her vision was tunnel vision. It had been this keenness that had allowed her to succeed in previous endeavors and it was that focus which just might save her now. With a rush of new strength she summoned from deep within, she pulled, clawed and flat-out willed herself all the way to the top of that second embankment. *Hooray*, she thought. *Thank God . . . I made it.*

There was just one small problem. A small problem in some other universe maybe, but it seemed like a deal breaker right now. There was a guard railing - a two and a half foot high metal guard railing - that stood between her and Interstate 40. Glorious, glorious Interstate 40, with all of its possible rescuers, lay just on the other side, but what possible strength did she have left to get herself there? Even as she lay completely prone in the weeds, she knew that she *had* to get over that railing, but she also felt a coolness beginning to encompass her body. Gray and white dots danced in her eyes. The great seducer "unconsciousness" was calling to her, urging her to slip into peaceful blackness. With all of her will, she fought back.

"Have to stay awake. Have to stay awake," she rasped. She began counting numbers out loud again so she wouldn't pass out. She knew that passing out meant certain death.

"1, 2, 3, 4," she said, very deliberately. "1, 2, 3, 4."

"1," she said, and lifted her good arm with the bad hand to the top of the rail.

"2," she said, and lifted her bad arm with the good hand to pull her body upright, even with the rail.

"3," she said, and lifted her left leg which pulled on her backside which still had the tip of his knife stuck in it, over the rail.

"4," she said, and dropped to the other side as gently as she could.

"Made it," she said, with a smile that nobody saw.

The car headlights whizzed by her now. They were very, very close. She heard their loud engines, felt their powerful vibrations in the ground. She lay on her side, trying to stay functional, lifting her arm to catch a passerby's attention. Initially, the drivers of the cars and trucks most likely did not see her and thus did not come to her rescue. One bright light after another zoomed by.

Stop . . . damn it, she thought. But they did not stop.

With all that was left in her, she inched ever precariously closer to the painted white line - *like "suicides" in basketball,* she thought. *Go a little bit farther than you think you can go,* she could hear her coach saying. Later, no one was ever able to explain it, but somehow she managed to "go a little bit further than she thought she could go" right across three lanes of Interstate traffic.

So there she sat, propped up on the median of I-40, her hand held high, as if hailing a cab in New York City. Now, in her new, eminently more visible position, she got her rescuer. She saw the very next car slam on its brakes, reverse itself and then screech to a stop right in front of her. Two young guys jumped out of a two-door coupe and rushed over to her.

"Holy Fuck," she heard one of them say.

***

MONICA'S APARTMENT, CENTRAL & TRAMWAY   APRIL 6, 1981 1:10 AM

Mike arrived at Monica's small darkened four-plex, located just above Tramway, near Central. He knew Monica would probably be a little bit pissed at him for getting home so late, but he would make her understand. Reaching over for his cigarettes, he realized that he didn't have them. "Shit," he said and slammed the palm of his hand against his forehead. He realized that there was a 99.9% probability that he had left them in Tijeras Canyon. "Shit," he said again and got out of the car.

He rang the doorbell but there was no answer. He wondered why Monica didn't answer. A little bit of panic washed over him and he leaned on the doorbell without pause.

"Use your damn key," Monica yelled angrily from the upstairs window. Calming himself down, he fished in his pocket, opened the door and slowly walked up the stairs.

Monica had already fallen back into a deep sleep by the time he reached her and he had to shake her awake.

"Monica, Monica wake up . . . I just killed somebody," Mike blurted out and fell to his knees crying.

Monica blinked and looked into his large contorted face. "What are you talking about?" she gasped. "Where have you been?"

"Did you hear me, babe? I killed somebody."

"What are you talking about?" She sat up. "I don't believe you."

"I killed some girls in the mountains, Monica. I don't know what made me do it, but I killed two girls up in them mountains. Look at me; I got their blood on me."

She turned on the light next to the bed and stared at him. His shirt, jeans and shoes were completely covered in dried and not-so-dried blood. She felt sick, deep down sick because she knew what she had seen him do before and she knew that he had it in him to kill. She wished very hard that what he was saying wasn't true.

"What? What two girls? Who were they? No way, you wouldn't do that . . . I don't believe you. I don't want to believe you. What girls? Who were the girls?" She knew she was talking just to talk. She knew there were no good answers.

Mike got mad. "Too many questions, I don't need that shit. Shut the fuck up." He glared at her and then suddenly hung his head in submission. "Sorry. I'm sorry Monica . . . I did it. Here's the knife. I love you." Mike pulled the bloody weapon from his back pocket and presented it to her.

Her eyes widened and she bit her bottom lip as she looked in horror at the blood-covered knife. "Oh, my God," she said at last. "You did it." She collapsed back onto the bed. "What have you done? What are we going to do? Why did you have to do that now?"

Mike just shook his head and silently got to his feet, pulling Monica with him. They went into the bathroom together and Mike asked her to help him wash his hands. Numbly she did what he asked.

He stood like a child as she lathered up his large hands and then patted them dry. He dropped the bloody knife into the sink and watched in silence as the victims' red blood spiraled down the drain. Finally, when Mike was satisfied that the knife was as clean as it was going to get, he placed it inside the front cover of Monica's family Bible that sat on a stand at the top of the stairs.

"Monica, I don't know what went through my head up in those mountains," Mike explained as they walked back to the bedroom. "I got upset. I went berserk . . . that girl, the one next to me, she made me go berserk. She was staring at me. She poked at me. You know I love you so much. You got my baby in you."

"No, no, Michael, you didn't do it," she said. She shook her head and blinked. "Did you?" trying to will a different answer out of him.

"I did it, babe. God was there with me. I did it cause I love you. That's all I can say . . . cause I love you."

"I love you too, Michael," Monica said, but did not feel. She felt only the continuing roller coaster of her emotions as his story unfolded. She put her hands over her mouth, sank back onto the bed and started rocking back and forth, trying to comfort herself, trying to keep from screaming.

The bed-stand light flickered on her young round face and her anguished body shook. She cried and cried. Their baby was to be born in a couple of weeks and she couldn't imagine how things could get any worse.

Mike hunched over, cried along with her. They wailed together for a long time, like a pack of unhappy bloodhounds. Finally, Mike stopped crying, framed her face with his hands and said in a husky voice, "Monica . . . we gotta go back. We gotta go back to those mountains."

She gaped at him and mouthed, "What?"

"We gotta go back, Monica. My cigarettes and lighter is out there. They must a fell outta my pocket," he said, his composure regained. He stood up, walked downstairs to the refrigerator and gulped down half a container of milk straight out of the carton.

"Michael, you're going to get in trouble . . . no, you're going to get *us* in trouble," Monica said, following him downstairs.

"That's why we gotta go get 'em, babe. We gotta go back to them mountains and get 'em. So they don't know it's me . . . we gotta go back now."

"Why? Why, did you have to do that now? Why did you have to kill somebody?" she cried.

"Sorry, babe. I don't know what went through my head. I love you so much. I'll make it right. You know what a hard worker I am."

She shook her head. "This doesn't make any sense, Michael. I don't want to go with you . . . I'm scared."

"I'm scared too, babe . . . but I don't want the cops to know it was me. It'll be alright. Come on Monica, we'll just go get 'em and come right back. You won't even have to get outta the car."

Monica knew that this was not the time to argue with her boyfriend. Maybe he didn't just kill two women, maybe he was just talking crazy or joking or something. Monica had no idea what to think. Maybe it would be better if she just went there and saw for herself.

"Okay, Michael, let's go get your cigarettes," nMonica said and grabbed her coat while Mike changed. When she got to the car, she saw women's clothing in the back seat.

"Michael, what's this?"

"Those are them girl's clothes. Take 'em out and put 'em in the house before we go. So no one sees 'em." Monica shook her head but took the clothes out of the car.

After the bag was stashed inside the apartment, the couple got into Mike's light yellow Ford Galaxie 500 and drove back to Tijeras Canyon.

***

TIJERAS CANYON   APRIL 6, 1981 1:40 AM

Mike and Monica traveled the entire distance to Tijeras Canyon without talking. Monica, so very pregnant, was unable to get the seat belt across her bulging waist, so she sat partially spread-eagled in the front seat, her hands resting lightly on the dash. Due to her recent weight gain, she felt uncomfortable most of the time. But her physical problems didn't compare to the new problems Mike had just laid on her. She was still hoping that Mike had made up the entire story . . . or at least the part about killing those girls. She hoped that this was one of his sick little jokes. She did not want to see any dead bodies.

Mike knew that Monica was upset with him, but she would get over it. Didn't she understand that he had done the whole thing just for her, to get back at those Anglo chicks at that party? The ones that had humiliated them?

Didn't she understand that he wanted to show her how much he loved her? No one would miss those dumb, uppity bitches anyways. Right now, he was hyper-focused on retrieving his cigarettes and lighter. Once he got them back, no one would have a clue that it was him. Of course, he knew what he was doing, and besides, he had guidance from above. "The Lord just sent me back," he would say later.

Just as he had done earlier that evening, he exited the freeway at Carnuel and headed east on Old Route 66. He again drove by the trashy double-wides, Dead Man's Curve and onto the flat toward Tijeras. On the first pass, he missed his turn. He also missed the figure crouching low behind a post.

"I know it's around here somewhere," he said and U-turned back in the other direction. This time he looked harder and with more determination. He drove v-e-r-y slowly. "I see it, there it is," he said, turning onto the correct dirt side road and rolling down into the arroyo. As Mike and Monica slowly bumped down the unpaved path, Monica

felt sick before she even got there. With the headlights illuminating the road, she saw what looked like a puddle of blood. That was it for her. She closed her eyes and sank down in her seat.

Once into the arroyo, Mike drove the car back and forth, back and forth, trying to locate his cigarettes. Finally, he parked roughly in the same location he had parked earlier. He left the engine running and the lights on.

"I think I left 'em right over h—," stopping in mid-sentence. The cigarettes and lighter were there, but the girl that he had left for dead was gone. "What's going on?" he screamed.

"I can't see them," he said, moving his head in alternating directions. "Where are they?"

Mike got out of the car. "Where is she? I need to go look for them," he said and spun around wildly. "Shit. Shit. Shit," he repeated.

"No!" Monica yelled. "Don't go looking for nobody. Just get what you gotta get and let's go. I'm scared."

Monica stayed inside the car crying, her hands pressed together, in the praying position.

Finally, it dawned on Mike. Someone must have found the dead girls and took them somewhere, maybe to the police. The more he thought about it, the more he decided he better get the hell out of there. ASAP.

In close to total panic, he grabbed his cigarettes and lighter off the ground and jumped behind the wheel. "We gotta fucking get out of here, Monica," he said and backed up the car. He backed up so fast, he hit a tree. Monica wailed ever louder with each lurch of the car. Frantically, he pulled forward, turned around and screeched out of the arroyo. Once he got back on Old 66, he sped away, swerving from lane to lane. Monica screamed at him to slow down.

"You want to get stopped by the cops?" she lectured.

Her words hit Mike like ice water to the face and he slammed on the brakes, significantly slowing his speed down. Even though he desperately wanted to drive 100 miles an hour to get home faster, he realized he could not. He knew that he must obey all traffic laws and drive exactly the speed limit. Tonight was not a good night to get pulled over by the cops. It occurred to him that the police might be waiting for him at his house, but luckily his driver's license listed his mom's address, so for sure he wouldn't be going there.

As he drove, he tried to collect himself. He knew he needed a plan. However, before any sort of plan could be formulated, he saw flashing blue and red lights in his rear-view mirror.

"What the fuck do they want?" Mike said. He thought he might throw up. Monica was freaking out too. Hyperventilating, actually. "Take it easy," he told her, as well as himself. Maybe he had been right before and someone *was* following him the whole time. The police must already be on to him. "Fuck, fuck, fuck," he said, looking for something to bang his head on.

The flashing lights were closer now, the siren louder. The squad car was closing in, about 300 yards behind them. He held his breath, wiped the giant drops of sweat from his forehead and changed lanes. He couldn't decide if he should make a run for it or pull over. When the police cruiser pulled within two car lengths, Mike knew he was screwed. Then just as quickly as it had begun it was over. The cop car sped right past him in hot pursuit of a different criminal.

PART II

THE HUNT

CHAPTER 7

Patient "Jane Doe's" gurney rushed down the ER hallway amid a cacophony of directives. Burly hospital medics lifted her battered body directly from the ambulance gurney onto the operating room table at Presbyterian Hospital. Shortly after 2 AM, the paramedics had called the emergency room physician. They reported that they were transporting a patient who had been badly stabbed and was suffering from a life-threatening chest wound. A staff of two trauma surgeons, an anesthesiologist, three nurses and two techs awaited her arrival in ER Room C23. More doctors were assembling in the operating room as well, but before she went into the OR she had to stabilize in the emergency room first.

The ER doctor had mobilized the backup trauma surgeon by phone, the surgeon arriving only moments before the patient. Presenting as an unidentified, pulseless, unconscious victim of penetrating injuries, she was given little chance of survival. She had no blood pressure whatsoever and combined with a host of other adverse findings and a blood pH of 6.68; she was, in fact, already dying.

Bright hospital lights illuminated her motionless body. Two IVs were started. One warmed for fluids and drugs, the other attached to a blood transfusion pump. The patient was in imminent danger of bleeding out, so they infused her with type O blood to increase her blood volume. A cardiac monitor was attached to her chest.

So many things needed to be done ASAP. She was full of holes and bleeding, bleeding, bleeding. Her face, her neck, her back, her upper extremities, her thorax and her abdomen had all been slashed. The paramedics had addressed the most egregious of her wounds during her ambulance ride, but some required renewed attention. Her body temperature was 28 degrees Celsius (82 degrees Fahrenheit) which needed to be elevated dramatically and immediately. A nurse covered her body with heated blankets. The numerous throat lacerations had made her windpipe unusable and both of her lungs had been punctured multiple times. A tracheotomy needed to be performed immediately because she couldn't breathe on her own. But . . . before any of these tasks could be accomplished, the beeping line on the cardiac monitor went flat.

Everyone in the room paused for the millisecond it took to realize what had just happened, and then, in unison, they accelerated into the motions they had been trained to do. Madly, they tried to bring her back to life. It was a Code Blue. The nurses, techs and doctors kicked into get-it-done mode. More medical staff poured into the room. It was an orchestrated frenzy.

Jane Doe, though clinically dead, was well aware of her surroundings. Climbing out of her useless body, she floated upward. She was on the ceiling now, observing the proceedings below. She watched the doctor inject her body with epinephrine and then saw him gingerly brace his hands on her damaged chest and begin compressions. Jane Doe knew from a CPR class she had taken that 100 compressions per minute were required to get the job done. She further knew that you were supposed to time the compressions to the beat of the Bee Gees' song "Staying Alive." She could not decide if it was a good or bad thing to have that song stuck in her head.

The medical personnel were giving everything they had to resuscitate her. They all looked so terribly grim and worried, which was kind of weird because she felt so darn great. Her pain was gone now and she was more optimistic than she had been all day.

She felt so good in fact, she left the room altogether and went for a walk on the beach. It was sunny out and even though the raw salt breeze burned her face a bit, it felt wonderful. The waves crashing, the seagulls flying, it was actually kind of noisy, but still wonderful. She saw a woman wearing a black baseball cap, weeping. The woman stood alone, maybe a half mile down the shore at the edge of the water, letting the waves break over her bare legs. She ran towards the woman in the black hat. The coarse sand slowed her progress, but it didn't matter. In all honesty, she was in no hurry at all.

The wind kicked up and shrouded her goal. No worries whatsoever, she adroitly changed directions and ran straight into the ocean. She continued running until the water covered her head altogether, but that didn't matter either. The warmth, the weightlessness, the freedom, it all felt so refreshingly delightful. But, then . . . while enjoying herself underwater, she heard a voice. Her face crinkled in puzzlement as she realized it was someone calling to her.

"Come back, Miss," a woman's voice whispered sweetly into her ear. At the same time, the doctor pushed on her chest yet again. This time he saw an eyelid flutter. "Come on back, Miss," the nurse said again and Jane Doe was back on the table - with a pulse.

***

Mike's mind was troubled as he sat at the dilapidated kitchen table, smoking cigarettes and drinking beer, working on his next move. He did not want to get caught for what he did, but according to Monica, "he had got himself in some deep shit."

So many questions that he couldn't answer. Very perplexing about that dead girl - the one that was sitting next to him. Where the fuck was she? Had someone found her before he went back to the mountains and taken her body somewhere? Had she risen from the dead? Zombie-like? Was *she* now stalking him? Was the other one missing from the arroyo, too? Were they both stalking him? Would the cops figure the whole thing out and show up any minute to arrest him? The possible answers were as unsatisfying as they were unnerving.

Monica would be back from the store shortly and she expected him to have a plan. He was thinking about leaving town, but maybe he wouldn't have to. He also knew he needed to dispose of the knife and the dead girls' clothes. Everything most likely would have to go. Monica walked in the back door and threw the carton of cigarettes on the table. She sat down and glared at him.

"Well?" she asked disdainfully, arms folded across her chest.

He ignored her and picked up the brown paper bag containing the girls' clothes. With drool drying on his partially opened mouth and pupils dilated in anticipation, Mike dumped and spread the contents of the paper bag onto the kitchen table. Monica sat nearby, mildly interested, as he inventoried the items. $13.56 in bills and coin, two jackets, one UNM sweatshirt, one striped sweater, one pair of blue jeans, one pair of socks, two pair of shoes, a couple of IDs and two black pills from the pocket of one of the jackets. Mike immediately scooped up the money after counting it and put it in his wallet.

Monica highly disapproved of Mike's felonious actions, but, on the other hand, he had already did what he did, and she really wanted that UNM sweatshirt. It was right there for chrissakes. She asked Mike if she could keep it and with a disgusted look, Mike vetoed the idea. He did not want her wearing any of the evidence around town. Why were chicks so fucking dumb? He didn't know why he even put up with them – except for the sex, of course.

Now the pills. That was a different story. He was delighted. They were Black Beauties for fucking sakes. He knew what they were because he had once worked as a truck driver and a fellow driver had turned him on to their benefits. The pills gave you a sweet buzz and kept you awake when you needed it most. They were righteous. Almost made this whole thing worth it.

Almost. Anyways, he would put them to good use. He wrapped them up in tin foil and also placed them in his wallet with the newly found money.

The IDs were probably not valuable, but you never knew. The UNM ID said the name Julie Ann Jackson on it. Mike recognized the picture as the girl with the glasses. He informed Monica that she was the first one that he killed. He told her in the same tone of voice that one might use when discussing the weather. He decided he would hold onto the IDs for now and see if he couldn't think of some monetary use for them later.

Mike was about to get up and go to bed when Monica spoke to him.

"Did you rape them, Michael?" she asked in a soft but steady voice.

Mike's brow furrowed and he slammed his hand down on the table. "Why the fuck you asking me that?" he demanded loudly.

Monica, realizing her mistake, cowered. After a long pause, she replied, "I'm just curious." *Curious?* Mike's brain tried to process that word. *Is she trying to make me mad? That's none of her fucking business. Has she been drinking? Is she coming on to me?* He decided the best defense was a strong offense, so he replied, "Fuck you. I'm not telling you nothing about that."

He got up, picked up the two six-packs of beer, dumped three of cans down the bathroom sink, then took the rest and threw them into his car. "That's *your* beers I poured out, bitch," he declared, returning to the living room. He stood in the doorway and glared at her. "I'm going to bed," he said.

Monica started to ask how he could sleep after what he'd done - but he was already on his way up the stairs.

***

DOWNTOWN PRESBYTERIAN HOSPITAL   APRIL 6, 1981 2:55 AM

The odds of surviving flat-lining in a hospital setting are one in twenty. Arriving pulseless with over thirty penetrating injuries? Unheard of. The injured girl didn't have much going for her, but she did have a couple things.

One, she was young and in excellent physical condition.

Secondly, hypothermia, an abnormally low body temperature which can cause death, actually helped her. Hypothermia is a state where external conditions cause the body's core temperature to drop below 95° F. When the core temperature is lower than 85°F most victims become comatose, and below 82°F the heart's rhythm becomes dangerously disordered.

However, in some instances, such as this one, hypothermia can *save* lives by inducing virtual hibernation, lowering one's metabolic rate and allowing the body to stay alive at an nth of its normal requirements. Jane Doe's body temperature, when she arrived at the hospital, was a frigid 28 Celsius or 82 Fahrenheit, the lowest end of survivability. The low temperature required less circulating blood, benefiting her vital organs.

The third thing was that she was young and in excellent physical condition.

***

NORTHEAST HEIGHTS, ALBUQUERQUE   APRIL 6, 1981 3AM

"Aragon." Wakened by the phone, Agent Manny Aragon of the New Mexico State Police said groggily.

"Agent Aragon, an injured person has been found in Tijeras Canyon," Miss La Rue said. "You've been assigned to this case. Please meet Officer Juan Chavez downtown at Presbyterian Hospital. He is the responding officer and can fill you in."

"Okay," Aragon said. "Can you tell me anything?"

"Not much, just that a young female victim was found in Tijeras Canyon and she's been viciously stabbed."

"I'm on my way," Aragon said, slipping on his shoes.

***

DOWNTOWN PRESBYTERIAN HOSPITAL   APRIL 6, 1981 3:30 AM

"Okay, she's ready. Take her to OR," Dr. Phillips directed. The orderlies wheeled Jane Doe thirty yards down the hallway to a waiting operating room. The monitors had already been rolled in, the instruments laid out and the ultra-bright operating room lights turned on. There was no time to spare.

Doctors, nurses and technicians stood ready to attempt to save this girl's life. The number of personnel fluctuated as the surgery wore on, but no one wanted to leave. When the surgery began, Jane Doe was listed in "very critical" condition.

Initially, the doctors worked on her neck to stop the profuse bleeding from the left external jugular vein. Jugular veins are located on either side of the neck and are essentially huge drain pipes that empty blood from the head, brain, face and neck and take it back to the heart. Because of the immense amount of blood that the head requires, particularly the brain, a corresponding immense amount of blood must exit the head via the jugular veins.

After sewing up the deep jugular gashes, the doctors then focused on controlling the heavy venous bleeding from the other deep slashes located on the front and back of her neck. A technician placed a catheter in her left forearm artery which monitored her vital signs during resuscitation.

***

JAMES AND JULIE'S HOUSE, GARFIELD AVENUE, UNM AREA   APRIL 6, 1981 3:30 AM

James tried to sleep. He really did. He thought he might be able to doze while waiting for Julie in the chair by the front door, but he couldn't shut his mind off. Where was she? Why hadn't she called? She was always so responsible, so thoughtful. That was one of the many reasons he had fallen in love with her in the first place. He had met Julie on a blind date in the bowling alley, right after high school. They were crazy about each other from the start.

Initially, it had been a little complicated, him being in the Navy and all, but they made it work. James was stationed in Guam, so they mailed each other books that they thought the other might like to read. He sent her poetry and she sent him Herman Melville.

James didn't know who to call that he hadn't already called. He wracked his brain, trying to think of someone that might have any kind of information about her whereabouts. He had tried Colene's number umpteen times. All the calls he had made came up with no, no and no. He called the police again. They gave him the same line about "must be missing for at least 24 hours."

James had a sinking feeling in his heart. He knew Julie wouldn't intentionally put herself in danger, but that didn't mean she wasn't in danger. Nothing assuaged his apprehension. He tossed and twitched all night and when he slept at all, his dreams were filled with pain.

***

DOWNTOWN PRESBYTERIAN HOSPITAL   APRIL 6, 1981 3:30 AM

New Mexico State Police Officer Juan Chavez traveled to Presbyterian Hospital to obtain information from the victim. The victim had gone into surgery, he was told, and wouldn't be out for hours – if ever. Agent Manny Aragon, also of the New Mexico State Police, arrived at Presbyterian Hospital about the same time as Juan Chavez and after purchasing two vending machine coffees, sought out Officer Chavez. Chavez updated Aragon as to what he knew so far and then called his supervisor at the main office to update him as well.

"Hi Sarge. This is Chavez. I'm at Pres, checking on the victim. She's in surgery right now. Aragon just got here."

"Yeah, I talked to three witnesses."

"They were a couple of college kids from Texas and a truck driver going to California. They all stopped to help the girl. They didn't know much. I ran them through the computer and they came out clean. I have their statements and their contact info."

"We couldn't really see anything, evidence-wise, it was too dark. Lotta blood, though. Lotta, lotta blood. I followed the blood trail down to Old 66, but I stopped because it was so dark. I'll go back when it gets light out."

"Okay. Yeah, we'll go back now. We'll go protect the crime scene."

"I'll radio in when we get there."

***

MONICA'S APARTMENT, TRAMWAY & CENTRAL   APRIL 6, 1981 3:45 AM

Monica listened to Mike snore. She couldn't sleep at all, but it wasn't because of the noise. The baby was kicking her too, but that wasn't it either. She was kicking herself for getting involved with this guy in the first place. He had a terrible temper. She knew that. His temper had flared up endlessly since she had met him. The slightest thing could set him off. He was always getting into fights with other people and he regularly beat her up – even while she was pregnant. But tonight he had gone ahead and done the worst thing possible. He had killed two girls that he didn't even know. Two white girls. She assumed something bad would happen as a result, but she had no idea how terrible it was going to get.

But what options did she have anyways? Nine months pregnant and nowhere to go. She couldn't tell anybody about what happened or Mike would kill *her*. As she lay there staring at the ceiling, she hoped that he would come up with some kind of plan that would get them out of trouble. She prayed for it.

***

DOWNTOWN PRESBYTERIAN HOSPITAL   APRIL 6, 1981 4:30 AM

Well into her multiple surgeries, the doctors were still concentrating on sewing up the worst of the worst. Finally, with her neck stitched up and her vitals somewhat stable, the doctors took a hard look at the five-inch gash on her abdomen. They performed an exploratory laparotomy which involved a lengthy cut straight down the middle of the stomach. Because of the nature of abdominal organs - potential nasty bacteria and all - infection is a real risk if the surgeon accidentally punctures any of these organs. In general, bleeding in the abdominal cavity is considered a medical emergency. Luckily, the doctors discovered that the abdominal cavity was okay.

Two hours after arriving at the hospital, Jane Doe was still in a state of shock. To relieve this condition, a left chest tube was placed inferiorly and proximally. Ultimately, 2.5 liters (equivalent to 5.25 pints or two-thirds of a gallon) of blood was removed from her left chest. After draining the blood, the doctors positioned her for a thoracotomy - an incision into the chest to gain entry to the heart, lungs and/or thoractic aorta - where they found even more blood. This particular surgery requires that the patient have an ET (a tube inserted into the trachea for the purpose of establishing an airway) and mechanical ventilation when performed. The thoracotomy is a four hour operation, if all goes well. The procedure is regarded as both risky and painful for the patient.

Probing further, the doctors found four to five separate stab wounds to the lung, one of which was a "through and through", that is, it both entered and exited the lung tissue. The doctors were able to ultimately repair all of these wounds and stopped the bleeding from the lung. There was no further bleeding from the chest wall or from any of the major vascular areas after the fixes were made.

CHAPTER 8

New Mexico State police lab technicians Art Craig and Larry Renner arrived at the four mile marker on Old 66. Officer Juan Chavez and Agent Manny Aragon were there waiting for them. The technicians were quickly briefed and a plan of action was formulated.

Step one: Agent Aragon would drop Officer Chavez at the Interstate 40 median where the victim had been found. Step two: Officer Chavez would retrace and continue following the blood trail that he had discovered earlier that morning. Step three: Document everything. Step four: Craig, Renner and Aragon would protect, inspect and respect the entirety of their current location as a potential crime scene while they waited for Officer Chavez to learn where the trail ended.

Beginning his search in the area where the victim had been found, Officer Chavez noticed a partially frozen pool of blood. Chavez scooped up a sample of the blood and dropped it in a sterilized container which he labeled. He saw no signs of a struggle in the immediate area. The State Police officer wrote these details in his field notebook, took pictures and drew a diagram as he progressed.

Commencing from the median, the blood path guided him south across three lanes of freeway traffic and continued to the guard railing. Officer Chavez peered over the guard railing and down the steep embankment where the blood trail continued. Questions kept popping up in his head that didn't seem to have answers. *How did this severely injured person get across three lanes of traffic?* No answer. *How did she end up on the interstate?* No answer. *What kind of monster would do such a thing?* No answer, no answer, no answer.

He hopped over the two and a half foot guard rail and followed the bloody trail down the sheer 70 foot slope to Old 66. Dark splotches were apparent everywhere. The terrain was trashy, weedy and precipitous. Due to the extreme steepness of the grade, Juan Chavez basically had to do a controlled slide to get down the hillside. Upon reaching the bottom of the embankment, he snapped additional pictures and sketched a map of the whole area for reference. In his notebook, he recorded measurements of various distance relationships and estimated the degree of the slope. Chavez noticed something as he looked up from the bottom of the slope. He saw a *double* blood trail on the embankment. The girl had obviously slipped and had to climb up twice. *Unbelievable!* he thought and paused to write this down in his notes, as well as photograph the sliding marks.

Chavez also noted the width of the swath of gore. It seemed like too much blood for any one person to lose and remain conscious . . . let alone mobile.

His mouth dropped open as he realized that the trail went on further than he could see. It continued across the four lanes of Old Highway 66, then went about forty yards west on Old 66, over another guard railing and down yet another - even steeper, even rockier seventy foot slope into the arroyo far below. Even though it was cool outside, Juan Chavez was sweating. He radioed Agent Aragon before making his next slide down.

"Manny, drive the squad car down into the arroyo. This trail just keeps going. It goes into the arroyo. I've got another hill to slide down and this one's way worse. Very brushy."

"Okay. Do you need any help? A rope or something?"

"Nope, I'm okay. I'm sliding down. Good thing I got my leather gloves with me, there's all kind a cactus and scratchy shit on these embankments. And just so you know, there's still a shitload a more blood. I don't know how that girl made it. Okay . . . I'm going down. Get plenty of pictures of whatever you can. I got a bad, bad feeling." And down the slope Officer Chavez went. When he got to the bottom, though it was hard for him to believe, the trail of blood continued.

"What the fuck?" Chavez said as he walked past the other men waiting for him in the arroyo. Silently, they fell in a line behind Chavez, careful to step in Chavez's footprints as he followed the bloody path.

Abruptly, Officer Chavez came to a stop and stared in shock at the scene laid out before him. He saw signs of what must have been a tremendously violent struggle. Bushes trampled, branches ripped off, dirt gouged out - and again, lots more blood.

In one spot, he found an immense reddish discoloration and a body imprint on the ground. Technician Craig shot pictures of the large red-brown stain from different angles. He scraped a blood/dirt sample from the ground and put it in an evidence envelop and labeled it.

But the blood path did not end at the body imprint, it continued. It followed a dirt road along the river bottom, leading west to two distinct areas.

Again, both areas were saturated with large blotches of dried blood. From there, a faint blood trail continued west about ten yards further and then finally it stopped. The men looked at each other with question marks in their eyes.

***

JAMES AND JULIE'S HOUSE, GARFIELD AVENUE, UNM AREA   APRIL 6, 1981 6:30 AM

Julie was still not home and the countless phone calls James had made turned up nothing. So after virtually no sleep, he got on his bike and pedaled the two and half blocks over to Stanford - to Colene's house. Stopping directly in front of the pink triplex where Colene lived, he stared into her apartment, #B, searching for signs of life. His sick stomach got sicker when he saw no people, no movement inside. He walked his bike over to his buddy Nick's house, Colene's next-door neighbor, and banged on the door.

James had known Nick since high school. They were both musicians and had been in a few parades together. Different marching bands, of course, since Nick went to Albuquerque High and James went to Farmington High, but they were both brass guys, so they were bonded.

Opening his front door, a bleary-eyed Nick, dressed only in a striped green bathrobe, saw a frenetic James, his shoulder-length, reddish-brown hair tangled up, pacing the porch. "James, what's wrong, man?" Nick asked.

Bypassing all amenities, James blurted out, "I can't find Julie . . . we need to get into Colene's house now. I need to find her. I haven't seen her since yesterday." Seeing the near panic in his friend's face, Nick left his house to help James, still wearing only his robe.

The two men went first to the back of Colene's apartment and nosed around. Fogging the window looking in, James saw Julie's silver bike leaning against the kitchen counter. But no people. Maybe they were passed out or something, Nick reasoned. James felt he had no choice but to enter the house. Nick jiggled the doorknob but it was locked. James then tried the window and felt some movement. It was stuck but not locked. With a mighty shove, James forced the window up and they shimmied in. Careful not to disturb anything, they crept through the house like burglars. They did, however, call out the girls' names as they slipped from room to room.

"Colene? Julie? Are you here? HELLO?"

The response was a stabbing silence.

***

As the hospital staff attacked her multiple medical problems with precision, surgery proceeded wound by wound. So far everything was going well; the girl was becoming more stable. As members of the surgical team finished her thoracotomy, other doctors were preparing to move on to "lesser" injuries such as the repair of the left hand flexor tendons, which had been completely severed.

A buzz grew throughout the hospital as the surgeries wore on. Presbyterian employees throughout the facility were talking about the girl that had been brought in early that morning, cut to ribbons - dead really - but somehow still hanging on. As nurses and techs drifted in and out of OR they provided updates to the other staff members, the hospital version of listening to the World Series on the radio.

"Mary told me to check, how's she doing?" one nurse asked another in the cafeteria.

"They've sutured her lungs and now they're working on her back. Her blood pressure's finally stable," replied the tech. "She's a tough one."

**

Deep in the arroyo, the four officers from the New Mexico State Police Department continued their investigation of the bloody crime scene. They discovered tire tracks. Three of the tire prints were of the same tread but tread number four was different. The vehicle appeared to have been driven in and out twice. Technician Craig molded impressions of the tire tracks.

Officer Chavez looked specifically for clothes. He knew that the victim, who was found almost naked, likely did not arrive in the frigid canyon that way. He found only one forlorn white sock. That was it. The sock was cataloged and photographed but Chavez was puzzled.

"Where's the rest of her clothes?" he said out loud. Despite the battle that had obviously taken place, they found very little in the way of physical evidence.

Meanwhile, Agent Aragon was walking his walk, performing an outward spiral search pattern, making ever wider circles from ground zero – the body size splotch of blood – looking for evidence. His progress was purposefully slow to ensure that he missed nothing.

About seventy-five yards out, and at approximately 8:40 AM, Agent Aragon saw something. He stopped, drew a breath and stared straight ahead. Even though his training has taught him to always suspect that there might be other victims, he was still taken aback. It took his brain a moment to comprehend what he saw. Up ahead, behind the large cedar tree, a young woman's nude body sprawled face-down in the dirt.

***

DOWNTOWN PRESBYTERIAN HOSPITAL   APRIL 6, 1981 9:30 AM

With the patient's blood pressure stable and the thoracotomy completed, repair of the multiple wounds over the back, posterior chest wall, arms, shoulders and neck began.

***

TIJERAS CANYON   APRIL 6, 1981 9:35 AM

Morning dew dampened the ground and mountain blue jays chattered cheerfully. Rabbits hopped about and spring saplings blew in the breeze. Life was about the same as always for the creatures that lived in Tijeras Canyon Quarry. The quarry itself, however, had changed. It would not be open for business today, probably not tomorrow either. A horrific crime had been committed there.

Bill Slease, a deputy investigator from the New Mexico Office of the Medical Investigator, had been summoned to the scene regarding a body discovered earlier that morning. As Mr. Slease approached, he observed the lonely form of a nude young female, procumbent in the weeds.

A serious young man with close cut dark hair and bright eyes, Mr. Slease walked over to the deceased female and squatted next to her. Even though it was obvious that rigor had set in, his hand dropped down for a pulse check just the same. He found none, looked at his watch and in a somber voice pronounced her dead at 9:50 AM.

Opening his kit, he pulled out the waterproof plastic bag, vacu-containers, needles and collection tubes. He set them neatly on a plastic tarp he had placed on the ground. He studied the body where it lay. There was a moderate amount of blood and some dirt on her back. He scribbled copious notes and took a multitude of photographs. Thoroughness was a job requirement.

Eventually he gently rolled the body over onto the plastic bag to observe the anterior side. He observed a single stab wound to the chest. Based on experience, he had expected something like that. He also observed dirt compacted into the nostrils and mouth and that was little unusual. He then noticed a complete imprint of the young woman's face imbedded in the dirt and that . . . that sent shivers down his spine. He was aware of the other victim, of course, the one that been stabbed dozens of times and left for dead. He had already supposed that this perpetrator was a very angry man. His experience at OMI told him that when killers behave as savagely as this one, something had lit a long simmering ember and a scorching rage resulted. Mr. Slease would find out later how right he was.

***

DOWNTOWN PRESBYTERIAN HOSPITAL   APRIL 6, 1981 10:00 AM

Six hours after medical procedures began; Jane Doe's was still in surgery. The doctors had to be both meticulous and thorough and, indeed, the sheer volume of life-threatening injuries took time.

***

TIJERAS CANYON   APRIL 6, 1981 10:30 AM

Cops were everywhere now and the cheerless atmosphere silent as law enforcement went about the gloomy business of assessing what was now a murder scene. Yellow numbered evidence flags dotted the arroyo, their bright color starkly contrasting with the darkness of the circumstance. A news truck was parked out on Old 66 but media was not allowed in.

The majority of officers present encircled the perimeter of the crime scene. With so many cops in the area, it was lead investigator Manny Aragon's job to preserve the integrity of the crime scene and ensure there was no cross contamination from his own men. When recording a crime scene, the more pristine and the more specific the details, the more useful that information will be later, for the successful capture and prosecution of the perpetrator.

Three methods of recording the crime scene were typical in 1981: writing, photos and sketches. Every piece of evidence needed to be thoroughly documented. A written journal in the form of a field notebook was required to describe the scene in words, recording details of atmospheric conditions – e.g. weather and temperature, any vehicles or equipment present, accessibility of location and persons that might have knowledge of what occurred. Photographs needed to be taken of the entire scene using overall, medium and close-up shots and a log kept of all photos. Lastly, sketches and maps were drawn to scale so that evidence relationships could be made.

On this day, the following information was noted at the crime scene. The night of April 5th and the morning of April 6th were clear and cool. No moon – completely dark. Very isolated location. A vehicle had been at the location as evidenced by tire tracks. The only known witness to the crime was the as-of-yet unnamed surviving victim, currently fighting for her life at Presbyterian Hospital.

When the murder victim was discovered, both the size of the primary crime scene and the number of photos increased. Agent Aragon made a note that helicopter photographs of the area would be helpful and he would follow up on that later. Lastly, a police sketch artist arrived to accurately draw the scene.

CHAPTER 9

What goes through people's minds after committing what they believe to be a double murder? Are they haunted with guilt? Do they want to fly to Brazil? Would running down to the closest police station and confessing be the way to go? Or should one just get rid of the most damning evidence and hope for the best? Mike chose the last option.

Preparing for the short trip over to his mom's house, he loaded up his Ford Galaxie 500 with the paper bag of full of clothes, plus the murder weapon/knife from the hallway Bible and, of course, he could not possibly leave home without the eight remaining cans of Coors beer.

Before departing the apartment, but after a vision from the beyond, his brain directed him to break the knife in half, which he did.

Mike then drove over to Linda's house via Interstate 40. While driving on the freeway, he instructed Monica to heave the two parts of the knife out the car window. The first piece was thrown near Louisiana Street and the second just past Carlisle. And even though the feeling proved temporary, enormous relief washed over Mike after disposing of the murder weapon.

***

As a consequence of the attack and the many procedures that she had to endure, Jane Doe consumed 31 units of blood and 16 units of fresh-frozen plasma. Because they didn't have time to cross match her blood type, when she arrived in the ER she was given type O blood, the universal blood. After the type O blood was exhausted, they gave her whatever blood type they had.

It wasn't until eight hours after surgery began, that she no longer needed further blood transfusions. The doctors determined that she was no longer in shock and appeared to be clotting adequately.

Throughout the hours-long surgeries, it had been a fight for the medical staff to keep her blood pressure stable, and except for a couple of times where it dropped to borderline dangerous 50/60, they were successful. Adequate warming was also provided throughout the day, bringing her temperature from 28 degrees C (82F) to near 32-33C (90-91F) by the end of the procedures. As the many surgeries were winding down, the patient was upgraded from "very critical" to "serious condition and improving."

***

LINDA'S HOUSE DON GABAL, NW   APRIL 6, 1981 1:45 PM

Mike and Monica pulled into Linda's driveway arguing about why the sky was blue. As Mike got out of the car, an errant football from a nearby kid's game clocked him hard in the head. Pissed off, Mike picked up the ball and heaved a perfect spiral into the 10 year old's skull. Blood spewed. Mike glanced back at the fallen boy, flexed his lips upward and ambled into the house.

Inside, family members and neighbors jammed the messy two-story home. Mike's mom, Linda, presided. She held court from atop a blistered red vinyl dinette chair pushed up against the heater. A neighbor girl painted Linda's toenails, while one of her many nieces worked a dye job on her hair. The tangerine-colored nail polish coordinated nicely with her low-cut blouse, while her newly darkened hair matched her mood. When Mike walked in the house, Linda greeted him with a hug and a smooch while keeping her seat on the dinette chair.

Mike and Monica sank into the living room couch where his auntie, who hated him, sat. His aunt, a muffin shaped despot dressed in green velour sweats, struck a match. As she touched the match to the end of her cigarette she sneered in his direction, smoke curling out her nose.

The aunt had never liked Mike. When he was younger, he would filch her underwear, masturbate on them and then neatly fold them back into her drawers for her later unhappy discovery. More recently, Auntie blamed him for her son getting arrested.

It was widely rumored among the siblings that the aunt had put a curse on Mike . . . hexed him. Just thinking about this possibility shriveled his member. Mike fled to the safety of the garage. His brothers were already there, arguing about which car was faster - a Charger or a Camaro.

The women, seeing Monica without Mike, scurried over to touch her pregnant belly and to share their painful childbirth stories. One had been in labor for five days. One delivered a stillborn. Linda extolled the benefits of marijuana. "Smoke a joint on the way to the hospital," Linda advised. Sure the hospital had good drugs she said, but "a little weed in the car helps take the edge off til you get there." Linda also instructed, in no uncertain terms, that when she got to the hospital, she was to get hooked up to the pain killers immediately.

"Take the drugs," she advised. "Right away."

Out in the garage, one of the brothers passed around a Playboy for all to gawk at. The comments regarding Miss March, a blond with bountiful endowments, were predictably lewd and crude.

"I wouldn't mind gettin' a piece a her," a clever young Guzman said, followed by uproarious laughter. Mike said nothing and slipped away.

He went to his car and brought the remaining cans of beer into the house and placed all eight near Linda's tangerine toenails. "Thank you, honey," Linda said with an appreciative smile and popped one open. Mike knew that if he could continue showering his mom with presents, especially the inebriating kind, he might be able to tell her what he had done. Or, at least, maybe he could borrow some money.

***

JEFFERSON STREET NE, ALBUQUERQUE APRIL 6, 1981 2 PM

Delivery drivers rolled out of Albuquerque Tribune headquarters to deliver the day's paper. The Tribune, Albuquerque's afternoon paper, had a circulation of about forty thousand in the 1980's.

The papers were delivered to racks and doorsteps and the headline was actually kind of upbeat: "Reagan feeling better" referring to the assassination attempt on the president a week earlier. However, on page A-8, an article entitled, "Young woman crawls to freeway; rescuers discover stab wounds," was a little more ominous. The article described a stabbing, in general terms, which had taken place earlier that morning.

***

TIJERAS CANYON APRIL 6, 1981 2:15 PM

In view of the exigent need to identify both Jane Does, the search for evidence continued in Tijeras Canyon. The investigation had just gotten a big break - Manny Aragon was informed that victim number one had survived surgery and was now conscious. Upon learning this, Agent Aragon immediately drove to Presbyterian Hospital to obtain information from the girl. On his way there, however, he was contacted by the state police radio dispatcher and ordered into headquarters instead.

***

LINDA'S HOUSE DON GABAL STREET, NW   APRIL 6, 1981 2:30 PM

Auntie chopped up fresh green chile and plopped it on the kitchen counter with rice, beans and tortillas The smell of cooked food attracted the Guzman family into the kitchen like metal to a magnet. Mike used this distraction to pull his mom aside and present her with the "black beauties" he had in his wallet. Linda was ecstatic, which made Mike ecstatic. He also pulled a tiny joint from his pocket and gave that to her too. Linda did a little happy dance. Mike told her if she gave him $20 he could get her more black beauties. She was so delighted that she pulled a wad of cash from her bra and gave it all to him. Mike almost did a happy dance himself.

***

DOWNTOWN PRESBYTERIAN HOSPITAL   APRIL 6, 1981 2:30 PM

Recumbent on her hospital bed with a respirator strapped to her throat, Jane Doe's brain eased back to consciousness. Heavy fog lifting was needed before she could open her eyes. *Wow, I feel so groggy,* she thought. *What's going on?*

Then it hit her. She needed to get going . . . and fast. She had an exercise physiology exam this morning and she couldn't possibly miss it. She needed to hustle down to UNM pronto or face the wrath of her teacher, Dr. Huggins, who did not allow makeups.

She opened her eyes and simultaneously tried to sit up. Immediately a large hand reached out and pushed her back down. Her mind didn't comprehend why there was a hand in her sleeping area or, for that matter, why the hand was pushing her back down. She closed her eyes again to regroup. *I must be dreaming . . . wake up, wake up,* she told herself. She pushed more fog from her head and redoubled her efforts to get out of bed. While she made her mental adjustment, the hospital staff made its physical adjustment, and when she tried to sit up a second time, she got nowhere at all - her hands and feet had been tied to the bed.

"What the hell," she mouthed but no words came out. Her vocal cords weren't working. She struggled and thrashed, trying to free herself. Dimly, she remembered the violent battle she had fought the night before and she knew she had been hurt, but damn it, she had to get to school. A heavy-set female with kind brown eyes was speaking to her. She couldn't make out the words at first, but the voice – it seemed familiar. It was so soothing, so comforting.

"You have to stay still now, Miss. You're gonna be alright but you've had a bad accident - a very hard night. You've got to rest," the nurse said.

"I've got to get to school," the girl tried to say but couldn't.

"You can't talk right now, Miss, you have a respirator on, you can't get out of bed yet either. But if you are feeling up to it, there's someone here that wants to meet you."

The girl struggled to orient herself. She felt as if she had just awakened from a twenty year sleep. The nurse repeated that someone was there to see her. The girl nodded yes. The nurse nodded in simpatico and motioned for the person to enter.

A large, pale man with thinning blond hair, wearing a surgical gown, entered. The man sat next to her and tapped his chin in thought. Eventually, he held out a wooden board with letters on it.

"Hello, Miss," he said. "I'm Dr. Vail. I know you can't talk right now but I need to ask you a couple of questions. I'd like you to use this letter board, if you don't mind. Just point to the letters to spell out your answers. Don't worry, they are easy questions. Okay?" She nodded yes and he untied her.

"First of all, what is your name?" Both of her hands had been slashed severely and although she didn't know it yet, the right hand had been declared "dead." Her left hand was also damaged and attached to a wooden board but she could move it well enough to point.

Slowly, she tapped the letters C - O - L - E - N - E. Dr. Vail repeated the letters out loud and wrote them down as she touched them. She put her hand down after spelling her name. She was tired.

"Colene," he said. "Your name is Colene?" she nodded and blinked her foggy blue eyes "yes."

"What's your last name, Colene?

B-U-S-H.

"Bush? Your name is Colene Bush?" Yes.

"Very good," he said. "What about your friend's name? The one who was with you last night?"

After a slight pause, Colene spelled out Julie Jackson.

"Are both of you students at UNM?"

Yes.

"Thank you so much. We're going to contact your parents right away," he said.

Colene nodded.

Dr. Vail told her he would check on her later.

Outside in the hallway, he turned to his assistant, handed her the girls' names and told her to contact UNM police immediately.

***

JAMES AND JULIE'S HOUSE, GARFIELD AVENUE, UNM AREA   APRIL 6, 1981 3:30 PM

James still hadn't been able to locate Julie. Stress of the unknown was beginning to overwhelm him. He hadn't slept, hadn't eaten and hadn't had any thoughts other than finding his girlfriend. He had already contacted absolutely everyone. The police were no help at all.

It had been over 20 hours since James had last seen Julie. He didn't know if he should hit the streets or wait by the phone. At 3:30 PM, he received an anonymous phone call.

"Mr. Tuttle?" a toneless male voice said.

"Yes."

"I know this must be difficult for you, but you should call the UNM Medical Center right away."

"Who is this?"

"That's not important. Just call them and tell them who you are. They're expecting your call."

The phone went dead.

The hospital? Julie's in the hospital? James thought. *Something's happened. What could have happened?* The voice on the phone did not sound good.

James phoned UNM Hospital immediately, gave the operator his name and asked to speak to Julie Jackson. His call was transferred.

"Office of the Medical Investigator," the phone said.

Office of the Medical Investigator? As he comprehended those words, James' heart dropped to his feet.

"We don't have a contact number for the family," James heard someone say.

He was asked if he could come in to make a positive identification and was given directions to the morgue. Reality set in. His hopes evaporated.

✳✳✳

LINDA'S HOUSE DON GABAL STREET, NW   APRIL 6, 1981 4PM

Mike had missed the earlier newspaper story printed in the Albuquerque Tribune and he didn't normally watch TV news, but today he heard some chatter from the next room that caught his interest. Since no one was paying any attention to him anyways, he slouched down on the sofa and stared at the box. The story was about a UNM coed found stabbed to death in Tijeras Canyon, her identity unknown. The police had discovered the girl while searching the area for clues regarding a different stabbing victim, who was found alive on Interstate 40. The broadcaster said that the surviving victim's identity was also unknown but she had endured a night-long surgery and was now in critical condition at a local hospital.

"Fuck! Fuck! Fuck me," Mike said. "Alive? How the fuck is she alive? How the fuck did she get on I-40?" He crushed a beer can into his head. The pain he felt had nothing to do with his now bleeding forehead.

✳✳✳

DOWNTOWN PRESBYTERIAN HOSPITAL   APRIL 6, 1981 4:30 PM

The automatic doors opened wide to the ICU. Numbly, the distraught woman spoke to the busy nurse at the center desk. Entering the small room with bare white walls, she parked herself on the hard plastic chair next to the mechanical bed and exhaled. She couldn't believe it.

Colene was asleep, so she never saw those first expressions on her mom's face. Horrified. Staggered. Sad. Mad. So many emotions as she stared at her critically injured daughter. Tubes running to and from beeping machines, bandages everywhere, a ventilator covering her mouth. Carol had already spoken to the police and the hospital staff and they had filled her in on what they knew and how they knew it. All very bleak and perplexing. So far, Colene had been able to communicate very little.

Carol had never thought something like this would happen to one of her kids. Resting her hand on the unbandaged part of Colene's arm, she waited for her to wake up. Eventually Colene's eyes blinked open and registered recognition. Carol saw a thin smile underneath the respirator.

***

LINDA'S HOUSE, DON GABAL AVENUE, NW   APRIL 6, 1981 4:30 PM

Mike leaned against the oak tree watching his older brother change the oil on his beloved Dodge Charger. Behind the garage and far away from the others, Mike disclosed this new wrinkle in his life to his brother Raymond and his visiting Texas cousin, Sixto. They took the news badly.

"You done what?" Raymond said.

"What a dumb fuck! Why didn't you make sure they was dead? I woulda for sure made sure they was dead," Sixto lectured, with a slight Tex-Mex accent. "They had it on TV? Ooooh . . . you're so fucked."

Mike absently stroked a neighbor's mangy dog as he stoically absorbed the negative comments.

"You better get the fuck out of town . . . before the cops find you," Sixto said as he paced back and forth.

"Why the fuck did you go and do something like that? You're too stupid to be doing this kind a shit," Raymond said.

Mike generally didn't allow people to speak to him this way, but this was family. Mike felt like he could use some advice right now and there really weren't that many people he could turn to. He just had to accept the fact that Raymond and Sixto weren't happy with what he did and how it had happened. Mike also realized that this was not the right time to mention to his brother that he had used his name while committing the crime.

"Get rid of all the crap that you took from 'em," Sixto advised. "That's for sure gotta go."

"Fucking A . . . you stabbed two of 'em?" Raymond said, shaking his head. "Why'd you go an mess with white chicks anyways?"

"What a dumb fuck," Sixto repeated.

CHAPTER 10

Agent Aragon, arriving at New Mexico State Police headquarters, was told to write up what he knew so far regarding the coed stabbings. Effective at once, he was being taken off the case, due to a vacation conflict. This case required immediate and possibly long term attention, so Agent Tom English was sent out to the hospital to interview the victim instead.

Agent English rapped on Colene's ICU door. He knew she couldn't talk, so after waiting a respectful couple of seconds, he took a peek in before entering. A tall man with short sandy hair, a clipped mustache and watchdog eyes, Agent English entered her room and introduced himself.

"Colene," Agent English said. "I know you're tired but I need to ask you a couple of questions." He produced the letter board again and held it up near her. "We need to find out who did this to you so we can start looking for him and catch him. Okay?

She shook her head yes.

"Okay . . . do you know the guy's name that did this to you?"

Yes, she nodded.

"Spell the name for me, please." She gingerly touched the letters on the board.

"R-A-Y-M-O-N-D." Agent English said the letters out loud as she pointed, like the doctor had done earlier.

"Raymond?"

Yes.

"Do you know his last name?"

No.

"That's okay. Was he white?"

No.

"Spanish?"

Yes.

"Had you ever seen him before?"

No.

"Please point to a number for his height. How tall was he?"

Colene pointed to the number six.

"He's six feet tall?"

Yes, she nodded.

She proceeded to answer his questions letter by letter, nod by nod. She described how she and Julie were abducted at knife-point while walking home from the Frontier Restaurant. The man drove a black and white Chevy convertible. She pointed to the letters for "scared".

After a half an hour of spell and tell, not wanting to wear her out, the detective stood up to leave. Colene scrawled the word "Julie" on a pad of paper. He looked at her and realized she didn't yet know what had happened to her friend. He advised her to get some rest and left. Moments later the nurse arrived, added meds to her IV and Colene was out.

***

OFFICE OF THE MEDICAL INVESTIGATOR, UNM AREA   APRIL 6, 1981 5:00 PM

In 1973, the Office of the Medical Investigator, OMI, replaced the coroner's office in New Mexico. It became a special program within the Department of Pathology at the UNM School of Medicine. OMI investigates the cause and manner of death in sudden, violent or unexpected deaths in New Mexico. It is both a training and operational facility.

Earlier in the day, James had received an anonymous phone call that directed him to the brick building located near the University - OMI. He did not want to go, but a profound sense of duty dictated that he do so. He had been asked to come in to identify the body of his fiancée, Julie Ann Jackson.

His good friend Mark drove him down there, but James walked into the foyer by himself. Although his senses were somewhat impaired from lack of sleep, he noticed the odor right away – like a hospital smell, but worse. Suddenly, he felt dizzy and hoped the receptionist wouldn't notice his pale complexion. He needn't have worried; she didn't even look up from her phone conversation, instead pointing him to a sign-in sheet on the counter. He scribbled his name on the lined paper and then nearly fainted onto a nearby couch to wait his turn.

Finally, a thin, balding technician shuffled in to get him. The technician wore a white coat, black boots and a bolo tie. They entered a tiny pale-green room with two straight-back chairs and bare walls. The man, whose name tag read Ebbers, asked James questions. Where did Ms. Jackson live? What were the names and addresses of her closest relatives? What was her birth date?

Stuff like that. James responded as coherently as he could and Ebbers, his gray eyes showing no emotion, wrote the answers in crisp block letters on a sheet of paper attached to a clip board.

Eventually, Ebbers led James into an adjoining room filled with large drawers and a cold stainless steel table. James' head bobbed as he watched the technician pull open the drawer in front of him. With practiced efficiency, Ebbers unzipped the body bag and James found himself looking into the lifeless face of the woman that he loved. Time froze. There was dirt on her mouth, her lips were cut and her face bruised. The expression on her face etched itself into James' brain for all time. He didn't want this to be his last memory of her, or any kind of memory at all, but it was. At last, he gave the technician a nod indicating a positive ID and Ebbers pushed the drawer back into place.

***

BOBBY'S GAS STATION, 12TH AND CENTRAL, SW   APRIL 6, 1981 5:30 PM

Like a broken egg yolk on a Saltillo floor, orange and red smears formed on the horizon. The clouds and atmospheric particles manifested a panorama of uncommon beauty. Albuquerque, known as much for its ugly crimes as its beautiful sunsets; had no problem providing space for both.

Departing his mom's house, Mike motored over to the ratty little gas station at 12th and Central, where his light brown friend Bobby worked. He needed to chill out with the guys; they were way less judgey than chicks, or leastways they didn't talk so damn much.

The gas station's neon sign flickered to life as Mike pulled in. Bobby, gold tooth gleaming, muscles bulging in his too tight T-shirt, stood smiling in the office doorway, while the rest of the slouching regulars drank beer inside. As they drank, the tiny office, decorated with girly pictures and greasy car parts, seemed to sag under the excess weight of its occupants.

Bobby was happy because Mike had told him yesterday morning that he would bring him by a couple of six packs of beer. He walked over to Mike's car and looked inside. Mike realizing his transgression, decided to improvise. When he first acquired his case of Coors two days ago, it seemed like it was enough to last a lifetime, but then maybe he had promised some to one too many people and now he didn't have any at all. He also knew that he badly needed a favor from Bobby tonight and getting that favor had probably just gotten a whole lot more expensive.

"I don't have any more, man," Mike admitted.

"What the fuck?" Bobby's smile gone.

"I'll go buy you some more right now, Bobby. There's a place down the street that'll let me score without ID. I need some help with the cash though."

Bobby's smile returned. "Okay," he said, motioning to the guys inside. "Go get some donations from them."

Mike told Bobby he would go pick up the beer and then sheepishly asked him if he would rotate his tires for him while he was gone. Bobby flatly declined. "Fuck no," he said. However, Mike told him that he really needed to get it done today because he had gotten himself in a little bit of a mess. A possible problem with the law. Bobby, sensing opportunity, said "Okay," he would, but now Mike owed him a *case* of beer. Mike assured Bobby that he would definitely get him a case by tomorrow. He went inside the station office to collect funds for today's beer.

A fat guy rolling a joint looked up at Mike. The other three slackers, busy watching TV, ignored him altogether. "Hey guys, I need some dineros to buy beer," Mike said. An acrid cloud of gasoline and Marlboros permeated the ensuing silence. "Bobby said for you guys to give me money," Mike added. Their heads snapped up in unison and they immediately dug into their pants and fished out all the cash they had. They did not want to piss off Bobby. Not only did he provide them with an excellent hangout, his temper was epic.

Satisfied that he now had enough money to buy multiple six-packs, Mike handed Bobby his keys and again asked him to rotate his tires. Bobby shrugged and Mike hoped for the best as he trudged off to the liquor store. One could not push Bobby too hard.

When Mike came back about 30 minutes later with a six-pack under each armpit, his car was up on the rack, tires getting air gunned into place. Mike looked upward with a small smile and knew that his tracks had literally just been covered.

***

JAMES AND JULIES' HOUSE, GARFIELD AVENUE, UNM AREA   APRIL 6, 1981 7PM

The front door was wide open and even though it had turned dark outside, there were no lights on in the house. James and Mark sat in pain-filled silence. Earlier in the day, James had been a beehive of activity, attempting to locate Julie. Now that he finally had, he didn't feel like moving at all.

Mark asked James if he wanted something to eat, but James just shook his head. It would be a long time before he felt like eating again.

The pain that James had brought home with him began to take another form. He couldn't forget the expression on Julie's face. He didn't understand what kind of human being would do such a horrible thing to another human being. Anger was flooding his body like a tsunami hitting the shore. He began to pace the length of his house as the overwhelming depth of his grief and wrath sent out signal after signal for him to do something. To act. He knew now that he needed to pace elsewhere. Grabbing his baseball bat, he went outside.

***

BOBBY'S GAS STATION, 12TH & CENTRAL, SW   APRIL 6, 1981 8:30 PM

Monica got sick of waiting for Mike, so she walked over to the gas station on her own. Immediately, she began nudging him to leave. She felt crappy and edgy and wanted to go home and lie down. Mike was now slouched on the couch in Bobby's office, drinking beer and watching TV with the guys. He had no great desire to leave, but Monica was being annoying. Pregnant chicks could be such a pain.

Mike and Monica finally left the gas station and jumped onto I-40 towards their apartment. Almost as soon as they got on the freeway, the car engine started making bad noises. A grinding, screeching kind of sound. The kind of sound that made you want to get help right away. Monica thought she saw smoke coming out of the front of the car. Getting off the freeway at Carlisle, they found a gas station with a mechanic. The mechanic informed them that the motor was burnt out and the car needed a lot of work - probably a new engine.

Not having the funds to undertake such a large capital expenditure, Mike and Monica left the gas station and drove up Central. They hoped to make it back home where Mike would do the engine work himself. They got as far as Virginia Street when the car died altogether. Mike pushed it one block over to Zuni Road and parked it in what he felt was a safe place.

As luck would have it, Monica's parents lived nearby. The young couple walked the block and a half to her mom and dad's house hoping someone would be there. Her mom was home and insisted that they eat some beef tacos she had made earlier. Mike and Monica quickly gobbled up everything put in front of them.

Monica's mom was happy to see her because she had just bought the baby a cute red dress and wanted to show it to Monica. While the two women chatted in the kitchen, Mike drifted into the living room to watch TV. The 9 o'clock news had just come on and his crime was the top story. Again, the newscaster told about a girl found murdered in Tijeras Canyon. The newscaster asked the public for help. Anyone with any information should immediately call the police.

Trying not to freak out, Mike told Monica it was time to leave. Monica's mom took pity on her expectant daughter (even though she thought very little of her daughter's boyfriend), and allowed them to borrow her Ford Pinto. As Mike drove away from Monica's parents' house, he made a quick stop at his disabled car and grabbed the paper bag full of clothes.

102

***

BERNALILLO, NM   APRIL 6, 1981 9:30PM

Turned out Mike and Monica weren't heading home after all. It finally clicked in Mike's brain that he was a wanted man. He and Monica headed north to an apartment complex in Bernalillo, Mike's old stomping grounds. The complex had a bunch of dumpsters that got dumped early every day and he knew that whatever he put in the dumpster that night would be gone by 6 AM the next morning.

But before they even got to Bernalillo, Mike began destroying evidence. While driving the frontage road, he ripped one of the girls' shirts into tiny pieces and let the pieces flutter out the window one by one. Mike then grabbed a pair of blue jeans and using his teeth, like a dog, shredded the pants and tossed them out, too.

Arriving at the apartment complex, he slid the Pinto in next to the dumpster and used his car as a ladder to reach the top of the trash bin. Monica passed Mike the bag of clothes as he straddled the edges of the dumpster and the car, and he tossed the contents into the bin. When he got back inside the car he noticed the UNM sweatshirt still in the back seat.

"What the fuck, Monica?" Mike said.

"I know. It's just that it's practically brand new and there was nothing bad on it and I . . ."

"Shut up. We can't be fucking keeping none of this shit. Not none of it. If someone checks, they can't find nothing. You're so dumb sometimes. Give it to me." She handed him the sweatshirt and he wadded it up with disgust and threw it in the dumpster.

"We need to get the fuck out of here," Mike said.

***

ROUTE 44, BERNALILLO, NM   APRIL 6, 1981 10:30 PM

It occurred to Mike and Monica, after leaving the dumpster that they were hungry again, starving really. Mike drove over to a nearby burger joint where he and Monica consumed multiple burgers and sodas while plotting their next move. Monica suggested that they go back home and stay there until things cooled off.

"No," said Mike with an angry glare. "I need to go back and check on all that shit we just threw in the garbage . . . I gotta make sure it's covered up." The return trip took less than five minutes. When he got back, he saw a couple of homeless people flash in his headlights, but they immediately disappeared into the recesses of the apartment complex. To Mike's horror, the female of the couple looked to be wearing the UNM sweatshirt.

"Now look at what you did . . . Monica. I gotta go and get that back," he said and jumped out of the car, running after the homeless people. But it was too late. They were gone. He slammed his fist into the building. He realized he should have torn up the sweatshirt before he threw it in the dumpster. "Well, they're just bums," he said. "And ain't nobody gonna look for that shit out here anyways."

***

DOWNTOWN PRESBYTERIAN HOSPITAL   APRIL 6, 1981 10:30 PM

The plain clothes cop outside the room observed the following:

Colene, recovering from 12 hours of surgery, is temporarily alone. She is surrounded by a circle of machines and monitors. Her mom, constantly at her side since arriving this afternoon, is gone for the moment, searching for something to eat. Nurses and doctors, mainly nurses, circulate the ICU. Her primary nurse is assigned to herself and one other person, an elderly woman with pneumonia. The nurse cycles back and forth between the two patients - actually giving the older woman a little more attention.

The on-call doctor stops by during his evening rounds to check on her. He had heard about this patient on the evening news. One of the most vicious knife attacks ever seen, they said. Amazing that she had made it, was the consensus. From a distance, he sees a thin young woman sitting up in her hospital bed. Her brow is knitted and her head slightly bowed. Her eyelids are half-mast as the anesthesia continues to circulate. Nonetheless, since awakening from surgery her eyes have become clearer, bluer.

He approaches her and asks her how she feels. She smiles to the extent her stitched up face allows, still unable to talk. Pain medications flow from her IV. The doctor's eyes scan her chart and then he writes in the chart himself.

Pt alert & awake. Very stable and coping well with her horror.

***

MONICA'S APARTMENT, CENTRAL & TRAMWAY   APRIL 6, 1981 11:30 PM

"The rest of this shit's gotta go," Mike declared when he and Monica finally returned home. He grabbed the scissors from the kitchen drawer, pulled the girls' IDs out of his top shirt pocket and sat with only a bare bulb dangling above the kitchen table, readying himself for the task. His eyes rotated in opposite directions and his lips made a weird burring sound as he snipped the ID cards into tiny shreds. Regarding their ultimate disposal, he knew what to do. He recalled how dear old mom had taught him the convenient yet permanent solution of the toilet. Once, when he was younger and the cops showed up at the door at just the wrong moment, his mom used the john as her modus operandi to keep herself out of jail. So taking a page out of Linda's playbook, in a sort of family tradition, Mike flushed the shredded IDs down the can.

Returning from the bathroom, Mike head motioned to Monica that it was time for bed. Out of habit, she followed him up and lay down. He slept like a rock. She did not.

***

STANFORD STREET, UNM AREA   APRIL 6, 1981 11:30 PM

If anyone had been out there to look, James could have been seen striding up and down Stanford Street. But no one was. The street was completely empty and abandoned, just like it had been the night before. He'd been walking for hours now. Walking . . . patrolling . . . looking. He didn't have a gun but he did have a weapon – his small wooden bat. It might not be effective for anything other than point blank range, but that's what he wanted. Anything else would be unsatisfying.

Everyone, everything seemed suspicious. A dog at the gate, a paper bag blowing in the street, a kite stuck in the tree. James was a big guy, 6'4"with his boots on, and not the least bit concerned about his own safety. He was looking for the attacker, the killer. Would this guy be dumb enough to come back to the same place? He might. Maybe he lived nearby. James was ready.

CHAPTER 11

The unrelenting gusts from a spring storm jarred him awake, shaking his apartment building like a mild earthquake. Mike already had a headache and the rude awakening didn't help, but after a chug of flat soda, he felt better.

"Monica . . . Monica wake up," Mike said, poking her shoulder. "I got a idea." She cracked an eyelid and looked at him without moving.

"Whaaa?" she mumbled.

"We're gonna move. To El Paso. My family's there. I can hide out with them."

No response.

"You can have the baby there and I'll get a job. Then if nobody's lookin' for me, then we can come back."

No response.

"Monica, did you hear me? We gotta move. We gotta move today. We need to get outta here. The TV said one of them girls is still alive. She's gonna tell. We gotta go."

"I don't wanna go," Monica said at last. "I wanna have my baby here. My mom's here and she'll help me."

"No, babe. We gotta go. I'm too freaked to go by myself. You'll be okay." He began petting her stomach to convince her. She pushed his hand away. He pushed her hand pushing him away, away and continued petting her – a little more roughly this time.

"No, Michael. I gotta stay here," she said firmly.

He put his face next to hers and said in a low growl, "Monica, we gotta get out of here. The police might come and they might want you, too. I don't want my baby in jail." For the first time, Monica realized that she might be in trouble, too.

She rolled her body away from his. "Oh, no," she said weakly.

Mike smiled.

***

LEE'S GARAGE, ZUNI AND VIRGINIA APRIL 7, 1981 11:30 AM

Mike knew right away this auto repair shop was the perfect place to stash his car. Wiping sweat from his forehead, he surveyed the yard full of needy vehicles. There was an Oldsmobile rusting on its rims, a Mercury Comet with no engine and a primer gray Plymouth Fury with plastic for windows. His car would blend right in with the rest of the heaps.

Besides not running, Mike's car had dents in both its hood and back fender, and part of the interior was speckled with blood. This vehicle needed to be off the streets and out of sight. Someone might be looking for it. With the help of Monica's dad, Mike pushed his ailing Ford Galaxie 500 to the first bay door at Lee's Garage on Zuni.

"Hi," Mike said to the grease monkey who sauntered out to greet him.

"Whataya need?" the grease monkey asked with a frown.

"This car's not working. Motor's burnt or something. The insides need cleanin' too."

"The owner's not here. We're busy," the grease monkey told him.

"That's cool. Take your time, I'm leaving town anyways."

"Take it somewhere else."

"Hey man, I had to push it in. It doesn't run. I need to leave it here." Mike twitched. "Here's ten bucks. Help me out."

The grease monkey didn't like this guy but he had a strict policy of never turning down a bribe, so he said, "Okay, gimme the keys." And then added, "Chief knows you, right?"

"Yeah," Mike said and pressed the ten spot into his palm. The grease monkey nodded and Mike flipped him his keys.

***

COMME CHEZ VOUS RESTAURANT, LOUISIANA AND MONTGOMERY, NE HEIGHTS   APRIL 7, 1981 12:30 PM

"I came to get my check," Mike informed his boss at the French restaurant where he worked as a dishwasher. "I need it today."

"Payday's next Tuesday," the boss told him.

"I can't work here no more. I'm moving," Mike said.

"You mean you're quitting?" the boss said, starting to get angry. "You were supposed to work today."

"I can't. I'm leaving to Texas," Mike said blandly.

"Today?"

"Today.

"What am I supposed to do? I can't get another dishwasher at the last minute," the exasperated boss said. "You need to give me a couple of days to find someone else."

"I can't. I need my check. I'm leaving."

"Well, then you're just going to have to wait until Tuesday, like everybody else," the boss said trying to make Mike share the pain.

Mike, always at the ready with a quick con, replied, "I can't wait. I'm taking a plane tonight. I gotta buy a ticket. My uncle's got me a job in Texas and I gotta get there."

It began to dawn on the boss that this guy was a lying loser sonofabitch and it was most likely to his advantage to cut him loose, even if it did leave him shorthanded. If this deadbeat were to stay a couple of extra days, he would most likely cause problems. An unwilling employee was usually an untrustworthy employee. If, indeed, this employee had ever been trustworthy.

***

DOWNTOWN PRESBYTERIAN HOSPITAL   APRIL 7, 1981 12 NOON

James entered the ICU station of his friend, Colene. They locked eyes. A breathing mask covered his friend's mouth and the part of her face which was not bandaged, was puffy. She looked both terrible and amazing to him.

His new reality, the purgatory that he now carried with him, enabled him to see things that others couldn't. He knew that she had survived the unsurvivable, endured the unendurable. It took him one look into her eyes to understand the fury and the pain that she was experiencing.

He watched as people went in and out of her room: the nurse, the technician and what looked to be a couple of plain-clothes cops. The medical people adjusted dials and touched tubes, the cops sat in chairs and looked serious.

Others came and went, but James stayed. He had nowhere he needed to be and it gave him comfort to sit with Colene. He knew that if Colene had not found a way to stay alive, he would have been the cops' number one suspect.

***

MONICA'S APARTMENT, CENTRAL & TRAMWAY   APRIL 7, 1981 2 PM

Mike backed the U-Haul into the driveway. It was time to get the hell out of Dodge. Beat the feet. Vamoose. Last night, watching the news, he felt like a pot on a stove. Even though it was only spring, it was already way too hot in Albuquerque.

"Okay, babe. Start loading up. Throw everything you can into these boxes? We gotta get the fuck outta here," Mike said. "We're gonna maybe be gone for a while. That wasn't good, what's on TV."

"I know that, Michael, that wasn't good."

"We gotta go. Now."

"I feel dizzy Michael. I hardly slept for two nights."

"I know, babe, but we gotta leave. I'm gonna take care of you. You'll see . . . it's gonna be better somewhere else."

"What about the doctor? I'm supposed to go tomorrow."

"We'll get one down there."

"Yeah, okay," Monica said. She felt worse than dizzy, she felt sick. In her mind, a baby due any minute and on the run from the police for murder was definitely not "living happily ever after".

***

STANFORD STREET, UNM AREA   APRIL 7, 1981 4 PM

Agent English scoured Stanford Street looking for evidence. He knocked on every door of every house within a four block area to determine whether any of the residents had heard or seen anything unusual the previous evening. No one had. He located a discarded cigarette butt and scooped it up. Otherwise, he found nothing.

***

MONICA'S APARTMENT, CENTRAL & TRAMWAY   APRIL 7, 1981 5 PM

Moving day played out in slow motion. A couple of Mike's brothers came over and helped. They carried out the bed, the sofa and the table. That took two hours. Between arguing about who owed who money, whose old lady was the hottest and, of course, who could drink the most beer while simultaneously drinking a lot of beer, little was accomplished. Every now and then, the brothers would spontaneously break out in a wrestling match on the front lawn.

Mike's brother, Raymond, knew why Mike and Monica were leaving town but his younger brother did not know. Or care. Other "helpers" also showed up and that slowed things down even further. The "helpers" were really just there to shoot the shit and buy stuff. Mike needed money, so he was selling everything he could. The items that fattened his wallet the most were the Limbitrol and Emperin 3, narcotics which that helpful doctor had prescribed for him a couple of weeks ago without him even asking. Those pills brought in a bunch of cash. Thank God for that doctor.

Monica was the serious one of the bunch. She carried out as many boxes as her pregnant body would allow and in between boxes, she washed clothes. There were three regular loads and one "special" load: Mike's blood soaked clothes. Monica told Mike that he should throw those clothes away or burn them, but Mike said no. He told her that "all's she needed to do was wash 'em and nobody would never know." Monica sighed and did as she was told because, after all, Mike was always right. His right fist said so.

At the end of the day, the U-Haul was only half filled and the "helpers" were long gone. Monica just wanted to go over to her mom's house and sleep for a couple of weeks, but Mike declared that it was time to go. The sooner he left Albuquerque the better.

***

CENTRAL AND I-25, DOWNTOWN   APRIL 7, 1981 6:15 PM

Mike stopped at the Speedy Mart on Central and bought a carton of Marlboros and as an afterthought picked up the morning edition of the Albuquerque Journal. He thumbed through the paper impatiently and found what he was looking for in the Metro section, "Body Found in Stabbing Investigation."

"Shit," he said.

His crime was not being forgotten about as quickly as he had hoped.

***

After an on-air request had been made for blood for the UNM student who had been stabbed, United Blood Services was flooded with donors. The outpouring of generosity was overwhelming. Friends, family and strangers offered to donate to the girl who had needed over 55 pints of blood while in surgery. It was later calculated that approximately 95 pints of blood had been donated to United Blood Services in Colene's name.

***

NEW MEXICO STATE POLICE, DISTRICT 5, ALBUQUERQUE   APRIL 7, 1981 7:30 PM

Agent Tom English, a young and ambitious state policeman, had been out of the academy only a few years and had already worked his way up to the rank of detective. This case was one of his first big assignments and he was determined to track down the man who perpetrated these crimes. Since the story had gone out in the media about the suspect possibly having the first name Raymond, Agent English's phone had rung off the hook with tips about suspicious men named Raymond. He received just such a tip from the neighbor of Raymond #1. The neighbor was sure he was the killer. Raymond #1 was described as tall; he drove a convertible and had been acting funny.

Agent English drove over to APD on Roma Street and picked up a mug shot of Raymond #1. He then drove over to Presbyterian Hospital to show Colene her first photo lineup. She was watching TV when he arrived. Every day she looked a little bit better. He doubted that Raymond #1 was their man but he could leave no stone unturned. The public was frightened and the sooner the killer was apprehended the better everyone would sleep.

He handed Colene a photo array with five young Hispanic males. She studied them for ten minutes and then handed the photos back to Agent English.

She shook her head "no."

Agent English nodded, tapped his hand briefly on her shoulder and left.

He made the five minute drive up Central Avenue and paid a visit to the night manager of the Frontier Restaurant. Agent English showed him pictures of the victims, Colene and Julie, and asked if he remembered them. The night manager told him hundreds of students came in nightly and he did not remember these particular girls. Agent English thanked him for his time and gave him his card and said, "Call me if you remember anything."

Tom English called APD regarding this homicide. He asked the lieutenant to make sure the suspect's description was circulated throughout the department right away.

***

I-25 NEAR LAS CRUCES, NEW MEXICO   APRIL 7, 1981 10 PM

"Okay, throw em now," Mike said.

"You're paranoid," Monica replied.

"Throw the shoes . . . Wait. Just throw one. Throw the other one after we get *past* Cruces. Spread it out. Make it harder for the cops to find anything."

***

JAMES AND JULIE'S HOUSE, GARFIELD AVENUE, UNM AREA   APRIL 7, 1981 11 PM

James sat on his front porch playing his recorder. He knew he would go out shortly and search for the killer but right now he needed to exhale some of his grief. The notes he played were mournful tones of pain and he played the same unhappy notes over and over again. No one else was there to listen to his random, repetitive requiem of sadness. He was alone.

***

"Come on Michael, wake up. We gotta get out of here. We gotta find somewhere else to stay."

Snore.

"We gotta get over to your sister-law's that lives here and see if we can stay with her," Monica said. Mike continued to sleep.

"We can catch her before she goes to work . . . if we leave now. You gotta get up, Michael."

Snore.

The couple arrived in El Paso, Texas, late the previous evening and found a cheap, crummy motel to crash in. The bed was hard, the walls thin and the cockroaches brazen. Monica did not want to spend another night in this dump. She shook Mike repeatedly but could not rouse him. Out like a light. She decided to let him sleep in and left the room to find coffee.

Mike was far, far away from the motel, even further away from Monica. With his knees pushed up against his chest, he sat by an ephemeral stream filled with dark lazy water. Weeping willows thicketed the sandy shore, making it almost cave-like. As Mike rested on the water's edge, he observed a steady procession of freaky stuff drifting down the darkened ditch: car parts, toilets, dead bodies, stuff like that. Nearby, coyote pups yipped and dogs barked.

Suddenly, he felt hot. Burning up hot. Matter of fact, one of his shoes was on fire. He stood up and put the foot-afire into the nearby stream. Sadly, the stream did not douse the flame. It fed it, like gasoline, doubling the size of the blaze and completely engulfing his foot.

"Help," he shrieked in a girlish voice. "Help! Somebody save me." But then he remembered that he was alone, out in the middle of nowhere. No one to save him.

He tried covering his foot in dirt, but the flame stayed lit - like a festive tiki torch at a summer party. Panting and frothing at the mouth, Mike was running out of ideas. He looked again and saw his shoe had melted off and his foot was beginning to liquefy. In horror, he watched molten puddles of his own flesh form on the arroyo shore.

It finally occurred to him, that to have any chance at all, he would have to cut off his own foot. Reaching in his back pocket he pulled out his handy-dandy, 4" razor-sharp utility knife and plunged it deep into his ankle. Bright red blood spurted out like juice from a ripe orange, but he kept cutting. His entire body was awash in sweat and blood, yet he could not get the fire out nor the foot off. He badly wanted to run away, but how could he escape himself? In utter despair, he began to cry, not like a man but like a baby.

Monica had to shake him for a good five minutes before he finally woke up. Lying flat on his back in the motel room bed, he blubbered shamelessly until checkout time.

CHAPTER 12

Agent Tom English met with Julie's extremely distraught sister at his office. The sister, although anxious to be of assistance, could offer no information which might aid in the investigation of her younger sister's murder. All she could tell him was that Julie had no known enemies and that she had no idea who would want to kill her.

***

Colene didn't feel well enough to do anything other than watch TV. She had the choice of watching soap operas or games shows. She picked game shows. Her favorite game show, *Hollywood Squares*, was on. She laughed at the crazy answers the celebrities concocted, making her forget her troubles for the 30 minutes it was on.

Every day she improved a little, but she was still in a lot of pain and on a lot of drugs. This particular morning, Dr. Phillips came by to see her and was happy that she was doing well. He noted that her abdomen was a bit distended and gassy and he advised her to hold off on eating solid food for a day or two. He told her that her wounds looked good – no obvious infection.

And he had even more good news . . . the drains in her neck were coming out today. He also told her that someone would come by later to take a chest X-Ray in order to get a better picture of the knife fragment embedded in her ribs.

***

NM STATE POLICE, DISTRICT 5, ALBUQUERQUE   APRIL 8, 1981 5 PM

Tom English spent his entire day working the coed murder case. People in the UNM area, especially the women, were extremely apprehensive about having a murdering rapist on the loose. They wanted him caught.

Agent English returned to the Frontier Restaurant and spoke to the manager again. He showed him a composite drawing of the assailant. The manager said that it looked like a Spanish guy who occasionally loitered around the Earthrise Pool Hall, which was located directly behind the Frontier. The manager also said that this guy had worn a neck brace a couple of months back and he might go by the name Cisco, in addition to having the AKA of Raymond.

The detective then contacted Laura who worked at the Frontier on the night of April 5, 1981. Laura stated that she remembered seeing Julie that night. She said that she had spoken with her right before she and her friend left the restaurant that evening.

***

DOWNTOWN PRESBYTERIAN HOSPITAL   APRIL 8, 1981 11PM

"How's Julie?" Colene asked, via notepad, to just about everyone that came by. "Where's Julie?" It wasn't like Julie to not visit her in the hospital. Colene hadn't seen her friend in two days and she wanted to know how she was, how she had gotten away and if she had gotten hurt.

But nobody answered her. Every time it came up, the question was evaded or ignored. The response was either a large amount of silence or a giant amount of noise, but either way there was no answer. They thought they were protecting her. She had been through enough already, they told themselves. But, right now, her world was like the aftermath of a devastating earthquake. Toppled buildings and ruined futures be damned - the shaking stopped when it stopped.

Earlier in the evening, the police officer, Agent English, had been in to see her as usual and Colene wrote a word on the pad that she kept near her bed. "Julie?" the piece of paper said. She pushed it toward him. Agent English studied the paper with cheerless blue eyes, folded it in half and then shifted his gaze to meet hers. She had asked him this question before, he knew that. The first time he had avoided it like everyone else. But he was the professional, so after a very long pause and in a flat cop voice, he told her about Julie.

Colene's anguished eyes and quivering mouth gave him the reaction that he had expected. He did not enjoy dispensing bad news. Other cops that he knew didn't mind so much, but he would never get used to the almost blood-like taste in his mouth when he delivered the words that no one wanted to hear.

***

DOWNTOWN PRESBYTERIAN HOSPITAL   APRIL 9, 1981 10 AM

The next morning, Agent English proceeded optimistically from the Albuquerque Police Department ID unit to Presbyterian Hospital with a mug shot of Raymond #7, who fit the description of the assailant. Raymond #7 had previously stated that he hated Anglo cops and had a scar across his nose.

Colene took a long look at the new photo lineup containing Raymond #7 and shook her head no. Agent English was noticeably disappointed; Raymond #7 had seemed so promising.

Agent English explained to Colene that even though a simple composite had already been drawn, he wanted to create a more elaborate description of the suspect.

"I need you to write down everything you can remember, as detailed as you can, about what this guy looked like," he instructed her.

She had many details to convey but it took a while to get the information down on paper due to her poorly functioning right hand, but she kept at it. Colene vividly remembered every moment of her captivity and the extreme detail she had consciously attempted to memorize. She also remembered the fear. Remembering the incident required reliving it too and that was tough, but she felt it was her duty to help anyway she could. James entered the room and sat down near the foot of her bed. He watched as the blond cop confirmed aloud, detail by detail, what Colene was writing. James again stayed for hours. It was a little selfish and he knew it, but sitting with his friend Colene, blunted a bit of his agony.

After Agent English returned to State Police Headquarters that evening, he typed up an enhanced description of the suspect and sent out the updated bulletin along with the initial composite drawing to the New Mexico law enforcement community and the news media.

***

EL PASO, TEXAS   APRIL 10, 1981 9 AM

TruckStop City was just down the road from his sister-in-law's house. Mike could walk there if he had to. They told him he could start tomorrow and Mike said he'd be there. Even though Monica was back in Albuquerque, he still needed a job. That is . . . he needed money. For Monica and the baby, of course, but maybe a little for himself. He deserved it.

Moving down to El Paso had been necessary but it had used up all of his available cash. He had to borrow $50 from his uncle for the gas money to get Monica back home. Bringing her down to El Paso was a bad mistake. All she did was complain. She complained that she didn't feel good because she was pregnant. She complained that they didn't have enough money for the doctor. She complained that she missed her mom. She complained that she couldn't sleep because the police might show up, blah, blah, blah. On and on. Mike didn't have the patience or the time for that kind of shit. He would be better off just making the money and sending her some. He would go back to Albuquerque himself when the coast was clear.

***

DOWNTOWN PRESBYTERIAN HOSPITAL   APRIL 10, 1981 4 PM

"You're looking way too good to stay in ICU," Dr. Phillips said, looking at her file. "As soon as we can find you a bed in a private room, that's where you're going. And it will be today."

Colene smiled.

***

STANFORD STREET, UNM AREA   APRIL 10, 1981 11:45 PM

James was on patrol again, as he had been every night since April 5th. With the killer's composite picture burned into his brain, he scoured the neighborhood constantly, obsessively and with a vengeance. He circled for hours on end, stopping only when he realized that the citizens were looking suspiciously at *him*. He knew he would eventually buy a gun, but he hadn't gotten around to that yet.

James had been neglecting himself. His clothes were dirty, he kept forgetting to eat, and sleeping was a big, big problem. Hideous dreams haunted his sleep. He tried to stay awake, but a specific nightmare, of the most heinous and personal sort, regularly crept into his dreams and turned his slumber to anguish. It was always the same dream and it happened again this very night.

In his dream, ground fog swirled from the manholes, obscuring whole parts of the street. Steamy particles puffed from the ground like an old man's pipe. James and Julie strolled the sidewalks hand in hand as always, the baseball bat dangling easily from James' right arm, the bat now as much a part of him as any other permanent extension of his body.

As the young couple crossed the intersection at Vassar and Coal, a dusty brown car traveling at an excessively high rate of speed, raced perilously by them. James grabbed Julie and pulled her close and at the same time, raised the bat high over his head for protection. Darkened windows hid the driver's face and the car disappeared as fast as it had come.

Nothing had happened. The young couple was alright. It was just a scare. James kissed Julie and they resumed their walk down Coal. A quarter moon was up high in the sky and the misty fog gave the street lamps a languid milky glow.

James and Julie's pace quickened as a sudden drizzle caught them by surprise. It was time to head home anyway. James heard a car revving its engine and looked behind him. He saw the brown car. It appeared to be moving cautiously, maybe even nervously. It was a good five lengths away. James left Julie on the sidewalk, gripped his bat and stepped into the street, toward the oncoming vehicle. Like a western showdown, James and the car moved fatefully towards each other, both with deadly intentions. As he got closer, James saw the driver. It was the killer's composite drawing glaring at him behind the wheel. James saw pure evil, he saw white hate. Tire rubber screeching, the car accelerated, and then, at the very last second, it zigzagged past James, heading directly and without hesitation towards Julie. Horrified, James beat the side of the car with the fury of a wrecking ball, but it did not stop. The car drove forward and into the night.

James ran to the spot where Julie had stood just one moment earlier, but no one was there . . . just ground fog and silence.

***

DOWNTOWN PRESBYTERIAN HOSPITAL   APRIL 10, 1981 11:30 PM

Like the poor woman strapped to the log, propelling her inextricably towards the sharp, swirling blade, she felt sure her head was about to split open. Life inside a hospital room was a constant jolt to the senses. People coming and going, buzzing florescent lights, beeping machines, incessant, boring banter.

"How are we today, Ms. Bush?" Dr. "A" might ask and then without waiting, reply for her, "Yes, you *are* looking better, Ms. Bush." And so it would go - doctors "B" through "G" reciting the same script, or so it seemed. Very unrestful. At least twenty visitors conga danced through her room that day, mostly medical but others too. Curiosity seekers were kept out. The 24/7 cop at her door saw to that. A nice surprise did show up, though. An older lady with an even older black lab from the "Pooches for Patients" program was allowed in. The moment the big dog nuzzled Colene's face, she brightened and stayed that way for the ten plus minutes the lab was with her. It gave her a missing sense of humanity to touch the dog, to pet him. She didn't have to fake being cheerful. This was real and it felt good to do something "normal".

But that was the thing though, wasn't it? What *was* normal anymore? She could usually make it through the days, they were so busy, but the nights were a different story. At night, when all of the visitors were gone, she was back in the arroyo, trying to get away. She saw the man and he had a knife. She couldn't escape. What did he want? He hurt Julie . . . killed her. Why, why, why wasn't she able to save her?

Blue and red lights from the revolving motel sign across the street washed over her young, bandaged face like surf on a sandy beach. Oblivious, she cried and cried. Try as she might to suppress it, tears rimmed her eyes and muffled sobs crept from her throat. Her only thoughts were of her murdered friend and how to reconcile recent tragic events with her now uncertain future.

If it weren't for the night duty nurse, no one would have ever been aware of Colene's mournful late night weeping. The night nurse not only witnessed this girl's agony, she would say later that she ingested it. She never forgot the suffering that she saw in that girl. She told anyone that would listen, that she had never seen such brutality inflicted upon another human being – before or since. It stayed with that nurse throughout the years, like an uncured cancer.

***

DOWNTOWN PRESBYTERIAN HOSPITAL   APRIL 11, 1981 10 PM

"We have enough flowers in here," Carol said. Nurse Cindy scanned the room and agreed with Colene's mom that it was overflowing with flowers.

The piles of accumulated gifts made it seem like almost everyone in the world had heard about Colene's tragedy. There were countless flowers, plus non-stop phone calls and "get well" cards galore. She received cards from her high school basketball team, the ski patrol, school kids she didn't know, long lost family friends, even her school driver bus driver from the 3rd grade. She was surprised when she received a letter from William Davis, the president of UNM, telling her that her "spunky determination was inspiring to us all." Even Moriarty acquaintance, Mike Anaya, dropped her a get-well card. Nothing from brother Toney, though.

"What should I do if more arrive, ma'am? Throw them away or give them to other patients?" Cindy asked.

"But I like the flowers, Mom," Colene interrupted. "They make me feel better."

"No, there's too many," Carol said. "It's wasteful. Tell the hospital to ask the people to donate to the Crime Stoppers instead. Let 'em use the money to catch the bastard that did this."

Colene adored all of the flowers in the room but what her mom said made sense. "Yeah . . . okay . . . go ahead; tell 'em to give it to the Crime Stoppers."

***

FARMINGTON, NEW MEXICO   APRIL 11, 1981 11AM

It was a dark day in Farmington, New Mexico. One of their own, their neighbor's daughter, a young woman with a world of promise, had been murdered while walking home from a coffee shop.

The mourners poured into Trinity Lutheran Church. It was a Saturday but the church would have been filled any day of the week. There were hundreds of them. Some of them knew her and some just came to pay their respects.

Julie Ann Lovlien Jackson, age 19, was being laid to rest in front of friends and family.

CHAPTER 13

To increase her lung capacity she was constantly encouraged to cough. She needed to get the phlegm out in order to get her full breathing capacity back. Coughing was the ticket - she had been told - for a phlegm-free life. The nurses and her mom were continually on her case.

"Cough it up. You can do it, you can do it," they said, with the reassuring chatter of a little league coach. The only way she had to "cough it up" was through her breathing apparatus, a tracheotomy tube. The trach tube was a life saver, no doubt about it, but also it was a pain in the ass. The tube protruded from a hole located at the bottom of her neck, enabling her to breathe and talk. In order for her to talk, she had to suck in a large volume of air, plug up the tube with her finger and then immediately speak in short airy bursts.

Colene was sick, as in very sick, of being in the hospital. She was ready to leave. But her doctor had told her, that it was going to be a few more days. The trach had to come out first, and she wasn't quite ready. Even after eight days in the hospital, her face and neck were so swollen from the savage attack, that she looked like she had the mumps. The spirometer, a nifty little hand-held device that measures breathing volume, reported that her lungs were not yet to full capacity. She could only get the needle on the spirometer up about halfway. The doctors and nurses reminded her again that the fastest way to improve her lung function was to cough. Cough early and cough often.

As the days wore on, she had taken to staring out of her hospital room window. She reflected often on the fact that this was both the hospital that she was born in and "born again" in.

Her room was located directly across the street from the Crossroads Motel, a nondescript little two-story stopover on Central and I-25. She noted that the "L" in motel was barely flickering. Absently, she wondered if either the motel name and/or the missing letter had any sort of symbolic implications regarding her future. Was she really at a crossroads? And what the "L" did it all mean?

While looking out the window on this particular day and watching the motel patrons scurry from room to parking lot to room again, she saw an entire family of eight dressed in bunny costumes. Even though it was almost Easter, this struck her as funny, and she laughed. In fact, she laughed and laughed again. This excessive chortling generated some mild coughing. Optimistically, she hoped that she might be inducing some major mucus motion. And then, all at once, instinct told her that a mighty cough was a-comin. Cough, cough, cough. She could almost hear a tiny voice inside of her lungs say the words, "Passengers, the captain has now turned on the fasten seat belt sign." She knew a large loogie was about to get hocked. However, at this point, she could no more control it or prevent its eruption than the Italians could have stopped Mount Vesuvius. It was time for the villagers to scramble or die. Earth moving-like rumblings continued to stir deep within her chest.

Then it blew. A giant blob of snot projectiled outward and upward from the trach tube, landing at the intersection of wall and ceiling. It was as odious as it was odorous. Colene, attached to an IV, stared helplessly as the gross green glob of gunk slimed its way down the hospital wall. Following a brief moment of baseless embarrassment, she laughed her head off.

The next thing that happened wasn't so funny though, at least not right then. Another urge to cough overcame her almost immediately. And this cough, as hard as it was for her to believe, would be even mightier than the previous one. Oh well, she thought, the last one was funny, so this one should be fucking hilarious. About that last part, she was quite wrong. This time, when she coughed, the entire metal trach tube ejaculated out of her neck.

Her first thought was -*WHAT?* Her next thought was – *I can't talk. I can't even scream for help. A*nd her third thought was – *holy shit, not only can't I talk, but I can't even breathe without that darn tube.* Sweat drenched her body. Panic set in. Finally, she thought to push her little blue "nurse" button and an RN arrived immediately. The nurse calmly wiped off the tube and stuck it back in. Emergency over. Colene sucked in some air, covered the hole in her reinserted trach and gratefully huffed the words, "Thank you."

***

CENTRAL AVENUE, UNM AREA   APRIL 12, 1981 6 PM

Albuquerque women, especially college-age women living in the UNM area, were on edge. The recent attack at knife-point on two female university students troubled some of the residents enough to take extra precautions. The killer was still on the loose and the police believed that the man was armed and extremely dangerous.

Since walking with a friend obviously offered no protection, many women took the task of protecting themselves into their own hands. UNM's Daily Lobo echoed the fears of its students stating, "God only knows what kind of riffraff is waiting behind the next bush." In an attempt to quell the rising level of anxiety, the campus karate club offered a free self-defense seminar for all students.

But it wasn't just UNM students that were worried. The at-large killer worried Sherrie and her fellow workers at the Central Avenue Credit Union enough that they began packing pistols in their purses. "It concerns me," Sherry told a member of the media. "It scares me and I don't want to be an easy target for this maniac."

In the break room, at the Credit Union's main office on Central, Sherry and her two female co-workers were preparing to leave for the day. The women felt jittery walking down Central Avenue, even in broad daylight

Suddenly, a loud noise shook the room and the three women simultaneously reached into their respective purses and pulled out their weapons.

Standing frozen with their guns drawn, the co-workers looked at each other and laughed . . . nervously. They realized, belatedly, that the noise they had heard was a car backfiring out on the street.

***

DOWNTOWN PRESBYTERIAN HOSPITAL   APRIL 12, 1981 7 PM

"Get up! Get up!" her dad shouted. "GO, GO, GO." Colene had been sleeping while her father sat with her. Her peaceful face morphed into a horror mask. A thick-bodied nurse raced in and grabbed Colene by the arm and yanked her out of bed and rushed her down the hall as quickly as possible.

Two minutes earlier, Ina Gonzalez, a very thin nurse originally from Miami, had picked up the phone on the second ring. "Presbyterian Hospital, Ward 7C," Ina said in a friendly voice.

She heard only slow, heavy breathing. Her blood quickened. A man with a deep voice whispered ominously, "I know you have Colene Bush up there."

"What?" was all she could say. The hair on the back of her neck stood up and her own breathing got heavy. She fumbled unsuccessfully with her free hand to press a nearby security buzzer.

The deep-voiced man continued whispering, punctuated with long breathy pauses. "There's a bomb in her room . . . you have 20 minutes to get everyone the hell out of there . . . or you're all dead." Click.

"Aaahyyyhahhhah," Ina screamed and dropped the phone. The other nurses rushed over and surrounded her.

"Bomb." she said in a muted voice and then began screaming in short sentences, "BOMB!" "Colene Bush's room. 20 minutes. It's going off in 20 minutes. Somebody call security. Call the police. Get her out of here. Clear the area." Like a sudden storm, a cloud of personnel descended upon Colene's room.

Colene could not believe that her safety had been violated yet again. They told her she would be safe in the hospital. A New Mexico State police officer sat in front of her room at all times. Terror gripped her as they pulled her out of bed and hustled her down the hall.

Mounted Patrol Trooper Glen was the closest officer in the vicinity and the first officer to respond. He cleared the area of people. APD's bomb squad soon arrived and thoroughly searched the entire hospital floor for explosives. Dogs sniffed Colene's room but found nothing. Ultimately no explosion occurred and no bomb or suspicious device was located. APD gave the all clear to return to that part of the hospital at about 9 PM. Colene had to be given sedatives and many promises before she would agree to return to her room.

***

DOWNTOWN PRESBYTERIAN HOSPITAL   APRIL 14, 1981 2PM

Presbyterian Hospital was tight lipped about where Miss Bush was to recuperate. They did say that she would not be recuperating at another hospital. They further stated that she was released in fair condition.

Even though she arrived at the hospital with nothing, her mom had to make three round trips to the car when she left. The request to stop the flowers had made no difference; they still arrived by the pallet. Various medical equipment had to be brought along as well. It was a lot of stuff and Colene couldn't carry any of it. Her little sister was there as her personal slave. Colene enjoyed that part.

She said her goodbyes and thank yous to the hospital staff. Everyone had gone out of their way to be kind and helpful during her stay. The Presbyterian Hospital personnel, along with the college guys, trucker and paramedics that had gotten her there, had saved her life. Grateful was not an adequate word for how she felt about them.

A wheel chair was brought to her room and her mom pushed her through the hospital as well- wishers bade her farewell and good luck. She did not realize then that the healing process had only just begun.

***

STATE POLICE HEADQUARTERS, CARLISLE AVENUE NE   APRIL 15, 1981 1:30 PM

Crime Stoppers was flooded with tips regarding the "UNM Co-ed Killer". All tips were passed to the State Police. One confidential tip stated that a man named Raymond, this would be Raymond #18, matched the composite drawing of the suspect that Agent English had been circulating. The informant stated that Raymond #18 had been acting strangely of late. Agent English immediately showed a photo of this man to Colene but she was unable to positively identify him.

Despite the fact that Colene couldn't identify him, Agent English spent a fair amount of time delving into this particular Raymond. He was 5'10", with dark hair and eyes and had acne scars . . . but no scar across his nose. He was, interestingly though, born in El Paso, Texas. The assailant had told Colene that he was from El Paso. Agent English intended to find out as much as he could about this man. Raymond #18 was on now his short list.

***

DOWNTOWN PRESBYTERIAN HOSPITAL   APRIL 15, 1981 3:30 PM

Colene went to see the neurologist as an outpatient. She reported that the sensory loss in her legs had faded completely, but her hands, especially on the right side, tingled constantly.

"I can't button my buttons," she told the doctor. "My hands aren't working right." She told him she couldn't open jars, turn doorknobs, or tie her shoes. She wanted to go back to school as soon as possible but the only way she could hold a pencil was in her fist, like a first grader, and her signature was illegible.

Despite her frustration and the negative function of her hands, the neurologist told her he was impressed with how well she was doing.

***

SANTA FE, NEW MEXICO   APRIL 16, 1981 12 NOON

Spearheaded by the Crime Victim's Assistance Organization, $1.8 million was approved by the New Mexico state legislature for compensation to victims of violent crime. However, only violent crime victims after July 1, 1981, were eligible. Colene Bush was out of luck.

***

UTAH STREET, "WAR ZONE" ALBUQUERQUE   APRIL 18, 1981 3PM

While the police searched for a suspect, Colene hid out at a relative's house. Virtually imprisoned, she tried to make the best of a miserable situation. Her mother brought her magazines and drawing pads. The magazines were good while they lasted but Colene plowed through them quickly. The drawing pad was a nice idea too, but not practical, since both her hands were severely damaged. Mostly she watched TV.

Agent English brought over another photo lineup for Colene to scrutinize and it was another negative. Because his diligence was ceaseless and her patience infinite, they slogged through as many of the suspicious Raymonds as Agent English could find.

Today, however, Colene had something for Agent English. She had retrieved a very particular knife from her mom's house and she gave it to him to scrutinize. Colene told him that this was the same type of knife that the killer used. It was a 4" long JA Henkel knife, considered by many professional chefs to be one of the sharpest knives in the world.

Agent English thanked her for the knife and deposited it in his bulging briefcase. He made a note to himself to have one of his technicians evaluate it.

***

EL PASO, TEXAS   APRIL 20, 1981 10AM

"Mom, it's me," Mike said.

"Where the fuck you been?" Linda yelled into the phone. "I got cops all the time calling here. They keep calling. They want to talk to your brother, Raymond, about some white girls that got stabbed. He says he didn't do it. They got his name. They said some girl gave 'em Raymond's name. Raymond said that you said that you did it. Why didn't you tell me already?"

"Mom, would you shut up for a minute. Yeah . . . I did something. I messed up. I don't know why. The devil was in me Mom. I been in Texas trying to think."

"Listen, you dumb fuck. Get back here right now and tell these damn cops. Tell 'em it wasn't Raymond. I can't believe you messed your brother up like that. God damn you . . . you're so fucking stupid. Get your fucking ass back to Albuquerque now."

"Mom, I don't wanna go to jail."

"Get back here now and tell them cops that you did it, not Ray. Otherwise *he's* going to jail. Just tell the cops you didn't know what you was doing . . . tell 'em God said to do it or something like that. They'll probably just give you a couple of years anyways. But get back here now dammit and take care of it. You hear me, Michael? *Now!*"

"Okay, Okay. I'll be back in a couple a days. I gotta get a ride or get money to get there."

"You get up here now, boy. You hear me? Or I'll get someone to go down there and get your ass."

"Yeah, Mom . . . Okay."

***

UTAH STREET, "WAR ZONE", ALBUQUERQUE   APRIL 21 11:15 AM

Colene was presented with another photo lineup by Agent English. She could not positively ID anyone. Depression was beginning to gnaw at Colene. She did not want to be held captive indefinitely.

***

UNM HOSPITAL   APRIL 21, 1981 8 PM

It was a pretty uneventful delivery. Mom did as well as could be expected. She had given birth to a bouncing baby boy at the University of New Mexico Hospital maternity ward. Dad was unable to make the blessed event, but he did call. He said he would be leaving El Paso shortly. He told her that he bought the baby a toy truck at the truck stop gift shop where he worked. He said that he liked his new coworkers; they weren't all snotty like at the dumb fancy restaurant. He said he was making good money too. Mike's boss had already told him what a hard worker he was. Mike told her that he couldn't wait to see his new baby boy and asked if he looked anything like him. Even though he really didn't, she told him that he was a spitting image. He laughed a small laugh, then asked her how she was. She said she was feeling pretty good considering but she was worried all the time because of the terrible trouble he had gotten himself into. She told him there was stuff on the news every day and that his mom kept calling asking her what was going on and when was he getting back to Albuquerque. She told him the police had come by his mom's house more than once. The cops had brought his brother Raymond in for questioning and were trying to get him to confess. Monica told him she needed him to get home right away. He told her he would be there as soon as he could.

CHAPTER 14

In order to more fully recall the events of April 5 and 6, 1981, Deaf Smith County Sheriff Travis McPherson and New Mexico State Police Sargent Dean Smith took Colene to the Four Seasons Motel where NMSP had rented a room. Colene had agreed to be hypnotized.

Sargent Smith was the hypnotist and he softly began intoning to Colene.

"Colene, I'm going to be asking you to do some things and I want you to listen just to my voice, and try in your mind, to picture the things that I paint for you. First, I want you to close your eyes. With your eyes closed, I want you to imagine that up in the top of your forehead there is a bluish-white light. While you are looking at that bluish-white light, in the top of your forehead, I want you to concentrate on the muscles in your forehead and tell them to relax. Relaxation is the absence of effort; you don't have to do anything to relax."

Sargent Smith continued speaking in low soothing tones, calling upon her to relax." You are on the elevator of relaxation. You start on the tenth floor and as you go down, you go deeper and deeper into relaxation. In a few minutes you will hear the voice of Mr. McPherson and upon hearing his voice you will go into an even deeper level of relaxation."

"I want you to act as if you're a reporter. You have a TV camera." McPherson said and asked her about the details of that night. Colene, while under hypnosis, was interviewed for two hours as McPherson tried to glean as much additional data about the criminal as possible.

As the hypnosis session completed, in an act of pure coincidence, a man who had not previously been considered a suspect, turned himself into police.

***

SANDOVAL COUNTY SHERIFF'S OFFICE, BERNALILLO, NEW MEXICO   APRIL 23, 1981 10:30 AM

"Good morning, Sandoval County Sheriff's Office."

"Hi, I need to talk to Jimmy Gutierrez."

"Who may I ask is calling?"

"This is Michael . . . he knows me. He knows my mom, all my life. I need to talk to him. I need to get something off my mind . . . I did something."

"May I have you last name, Michael?"

"Ma'am, just get me Jimmy, okay? I gotta talk to him. He knows me."

"Hold on, one moment Michael. I'll connect you."

"Hello, this is Detective Gutierrez. How can I help you?"

"Jimmy . . . this is Michael. You known me since I was a kid. You known my family, my mom, Linda from Bernalillo. I was the really big little kid. We're over on Don Gabal now. You helped my brother last year . . . 'member?"

"Oh, yeah. Yeah, I remember you Michael. What do you need?"

"I killed somebody, Jimmy. I killed a girl up in the mountains about two weeks ago now. I thought it was two I killed, but I guess it's only one. I need to talk to you, Jimmy, so I can get this shit off my mind."

Detective Gutierrez took a deep breath. "Sure, Michael, that's a good idea. Why don't you come down to my office and tell me about it. I have some time right now. I'll just wait for you."

"I gotta get this stuff off my mind, Jimmy. Can you come over to my mom's house? I don't want no other cops around. I only want to talk to you, cause I trust you, cause you known me since I was a little kid. I don't wanna get put in no handcuffs, Jimmy. You gotta promise me that. My mom said you always treated our family real good, so it's you I wanna tell."

"I'm going to put all my meetings on hold and I'll be right there for you, Michael. I'm leaving now."

"Okay Jimmy, I trust you."

***

LINDA'S HOUSE, DON GABAL, NW   APRIL 23, 1981 12 NOON

Sandoval County Investigator Jim Gutierrez drove over to Linda Guzman's house in northwest Albuquerque to interview Michael Guzman. Mr. Gutierrez came alone as promised. The interview was recorded on audio cassette tape.

JG: Michael are you giving me this statement of your own free will?

MG: Yes, sir.

JG: I have advised you of your rights haven't I?

MG: Yes, sir.

JF: And you still want to give me a statement?

MG: Yes, sir.

JG: Okay. You called me at approximately 11:30 AM at my office, is that right?

MF: Yes, sir.

JG: And you advised me that you were in trouble and that you'd killed somebody. Is that correct?

MG: Yes, sir.

JG: Okay. Why don't you tell me what happened?

MG: One night I was at work and ahh. . . .

JG: Where do you work?

MG: Comme Chez Vous.

JG: Is that a restaurant or what is it?

MG: It's a restaurant.

JG: Where is it located?

MG: It's located on ahh . . . Montgomery and Louisiana, the corner of Montgomery and Louisiana.

JG: Okay.

MG: And I had a hard day at work, I had got a knife from work already.

JG: What kind of knife was it?

MG: It was a small knife that I was taking home for my wife.

JG: Was it a cutting knife or . . .

MG: A cutting knife. And I was getting ready to go home and I stopped out there on my way with a hot plate of food by the side of me, I always used to take one home at night, almost, cause I get home at 1, 12, 11 o'clock at night . . . and I was going home.

JG: Were you by yourself?

MG: Yes, I was.

JG: What were you in?

MG: I was in a 1967 Chevy Ford yellow convertible. And when I started going home, I had beer in the back of my car that I had for a day in my car already.

JG: How much beer did you have?

MG: I had a case of beer. I had gave my mother a six pack, I had the rest.

JG: What kind of beer was it?

MG: Coors beer.

JG: Okay.

MG: It was tall cans. And I had it in there covered up with a plastic bag so nobody would see it, so I wouldn't get pulled over cause I didn't have no window in the back. The car that I was driving was a '67 Ford Chevy . . . I mean Ford convertible, it didn't have no back window, right now it's in the shop.

JG: Which shop is it in?

MG: It's in ahh . . . up on Zuni . . . Lee's Garage . . .

JG: Lee's Garage?

MG: . . . and I'm willing to show the car and how the girl got out and what happened from there. And the way this happened was that I, Michael Guzman, was coming down from work.

JG: You were driving, right?

MG: Yes.

JG: Okay, just take your time.

MG: I was coming from work and I stopped at the station, I don't know the name of the station, I think it was Vickers Station, right there by Stanford, like they say the murdered girls had been picked up. I did not pick up the girls. When I had finished, they been out in my car. They were coming down, I guess they were coming down. When I got in my car, I didn't notice them until I went around the corner by Stanford, stopped my car, and I looked back to get me a beer and the girls were right there and they said they wanted to party with me.

JG: They were in your car?

MG: They were in the back seat already.

JG: When did they get in your car?

MG: Pardon me?

JG: When did they get in your car?

MG: I don't know, they must have got in when I was at Vickers because I went to buy a pack of cigarettes and came back, I just got in my car like I normally do . . .

JG: But you never saw the girls get in your car?

MG: No, I didn't see them get in my car.

JG: Okay. Then you drove around the corner on Stanford?

MG: No, I didn't drive like that on Stanford. I went from Vickers like that . . . like that . . . I don't know how to say it Jim. I went . . . okay, Vickers is right there by Central, right?

JG: Uh-huh.

MG: I went straight out, right around the block, I took a left then I took another left, I was going to go down towards the frontage . . . what's the name of that place, the Frontage . . . where they have all the games . . . game rooms?

JG: I don't know.

MG: Well, I was going down there . . .

JG: When was it you noticed the girls in the car?

MG: When they came up an' said, "Can we party with you?"

JG: Is that what they told you?

MG: Yes. And ahh . . . I said, "No, I'm tired and I'm going home, I just got off of work." They said, "You can party with us, we ain't going to hurt you, we want to be your friends." And that's when I turned around and said, "No, I can't, I'm married." "What are you afraid of . . ." that girl told me, the one that's alive right now, the one that was sitting towards me . . . next to me . . . the other one was sitting . . . I even told the . . .

JG: Did they get in the front seat or what?

MG: Yes.

JG: They moved up to the front seat?

Linda Guzman: From the beginning?

MG: No, not from the beginning.

JG: When did they get in the front seat?

MG: Pardon me?

JG: When did they . . .

MG: When I stopped the car right there on the corner by a white house and I got out of the car and that's when I took my knife out and I told them to get up front.

JG: You pulled a knife on them then?

MG: Yeah.

JG: And you told them to get in the front seat?

MG: Yeah.

JG: Okay. Go on.

MG: And then I continued driving, cause I was scared, cause I had pulled out a knife. From there they just started talking to me, asking me questions and I was getting nervous and they were pushing me and pushing . . . and pushing and pushing.

JG: How were they pushing? What were they saying to you?

MG: They were asking all kinds of questions, questions that I can't really remember. I know some of the questions that really hurt my feelings were . . . "Why don't you party with us . . . I'll make you feel good." The one that was sitting next to me said that. They . . . they . . . after I had done everything . . . took them for a ride . . . riding around, we were talking . . . .

JG: Where did you go, just around town or what?

MG: Around town, yes. I didn't know my way good. I don't know my way good around this town and I asked the girl, "Where are we at?" and she said, "We're on Central" and then "We're on Zuni" and all the way up on Zuni . . . .

JG: Did they tell you their names?

MG: I remember one of their names, Jolene Jackson or something like that, but I can't remember the other one.

JG: Okay. And then what happened?

MG: And they asked me what was your name, and I said a different name, cause I didn't want to get in trouble, I said, "My name is Raymond." And ahh . . . from there, I continued going up Zuni all the way . . . they told me I was on Zuni . . . of course I knew once I seen the sign, cause I was just going crazy driving around. I finally came to a stop sign.

JG: Why did you pull the knife on them?

MG: Huh?

JG: Why did you pull the knife on them?

MG: Cause . . . I don't know, Jim. The thing is that I didn't want nothing to interfere with me and my wife anymore. I had been threatened that my baby was going to be taken away, and I was trying to do my best for my baby and I was tired. I used to mess around a lot on her and I . . . .

JG: You pulled a knife on them and told them to get in the front seat?

MG: Yeah.

JG: An then you were up by Zuni and what happened?

MG: I took 'em and they . . . before we even got to Zuni, let's put it this way, I started telling them, "I feel like killing myself," and they said, "Why?" and I said . . . and they started telling me . . . "Well, we'll be your friends," and I told them, "No, you can't be my friends, the only friend I got is God." All the friends I have back-stabbed me, I went through hell. I told them that God was the only thing that's doing this . . . like right now. I believe that God's doing this, making me do this, it ain't my mom, it ain't you, it ain't nobody, it ain't myself . . .

JG: Well, I think it is yourself thru God, don't you think so?

MG: Yeah.

JG: Okay . . . then what happened?

MG: I can't really remember much, cause I have so many things on my mind.

JG: Try and tell me, the best you can remember, Mike. Tell me what happened, don't be scared . . . tell the truth.

MG: An then I started going down, and I told them, "I'll take you home, if you want." They said, "No, no . . . it's okay." I guess they were scared, cause I already had the knife . . . showed 'em I had it on me. And I was driving with this hand and I had the knife under my leg.

JG: You were driving with your right hand and you had the knife under your left leg?

MG: Yeah.

JG: Okay.

MG: Okay . . . and then they said, "Just keep on driving, we'll talk with you Mike, just tell us what's wrong." . . . Oh, Raymond, I'm sorry . . .and ahh . . . my mind just started going berserk, I was getting pissed off. Why? I don't know. What was I doing with them girls, you know, in my car? My wife's mom, or my girlfriend's mom, had just helped us buy that car and me and my wife lived at our own house, we were doing real good until that night . . . all of this happened, then I kept going up . . . which was . . . is that, north?

JG: East.

MG: I kept going east and I wouldn't stop . . . I wouldn't pay attention to them. I stopped and I put the car in reverse. I seen that it was a dark alley . . . not an alley, but like a dark arroyo . . . and I went down the arroyo and they said, "What are you doing?" And I just told them, "Shut up, don't talk to me no more." And we got down there . . .

JG: Relax, relax, just take your time, relax.

MG: When we got down there . . . I told the girls . . . they told me, "What are you going to do, don't hurt us." I just told 'em to shut up. . . . "Take your clothes off before I put the knife on you, in your gut." And I had 'em strip . . . and I told them, "Throw your clothes in the back." I had the knife on the girl that was sitting by me . . . I mean I had it up on her . . . chest, right by her heart.

JG: Were you in the car or out of the car?

MG: In the car.

JG: And the girl was sitting by you and you had it by her heart?

MG: I had the knife pointed towards her heart and I tell her, "Strip, I don't want to talk no more . . . just strip." I don't know Jim; something was in me that night. I can't live with this all my life, you know . . . it hurts me; it hurts me for what I done. I don't even know the girls, to tell the truth. I really don't know what went on. I was not drunk. They'll tell you . . . I was talking. The only thing I kept saying was that God is my friend . . . nobody's my friend. And that's the way I see it Jim, nobody. I ain't got no friends. I've had a rough time all my life. I've been a runaway. I'm a nervous person. I've been nervous for years. I've had a nervous breakdown already.

JG: Just relax. Okay, then what happened, you were sitting in the car and you had them both stripped, completely stripped?

MG: I had both of them stripped.

JG: Completely?

MG: Yes, completely.

JG: Okay, then what happened?

MG: And then I got . . . I stepped out of the car . . . I opened the car door on my side and I told the girl that was sitting next to me, she kept saying something, I can't remember exactly what she said, and I told her, "Just shut up" and I got the keys out of my car and I opened the trunk and I told her, "Get in the damn trunk and shut up."

JG: Which one was this?

MG: The one that was sitting by me, the one that's alive right now.

JG: The one that is alive right now?

MG: Yes.

JG: And you put her in the trunk?

MG: She is the main one. Jolene Jackson, if that's her name, she was not saying nothing . . .she wasn't saying nothing bad, it was the girl next to me that kept poking me and poking me and making me get mad and how she was doing it, I don't know. I just couldn't take it no more.

JG: So the one sitting by you was the one that made you mad?

MG: All the way. She would not keep her mouth shut.

JG: Okay, then what happened? You opened the trunk and then what happened?

MG: I opened the trunk after they were naked and I told her, "Get in the trunk" and I told her . . .

JG: This is the one that was sitting by you; you told to get in the trunk?

MG: Yeah, and I told her to get in the trunk, and she got in there and she went, okay, okay . . . " and I shut the trunk and I went back to the car and that girl, Jolene Jackson was laying on the seat with her legs open and she goes to me, "Michael, is this what you want?" I just stayed quiet.

JG: Which way was she laying?

MG: Like . . . she was the one that was on the door, right?

JG: The passenger side.

MG: The passenger side. She had her head on the passenger. . . . and she was laying out towards me with her legs open and she goes. . . Mike, is this what you want?

JG: Mike or Raymond?

MG: Raymond . . . is this what you want? And I just stared at her and looked at her and jumped in the car and grabbed her like that . . . "Come on with me," I said, and I took her up around the tree and she goes, "Mike, don't hurt me please" . . .

JG: Mike or Raymond?

MG: Raymond . . . it's, I don't . . . That's my name, Michael . . . and I was using Raymond . . . and you know what I mean . . . and she goes, "Raymond, don't hurt me please." And at the time I put the knife in my pocket, my back pocket. And I hugged her so I wouldn't get nothing on me. And she goes . . . we were walking and she said, "It's cold out here." I said, "It won't be cold for long." And I pulled out the knife from my pocket and I just put it in her one time and went back. By the time I came back, the other girl was already dressing up, already dressing up. And she looked at me and she started running. When she started running, I started running and that's when I put the knife in her back. All I can remember is that I just stabbed her twice, once in the back and once in the stomach. She was trying to slap me; I pulled the knife out of her back. A little piece of knife got broken in her back. I had seen the knife. When I went home . . . well, I'll put it this way. When I went home, before . . . when I was stabbing that girl, what made me stop was when she got on her knees and said, "Oh God, let me die in peace." I right away got the knife, threw it in the backseat of the car, I got in the car with my lights off and just took off up the hill, turned them on when I got on the road, then I went home. I went to talk to my wife, I was all bloody, I was hurt, I don't know what I was doing . . . I talked to my wife.

JG: Did you tell her what happened?

MG: Yes, I told my wife what happened . . . like she loves me so much, she knows what I've been through . . . we're doing damn good . . . and I took my wife down there, I took my wife down there and I told her . . . she was asleep when I got home . . . this was about 11 o'clock Sunday night, cause we had got early out of work, it wasn't Monday, like they're saying on TV, it was Sunday night when I did everything . . . .and ahhh . . . I went home, I was crying . . . telling my wife, "Monica, Monica wake up, I just killed somebody." She wouldn't believe me, she didn't. When I showed her the knife and the clothes . . . she started crying, "Why did you do it?" "Cause I love you" that's all I could say, cause I love you . . . and she started crying, "I love you too, Mike." And I told her, Monica, we got to go back" and she goes, "What for Mike, you already did it; you're going to get in trouble." And I told her, "My cigarettes and my lighter is out there." And she goes, "Oh my God, what are we going to do now, why did you have to do it now?" Monica, I don't know what went thru my head. I was pretty upset. I love that girl so much, she's carrying my baby, I'm a hard worker, I just don't know what went into my head Jim, and ahh . . .

JG: What did you do with the clothing and the knife?

MG: The knife, I don't know, I just threw it Jim.

JG: Do you remember where you threw it; were you driving down the road or what?

MG: On the freeway somewhere.

JG: On the freeway?

MG: Yeah.

JG: You're sure it was on the freeway?

MG: Positive.

JG: How long of a knife was it?

MG: It was a little one.

JG: Was it like a streak knife or what?

MG: No, it was a knife, a very, very sharp knife, it had a handle like that, the size of my hand and I could draw it if you'd like me to draw it?

JG: How long was the blade?

MG: The blade was around like . . . that long.

JG: 4 inches, 5 inches?

MG: 4 inches, 5 inches.

JG: What color was the handle?

MG: Black.

JG: Black handle?

MG: Yeah.

JG: Was it sharp on both sides or just on one side?

MG: One side.

JG: What do you use them for at work?

MG: To cut meat.

JG: To cut meat?

MG: Yes.

JG: Okay. And what did you so with the clothes?

MG: I threw the clothes all over the place, I got in my mother-in-law's car and I drove off and I started throwing clothes in Bernalillo.

JG: You went to Bernalillo?

MG: Yes.

JG: Where about in Bernalillo did you start throwing the clothes?

MG: All over the road . . . I just started throwing pieces and pieces . . . you know . . . I . . .

JG: You tore them all up?

MG: I tore 'em all up.

JG: And you threw them away?

MG: Yes, and I threw . . . I remember throwing the clothes of that Jackson girl in the dumpster of Bernalillo where I used to live in the low-income projects. I threw the University . . . that it said, University Lobo New Mexico, something like that, I threw it in the dumpster and the next morning when I went to see how things look, there was an old man and an old lady taking stuff out of the garbage can.

JG: Did you . . .

MG: I'll tell you where we left off from Jim. When I took Monica back, all she could see and all I could remember is where the girl was laying, the one that was sitting by me, the one that I had stabbed in the back and in the front. I had ahh . . . I went back for my cigarettes, I don't know what made me go back, I just told Monica that I gotta go back.

JG: Did you find your cigarettes and your lighter?

MG: Yes, I did.

JG: And you picked them up and took them?

MG: Yes, I did and I looked for the girl and all Monica and me could see was a big blood stain, a big old pile of blood.

JG: And the girl wasn't there anymore?

MG: The girl was not there no more. This was around, I figure around 12:30 or 1:00 in the morning that we went back.

JG: On Sunday night?

MG: Yeah. And ahh . . . so, I stabbed the girls but I didn't know that I had killed them, and like they're saying 25 times, I did not stab them 25 times, that girl they're saying 25 to 50 times . . .

JG: Did you rape them Michael?

MG: No, I didn't rape them . . . I'm willing to even jack off, like I told you and give you some of my sperm to show you . . . .

JG: Are you willing to take a lie-detector test to that?

MG: I sure am.

JG: So, you didn't have intercourse with them or anything?

MG: No, I just grabbed . . .

JG: Any oral sex or anything?

MG: No, the girl that's saying that I raped her, she was put in the damn trunk. The one that opened her legs to me was that Jackson girl. I jumped in the car, right? And I grabbed her like that, "Get out," and I took . . . like I told you, I took her, I was shaking, I was shaking like hell, Jim. I, I didn't know what was going on or what I was doing. I 'm just a very high-tempered person and my mind goes crazy.

Linda Guzman: He's nervous.

JG: Okay, just relax, please.

MG: And ahh . . . I told her, "Get out of the damn car." I didn't even give her time to say anything, I just got her, she was barefooted, naked, she was naturally naked, actually naked, both of them were. And I just pulled out my knife and I stabbed her by her breast, right here, on the side or on the top of her breast, and she screamed, she screamed, and that's when my mind really went berserk after I did that, and I just went and I wanted do it to the other one too.

JG: Okay. This interview is concluded at 12:25PM

***

ALBUQUERQUE POLICE DEPARTMENT, ROMA STREET   APRIL 23, 1981 3PM

"Okay, Guzman, you're going for a very short ride," Bernalillo County Detention Center guard Tony Towers told Guzman as he snapped handcuffs around his wrists.

"I'm not supposed to be handcuffed, man. That's the deal. That's the deal I made with Jimmy Gutierrez," Guzman said.

"Deal is, Guzman, all prisoners are handcuffed when they get transported . . . for safety purposes. It's the law. So shut the fuck up." Mr. Towers, a large muscular black man, guided him towards the van parked at the curb. "You're going to get yourself booked at the jail. I heard you did some bad shit, so just relax and take it. You might be there for a while." Towers smiled, slid the van's side door shut and drove the few short blocks to the jail.

***

NM STATE POLICE DISTRICT 5, ALBUQUERQUE   APRIL 23, 1981 5PM

Agent Aragon told Agent English that Michael Guzman had surrendered and confessed to the crimes of murder and attempted murder.

Agent English stopped by Lee's Garage on Zuni to check out the suspect's car before he driving over to the jail. English found a 1967 white over yellow Ford convertible. He made sure the car was secured in the yard and free from tampering before he proceeded to the jail to see the suspect.

When Tom English arrived at the jail, Guzman was in the process of confessing for a third time. Upon arrival, English joined the interview and also questioned Guzman. Guzman gave correct, unpublished information about the crime.

***

JUAN TABO AND INTERSTATE 40   APRIL 24, 1981 8:30 AM

In the vicinity of the Juan Tabo overpass and Interstate 40, a partial knife blade was found on the shoulder of the overpass. It was located approximately five feet, six inches from light post C96. It took four officers 45 minutes to find it.

CHAPTER 15

Former dishwasher, Michael Guzman was arraigned in front of Metro Court Judge James O'Toole. The judge ordered Guzman held over for trial. District Attorney Ray Padilla asked for a one million dollar bond but that was deemed too high and the bail was reduced to $250,000 cash or surety. Guzman was charged with murder, attempted murder and kidnapping. His sisters wept as the arraignment was read.

***

While making herself a cup of tea, Colene heard Shorty, the black and white terrier, barking. She looked up and saw Agent's English's white, unmarked police car pull into the driveway. Thirty minutes earlier he had called and told her he was on his way over with another photo array.

He carried with him his ever-present, ever-expanding briefcase. It contained information about Colene's case. He needed to keep his notes nearby so that he could refer to them if need be. Every shred of evidence or plausible theory that had presented itself had been meticulously followed and/or investigated by Agent English until it did or did not prove useful.

"Sit down," she said and motioned him toward the kitchen table. She noticed the deepened creases on his forehead and the bags under his eyes. "Would you like something to drink?"

"Cold water," he said.

Placing the glass on the table, she sat down next to him. He had shown her many photo lineups over the past two weeks. Every probable suspect brought a new photo lineup and every time it had been a no-go. This time she hoped the results would be different – because the probability of a "hit" had gone up dramatically.

She knew that a man named Michael Guzman had turned himself in and subsequently confessed three times. She hoped that this man was truly the right man. Agent English had warned her early on that people falsely confessed to crimes all the time, especially high profile crimes like this one. But, Agent English told her, that this man had known details that only the killer could know. She also hoped that if her attacker was in this photo lineup, she would recognize him. Not having the criminal in custody wore on her and on her family.

"You ready?" Agent English asked.

"Yes, sir," she replied soberly.

The photo lineup had five pictures, as always, and Agent English made no comments one way or the other about the men presented. He had cautioned her ahead of time that the perpetrator might not be among those pictured. She nodded. As always, the photo lineups were composed of young, Spanish looking men.

She took a deep breath and stared at the sheet of photos and she knew. She pointed to photo #3 and said "Yes, definitely, that's him." A weary smile crept across Agent English's face. Seeing the man again caused Colene pain and fear, but relief as well.

Before Agent English left, he took a snippet of Colene's hair to be used as an evidence standard and placed it in a plastic bag. She almost didn't notice him cutting her hair; she was so consumed with thoughts of going back to her "normal" life. She didn't know it then, but thanks to Michael Guzman, she would never have a "normal" life again.

***

Don Gabal Street, NW   April 24, 1981 6 PM

Guzman's neighbor, Sandra Lucero, couldn't believe that the nice young man down the street had been arrested at all, let alone for murder. She was of two minds. On the one hand, she couldn't believe that he would do such a thing and on the other hand, she couldn't believe that her kids had occasionally hung out with him. It was nothing much, really. Once or twice he had driven her son to the market on Central to buy some soda. And, once . . . when it was someone's birthday, her daughter had gone down to his house for a piece of cake. The thought frightened her a little, but he didn't seem dangerous . . . at least as far as she could tell. She was just glad that this terrible thing, this kidnapping and murder, had not happened to her own kids.

But he seemed like a nice guy. He had even helped her when she needed some assistance. On a very snowy day, the winter before last, he shoveled her driveway so she could get to work. She did remember though, that when he had helped her, he had been very charming one minute, literally insisted on helping her, and then got disproportionately angry when another neighbor flipped him off because he had accidentally thrown some snow on the guy's car as he drove by. That was a little perplexing, but he did help her get to work on time.

Guzman would later be described as a charming and controlling manipulator with a violent temper and a need to dominate women. These were traits that Sandra hadn't identified in him at the time. She certainly was not aware that those are the very common traits of a serial killer.

***

2ND JUDICIAL COURT, ALBUQUERQUE   MAY 4, 1981

District Attorney Steven Schiff announced Monday that Michael Guzman had been indicted by the Grand Jury on six counts with sufficient aggravating circumstances that would permit the prosecutors to ask for the death penalty, if convicted of first degree murder.

Six innocent pleas were entered by the public defender and Judge Gerald Cole further lowered Guzman's bond from $250,000 to $100,000.

***

APD ROMA STREET, DOWNTOWN   MAY 6, 1981

The Mile High Optimist Club honored APD Officer Tim Kline of the Albuquerque Crime Stoppers with its fourth annual law enforcement plaque. Tim Kline and Crime Stoppers were instrumental in finding murderer/rapist Michael Guzman. A tip received regarding his brother, Raymond Guzman, led to Michael Guzman turning himself in.

***

JAMES AND JULIE'S HOUSE, GARFIELD AVENUE, UNM AREA   JUNE 1981

Lying propped up on his couch in a dirty, threadbare blue flannel robe, James stared at the ceiling. He saw images of people killing other people on the plaster. He wondered why the violence of the world kept invading his home. But it didn't matter anymore.

It had been days since he had eaten, shaved or bathed. Though he was only 21 years old, he looked more like an unpressed 40. A few months earlier, he had been known as a happy-go-lucky guy, almost a Disney-like character, but no more. Now he was in a dark, dank hole and couldn't get out. Matter of fact, he sank deeper by the day.

James held a loaded Smith and Wesson revolver in his hand. He was bone tired and wanted the excruciating pain to go away. Life had lost its luster.

Fiddling with a piece of lint on his bathrobe, while his mind contemplated black thoughts, he heard a distant noise.

Eventually he recognized the noise as his phone. Thinking it might be providence calling, he answered. It was his brother. James told his brother that he was about to commit suicide and hung up.

Silent and alone, James looked at the gun with the black matte finish and began reviewing his reasons why he chose not live. The phone rang again. This time James did not answer. It rang and rang. He did not pick up even though the ringing seemed to get louder and louder, almost screaming with urgency. James ignored it. He was busy trying to decide where to place the gun when he pulled the trigger. Finally, finally the fucking phone stopped ringing and James exhaled in relief. He slowly raised the weapon toward his head.

But the phone rang again. And it kept ringing. And ringing. And ringing. James looked at the phone and snarled. He made a mental note that in his next life he would not have such a machine.

Riiiiing, riiiing, riiiiing, riiiiiing, riiiiiiiiing. He couldn't stand it anymore, so he picked up.

"What?" James said disgustedly.

"What are you doing?" His brother screamed. "You can't kill yourself."

"Oh, yeah? Watch me," James replied and pushed the pistol into his temple.

"You have so much to live for . . . don't do it."

"I have nothing to live for. I have no reason at all."

"You have a *million* reasons," his brother argued.

"Name one," James said.

Quiet for a moment, James' brother spoke, "If you pull that trigger . . . I'm going to come over to your place . . . and kick your sorry dead ass . . . from one end of the house to the other . . . and there's not going to be a damn thing you can do about it . . . because you're dead."

James contorted his face as he pictured the scene his brother had just described. He sat up and laid the gun on the coffee table and a laughter that he didn't know he had left in him crept out of his chest. He laughed and laughed, almost to the point of barely being able breathe. James was still laughing when his brother showed up a half an hour later. Turned out there was a reason to live. James did not want his brother to kick his sorry dead ass from one end of the house to the other. Living was his only defense.

***

"Michael . . . Michael . . . I am going to put another curse on you." the eerie falsetto voice said through the vents. "It's me . . . Auntie! Can you see me Michael?" the voice said. "I'm on the ceiling again . . . no wait . . . I'm on on the wall. No, I was right the first time, I'm on the ceiling."

Prisoner Guzman lay on the bunk in his solo cell, seething, the stub of a cigarette clenched in his teeth.

"Remember me, Michael? This is Auntie and you've been a very, very bad boy and I'm putting a curse on you . . . I'm going to turn you into a three-headed rat and cut off your pecker . . . Michael . . . Michael . . . . No, wait . . . I'm turning you into a chicken instead. I forgot . . . you're in jail and they kill rats there." The eerie voice paused and was replaced with loud horse laughs and high pitched cackling, cascading off the jail house walls like a summer deluge.

The other inmates hated Prisoner Guzman and provoked him often. Prisoner Guzman succeeded in getting himself transferred to the psych unit, where he spent large amounts of time cultivating his crazy persona. The howling, the crying, the fake blood throwing up, annoyed his fellow inmates. To get back at him, they taunted him whenever possible.

***

2nd Judicial Court, Albuquerque   September 23, 1981

Jail guards escorted Michael Guzman into the District courtroom Monday, his handcuffs remaining on as he stood next to his defense attorney, Joe Fine.

Mr. Fine asked Judge Cole to declare Guzman incompetent to stand trial. One psychologist testified that Guzman suffered from depression, anxiety and hallucinations. He further noted that Guzman had frequent nightmares, drooled on himself and spoke to people who weren't there.

Another psychologist testified that Guzman thought his aunt was a witch and he was sure she had put a curse on him. Guzman said that she had put pins in the head of a doll and that he suffered terrible headaches as a result. Mr. Fine asserted that Guzman had lost nearly all of his memory and had thrown up blood repeatedly since being incarcerated. After listening to all of the testimony Judge Cole ruled Guzman incompetent. The Judge ordered periodic reports on his condition and canceled Guzman's October murder trial date.

***

FORENSIC HOSPITAL, LAS VEGAS, NEW MEXICO SEPTEMBER 25, 1981

Guzman was sent to the New Mexico Behavioral Health Institute-Adult Psychiatric Division in Las Vegas, New Mexico. This facility provides court ordered treatment to individuals suffering from mental illness. It is the most restrictive psychiatric setting in New Mexico.

Prisoner Guzman was very happy to be out of the jailhouse and into the nuthouse. His jail buddies, the few he had, told him life was much nicer in the loony bin. Nice rooms, therapy galore and lots of drugs. Not to mention, no murder trials and of course no murder verdicts while residing at the funny farm. What's not to like? The Bernalillo County Detention Center was oppressive and the people who ran the fucking jail were not nice at all. They didn't understand him. While at the jail, he had gone to quite a bit of trouble cultivating the crazy thing; even going so far as to cut a cross onto his chest with a paper clip and still they weren't impressed. Those dumb jail assholes were constantly questioning his insanity, said he was faking it, told him that they'd seen inmates do way loonier shit.

Turned out it didn't matter what those stupid jail pricks said anyways. It's what the judge buys that counts. Judge Cole fell for the "nuttier than a fruitcake" thing - hook, line and sinker, and now, Prisoner Guzman, at least for the foreseeable future, did not have to take responsibility for his heinous crimes. Sweet.

***

THE PLAZA, SANTA FE, NEW MEXICO SEPTEMBER 25, 1981

The crowd was in a tizzy. Amidst the patriotic bunting and hoisted flags, people had positioned themselves atop chairs to better see him. On this unusually warm day, standing at a podium on the east side of the capital building, Toney Anaya addressed a large assemblage of enthusiastic, almost exclusively Democratic, supporters. Dressed in his best blue pin-striped suit, he appeared tanned, almost regal. "He looks presidential," a few well-wishers whispered.

"Ladies and Gentlemen," he began. "Thank you, thank you all, for your support and for coming out here today in this heat. It's almost tropical," he said. "I don't usually feel this hot unless I'm answering questions from the press," he joked. Then, with a quarter-smile on his face, he went on to speak for another 35 tiresome minutes, discussing the excellence and benevolence of his backers, his dazzling background and his dedication to public service. The crowd hooted and applauded his every word. Ultimately, he got to the point. Everyone in attendance already knew the point, but the point was, they wanted to hear him say it.

"I'd like to announce my intention to run for Governor of the Great State of New Mexico." Toney Anaya said at last. The crowd was beside itself in ecstasy. "Toney, Toney, Toney," they chanted. "Anaya for Governor." Toney Anaya pins and bumper stickers were handed out to anyone that wanted one.

After the rally was over, the man of the hour got in a black sedan with his handlers, and headed to the Santa Fe airport. He owned his own plane and it had been prepped for his arrival. Anaya was going to repeat his announcement to run for Governor ten more glorious times in the next 30 hours. He intended to fly to Raton, Springer, Las Vegas, Farmington, Gallup, Silver City, Las Cruces, Carlsbad, Roswell and Clovis. He thought if doing it once was great, how much better would it be to do it over and over again. Plus, it gave the simple people of New Mexico something to remember. Plus, plus, someone else, which he didn't even know yet (but soon would), had also arrived in Las Vegas, NM, (campaign stop number four) that very same day. That person would not be at the campaign rally but would ultimately help shape Anaya's lasting legacy.

***

2ND JUDICIAL DISTRICT COURT, ALBUQUERQUE MARCH 23, 1982

A new set of psychologists evaluating Michael Guzman, the accused murderer of Julie Ann Jackson and attempted murderer of Colene Bush, found him competent to stand trial, District Attorney Stephen Schiff announced on Wednesday.

Jury selection was scheduled to begin April 16, 1982.

Joyce Nance

PART III

THE TRIAL

CHAPTER 16

TRIAL BEGINS

Originally, 143 people sat in the courthouse awaiting voir dire (jury selection) in the case of New Mexico vs. Michael Anthony Guzman. Four days later, twelve jurors and four alternates remained.

Because it was a major trial, one potentially involving the death penalty, a circus atmosphere prevailed. All three local television stations parked their vans in front of the 2nd Judicial District Court in anticipation of opening statements. With the courthouse looming large in the background, newscasters reported events live as they unfolded.

The media was inside the courtroom as well, but the judge had ruled that no television or photography equipment be allowed in court. The cameras made the defendant uncomfortable. The victims' families' comfort had not been ruled on.

The courtroom was jammed, many of them gawkers who wanted to see the killer up close. A side door opened, the handcuffs were removed and Guzman shuffled into the courtroom. He wore a light blue shirt with a white pullover sweater and was considerably thinner than his pictures in the paper a year earlier. He sat down next to his attorney, his expression blank.

Because the defendant had already admitted guilt to most of his offenses, he claimed innocent by reason of insanity. This tactic, the Hail Mary of defenses, is used in less than one percent of all criminal cases and is rarely successful. To this end, Guzman had worked diligently on his insane personality since his arrival in jail. His lifetime of unstable antics and his documented dysfunctional family, to be detailed throughout the trial, were a bonus.

Ray Padilla, an assistant district attorney for the State of New Mexico, shuffled papers at the prosecutor's table, as he readied himself for his opening statement. Before he began, Judge Gerald Cole informed the jury that since this case was "somewhat sensational," they should avoid any media accounts of the trial and not discuss any court proceedings until it was time to deliberate on a verdict. Judge Cole, a baritone voiced, no nonsense, veteran adjudicator read the charges against the defendant.

"The Defendant has been charged in Count One with murder. The defendant has been charged in Count Two with attempt to commit a felony, to wit, first degree murder. The defendant has been charged in Count Three with criminal sexual penetration. The defendant has been charged in Count Four with kidnapping. The defendant has been charged in Count Five with kidnapping. The defendant has been charged in Count Six with tampering of evidence. Each count is the charge of a separate crime. As to each count the defendant has pled "not guilty." He is presumed to be innocent. The State has the burden of proving the guilt of the defendant beyond a reasonable doubt."

***

PROSECUTION OPENING STATEMENTS

Mr. Padilla, looking fit and trim in a dark blue suit, his dark hair meticulously groomed, informed the seven women and five men of the jury that the purpose of opening statements was to provide a road map of what was to come in the trial.

"Ultimately," the assistant district attorney said, "it will be your responsibility, in your own minds, to piece everything together . . . and make the decision that you have to make."

Mr. Padilla recapped the case.

"You are going to be told that on the 5th day of April 1981," he began, "two University of New Mexico coeds . . . by the name of Julie Ann Jackson and Colene Bush . . . were studying for final examinations. You are going to be told that both of these students decided to take a break to have a cup of coffee . . . and they went to the Frontier Restaurant . . . and they had that cup of coffee."

The prosecutor told the jury that the two young women left the restaurant, were grabbed off the street by a man with a knife, forced into a car and taken directly to a remote location.

"You will see and you will be told," Padilla said, "that the route that was taken out there that night . . . was essentially a straight line."

"Once down in this arroyo-like area . . . the defendant parked the car . . . and he turned to the girls and he said 'Okay ladies, the fun's over now.'"

Mr. Padilla told the jury that both women were told to strip. Colene was locked into the trunk of the car where she stayed until she heard the defendant and Julie leave the car. Mr. Padilla told the jury how once Colene escaped from the trunk, she was chased and stabbed repeatedly by the defendant.

Mr. Padilla said that the stabbing didn't stop until Colene finally said, "My God, let me die in peace . . . please . . . what do you want from me?" The defendant responded, "You know what I want from you. You know that all of my problems are because of you Anglos." Mr. Padilla told the jury that the defendant then cut her throat yet again and left.

"Colene will tell you that . . . she decided that she was not going to die down in that arroyo . . . so she started crawling on her hands and knees. She crawled up an embankment which is approximately 60 feet high and at a grade of 80 to 90 degrees. She was successful in crawling up to Old Route 66. She crossed Old Route 66 and she crawled up another embankment, this time a 90 foot embankment . . . again, at an 80-90 degree grade. She crawled up that embankment, until she got to Interstate 40."

He told the jury that the witnesses included first responders, investigators, doctors and psychologists. The evidence would include the defendant's three taped confessions, medical reports, and psychological test results. Ray Padilla explained when and how Julie Jackson's body was ultimately found.

"At approximately 8AM, that morning, the sixth of April, 1981, the criminalistics people arrived. Officer Chavez will describe to you what was seen in that area. He will describe the blood that was seen. He will describe the search as it continued until the body of Julie Ann Jackson was found . . . west of where the car was parked . . . behind a tree. She was found face down in the dirt."

Ray Padilla explained how Colene communicated with police immediately following her surgery even though she was unable to talk.

"Agent English is going to tell you that he was the investigator who was in charge of this particular case. Immediately upon being assigned to the case, he went to the hospital . . . where Colene was in intensive care after her surgery. She was awake and was alert enough to be able to give some information . . . because she couldn't talk at the time . . . she either had to write it down as best as possible or she had to utilize a letter board and point out letters to give information to the police."

Mr. Padilla told the jury that they would hear testimony about the sanity of the defendant from experts in psychology and psychiatry. "They will tell you about how he acted, what he said . . . all of the tests that they ran on him . . . and each and every one of those doctors will tell you that it is his or her opinion that at the time of the commission of these offenses . . . the defendant was sane."

"After it's all over, ladies and gentlemen, the State is going to ask you to go into that room to deliberate and find the defendant guilty of the highest degree of every charge. To find that the aggravating circumstances, which would necessitate further proceedings to determine death or life imprisonment are present. We are going to ask you to find all of that, ladies and gentlemen . . . and we are confident that at the conclusion of this entire trial . . . that is exactly what you will do. Thank you."

***

DEFENSE OPENING STATEMENTS

"INSANITY!!!" Joe Fine screamed. "That's the only issue in this case at this point! With respect to the issue of insanity, there are two separate issues that I would ask you to consider. One – does Michael Guzman have the capacity for a psychotic episode in which he is unable to restrain himself? The second issue, my evidence will relate to – is not merely whether he has this capacity but whether in fact, there is a reasonable doubt as to whether Michael Guzman was in a psychotic episode at the time of the events in question."

Mr. Fine, a lanky man with a high forehead, massaged his temples while formulating his next thought. "With respect to whether Michael Guzman has this capacity, the answer is *yes* – based on the evidence. First of all, you will be exposed to Michael Guzman's background . . . and although we have two very, very innocent victims in this case, Mr. Guzman is to some extent an innocent victim as a result of what happened to him. During Mr. Guzman's youth, his parents had trouble. The mother hated the father and as a result, she took it out on Michael."

"It'll also be shown that this whole family is crazy and dysfunctional. All of his brothers appear to be experiencing trouble. One was recently institutionalized and has tried to kill himself on two occasions."

"The next factor," Mr. Fine said, speaking in the clipped tones of a slight New York accent, "is to consider whether Michael is preconditioned to act in a psychotic manner. The evidence will show that sometimes when Michael couldn't control himself, he would take his head and bang it against the wall as hard as he could. Monica Juarez will testify to this and she'll testify that Michael was always sensitive about people staring at him. He felt that they were staring at him and calling him, when in fact they were not staring and calling him."

"There will be testimony about suicide attempts by Michael Guzman. A gentleman by the name of Charles Mitchell will testify that he saw someone hanging himself from the Rio Grande Bridge. He went and took the individual down . . . he probably would have died if not for Mr. Mitchell."

"There will be medical testimony by Dr. Samuel Roll, a forensic psychologist in New Mexico. Dr. Roll will testify that Michael has had psychotic episodes, that Michael was paranoid and very, very deeply disturbed."

"Dr. Fink, the head of psychological services at the State Forensic Hospital, will testify that he feels that Michael has various problems, one of which is a borderline personality disorder with schizotypal features."

Guzman's defense attorney told the jury that after being found incompetent, the defendant was sent to the Forensic Hospital in Las Vegas. At the Forensic Hospital, Guzman continued his crazy behavior, such as eating toilet paper and talking to people that weren't there.

"With respect as to whether Michael was insane on the night in question," Mr. Fine said, facing the jury, "the following factors are relevant. First of all, Michael's common-law wife was going to have a baby. Every doctor who's going to testify in this case is going to say that this is a very, very severe stress factor. And this factor is even more severe in this case because the testimony will show how important that baby was to Michael. It meant being a man, having an object which he could love. He never received love . . . and having that type of relationship meant a lot to Michael. When he heard that Monica was pregnant, he shaved his head to look like the baby. When he turned himself in, it was partially as a result of the baby."

Standing a foot away from the jury box, Joe Fine continued. "Michael was very disturbed that night." "He came home; he was in an excited state and commented something to the effect that the whole world was against him. He wasn't climbing the walls insanely but he was disturbed. It is significant that one month before the incident, Michael went to a doctor, Dr. Hedges, and he told him of back problems . . . and was prescribed Emperin 3 and a drug called Limbitrol. Dr. Hedges will testify that when he saw Michael, Michael's condition – this is 30 days before the incident – was moderate to severe. He is not a psychiatrist; however, he does feel he can read people to a certain extent."

"The next item of evidence," Mr. Fine said, turning to a new page in his notes, "which relates as to whether Michael was insane on the evening in question will be Colene Bush's testimony. She will state that Michael spoke about God repeatedly . . . and that Michael said that God is his friend – that he compared the freeway to God."

"She'll further testify that she was probing to find out what Michael wanted . . . who he was . . . what makes him tick . . . and rightfully so. However, the testimony is going to show that when she probed Michael, Michael had a reaction towards her . . . he didn't like her. He was really bothered by her. And again, this is hard to understand, but you are not dealing with someone sane. And Michael referred to Colene Bush as poking him at him, poking at him."

Mr. Fine looked around the room, steepled his fingers and continued. "The next item of evidence which bears on whether Michael was insane or not at the time is Monica Juarez. She will testify that Michael came home, was greatly distressed . . . was severely shaken up. He put a knife on a Bible almost ritualistically. What does this mean? Is this the act of a sane person?"

"I would ask you, in closing, to take your journey and concentrate on the insanity issue. Really take a good look at it. We are admitting just about everything else. Look at all the facts, evaluate the witnesses . . . listen to the attorneys and return a verdict which is consistent with you inner feelings."

"Thank you," he said and sat down.

***

MOTIONS

With the jury out of the courtroom, attorneys from both sides stood before Judge Cole. Mr. Fine requested rulings from the judge on certain issues of law.

"At this time, I would move the court for a mistrial based upon the inflammatory and unnecessary statements in the district attorney's opening statement," Joe Fine said, his narrow face pinched in dismay. "His testimony that the girls were on scholarship, that they were honor students . . . is really just absolutely irrelevant here and can only serve to inflame the jury."

Prosecutor Ray Padilla shook his head. "Your Honor, these statements are perfectly admissible as the court is aware we are going to introduce three confessions of the defendant. In each of those confessions, he says that the girls got into the car, they were hiding back there. He attributes everything initially to the girls. The state has a right and a responsibility to show to this jury that those girls are not the type of person that the defendant paints them to be in his confessions. It is therefore relevant and admissible."

Judge Cole, pushing up his glasses with his middle finger, responded, "I'll take the motion under advisement."

"Your Honor," Joe Fine continued. "I am admitting that Michael Guzman killed Julie Ann Jackson. I am admitting that he attempted to murder Colene Bush – subject to an insanity defense . . . and specific intent defense. And I am admitting that great bodily harm was inflicted on Colene Bush by means of a knife. And I am also not going to contend in closing statements that the girls got into the car. And I'm giving the court notice of that. For this reason, I would like all of the surplus-age evidence out of the case, such as testimony that the girls were honor students or about the girls' character, which I personally know was very good. But I don't think that this is the reason for bringing about this testimony. It's just not relevant in this case."

Judge Cole peered down from the bench with dark expressionless eyes. "What else do you want to get in or keep out Mr. Fine?" he asked.

Looking at his notepad, Joe Fine said, "A lot of the doctor's reports regarding the serious nature of the injuries of Colene Bush . . . and also Colene Bush after the incident . . . what she did in order to save herself.

Again, I think that the inflammatory aspect of this evidence greatly outweighs the pro quid value."

"Mr. Padilla, as to the issue of guilt and innocence on any of the six charges, what difference does it make how far or how the steep the hill was that she crawled up?" Judge Cole asked.

"It demonstrates conclusively to the jury, the secluded nature of the area," Ray Padilla answered. "It demonstrates . . . we would argue . . . that a sane man would choose a secluded area to commit a rape and to murder two people. That a sane man would choose such an area to cover up his crime."

Judge Cole exhaled, and in a steady voice said, "As to her crawling up the hills, I will grant his motion. Direct your witness not to have her say how she had gotten down there. You've got plenty of police officers that can describe the secluded nature of the area. What was the other one, Mr. Fine?"

"The other issue, Your Honor, is how far the State can go with the medical evidence regarding Colene's condition and her recovery. To me this is not relevant at all. It's relevant, the initial wounds . . . any intent on Mr. Guzman's part, intent to kill or whatever . . . but how she recovered I don't think is significant."

"That's the limit of my ruling at this point," Judge Cole said, then turned to the assistant district attorney. "Mr. Padilla, you have a case where I don't propose to end up with a conviction based upon sympathy for the victims. There's a lot of difference between an officer describing that he walked up and down a 60 degree incline and the victim describing how she crawled up it and the question of prejudice in establishing your point."

CHAPTER 17

COLENE BUSH

Colene Bush, the surviving victim, testified first. The jury saw a composed young woman wearing a blue turtleneck shirt, sitting with perfect posture in the witness stand.

"Raise your right hand," Judge Cole said. "Do you solemnly swear that the testimony given in this matter will be the whole truth?"

"Yes," Colene replied.

"Be seated, Miss Bush," the judge instructed. "You are going to have to speak up so that my farthest juror can hear you." Colene shifted her eyes to the twelve jurors. They were staring at her. In fact, the whole of the courtroom was staring at her. As much as everybody wanted to get a look at the defendant, they really wanted to see the young woman who single-handedly fought off the knife-wielding, monster-sized killer.

"Can you give us your name please, ma'am?" Mr. Padilla asked.

"Colene Bush."

"How old are you?"

"21."

"Miss Bush, I would like to direct your attention back to the dates of April the 5th and the 6th of 1981 . . . at that time how old were you?"

"I was 20 years old."

"Miss Bush, if you would, I'd like you to tell us a little bit about yourself, briefly tell us about the high school where you graduated from and any highlights of your high school career if you would, please."

"I graduated from Moriarty High School in '79, I was in athletics . . . I lettered in three sports. Track and field . . . volleyball . . . and basketball. I was in the National Honor Society. I was a member of the student council . . . I guess that's about all."

"Okay, on the 5th and 6th of April, were you attending the University of New Mexico?"

"Yes, I was."

"Were you there on any form of scholarships?"

"Oh . . . yes, I'm currently on a Presidential Scholarship. Which is an academic scholarship."

"And you're back in school now?"

"Yes, I am."

"Alright Miss Bush, focusing on the 5th day of April of 1981 . . . we are talking about the evening hours. What were you doing?"

"That night I was drawing a picture for one of my art classes," Colene said.

"Was anybody with you?"

"No."

"Did you engage in any studying during the evening?"

"I was studying earlier and then I began drawing . . . on this one picture."

"Did there come a time during the evening when you got together with Julie Ann Jackson?"

"Yes, she called me in the evening and said she wanted to go down to the Frontier and get some coffee," Colene said and then recounted that Julie did, in fact, come over and they walked the block and half down to the restaurant for coffee. Colene told the court that they stayed there for a couple of hours.

"What time did you leave the Frontier Restaurant approximately?"

"About 11:30," Colene replied quickly and pushed her hair back behind her ears.

"And where did you go?"

"Back to my apartment."

Leaning against the podium, Ray Padilla said, "Can you explain to us the route that you were taking back to your apartment?"

Colene told him that they walked east on Central and then south, about two-thirds of the way, down Stanford.

"When you got two-thirds of the block down Stanford did anything unusual happen?"

"Yes, a man walked towards us. He was facing us . . . he was walking towards us. And after he passed us, he turned around and put his arms around both of our necks."

"Describe that man to us if you would please."

"He was very tall. He was fairly clean cut . . . he wasn't real shaggy looking. He had a dark blue ski-type parka with a belt. He was real muscular looking. Almost like a football player type."

"If that man were present in this courtroom today, Miss Bush, would you be able to identify him?

"Yes, I would," Colene answered immediately.

"Would you look around the court room, please? If he's here, would you point him out to us, tell us where he is seated? What he's wearing?"

Colene sat silent for a moment, her eyes scanning the courtroom.

"He's wearing maroon pants. He's seated over there," pointing at Guzman.

"What type of upper body clothing does he have on?"

"A white sweater."

"Okay, may the record reflect that the defendant's been identified," Mr. Padilla said.

"Miss Bush, the individual that you have pointed out in the courtroom today, does he physically appear the same in terms of height and weight and whatever as he did on that night?"

Colene studied Guzman then replied, "He looks a lot thinner."

"When you say he looks a lot thinner, can you give us an estimate?"

"Thirty pounds at least."

Colene explained to the hushed courtroom how the man had overpowered Julie and herself and forced them into his car.

"He had his arm—he was choking me with his arm and he had the knife at her throat . . . at her neck."

"When he initially grabbed Julie and you . . . did he say anything?" Mr. Padilla asked

"Yes."

"What did he say?"

"He told us just to keep quiet and not to say anything. He said, 'Don't scream.'"

"Just tell us, if you would, what was going on? What happened?" Mr. Padilla said.

"Um . . . we just said okay. He was walking very fast and I told him . . . I said, 'Hey, Buddy . . . slow down,' because I had hurt my foot about four or five days before . . . and I was basically limping because I had torn the ligaments in the bottom of my foot . . . and it was hurting me for him to walk so fast . . . and when I said 'Hey, Buddy, slow down,' he said, 'Don't call me Buddy. My name's not Buddy.'"

Colene looked over at the defendant, but he never saw it. His eyes were focused on the table.

Colene continued, giving her account of how the defendant forced Julie and her to walk to his parked car on Silver.

"What happened when you got to the car?" Ray Padilla asked.

"He asked if either one of us could drive," Colene replied. "And I said no immediately. Julie um . . . said no also, just following what I said . . . and . . . then he opened the door . . . and he told us to get in . . . he had the knife at my neck . . . and Julie immediately got in. She did as he said. So I had no other choice. I got in with her . . . er . . . I got in there too—with her."

Colene described the car that they were forced into as an older model, white convertible. She said that the inside paneling had been removed.

"How were you seated once you got in the car?" Mr. Padilla asked.

"Um . . . there was Julie . . . then me and then him."

"Where exactly was Julie seated?"

"She was on . . . I guess on the passenger side."

"You were in the middle?"

"Yes."

"What happened once you got in the car?" Ray Padilla asked.

"He asked us what our names were and Julie said, 'My name is Julie' and I told him my name was Pat."

"What happened next?"

"And that's the second time I asked him, 'Well, what's your name?' And he said it was Raymond."

Colene testified that the defendant told the girls that he was scared and lonely and he seemed nervous but nevertheless continued driving east. He told them he didn't have any friends.

"He almost, at one point, seemed like he was really sad," she said. "Maybe even crying."

The assistant district attorney ran his hand through his hair and then asked Colene if it seemed like the defendant had been drinking or if he might have been on drugs.

"I did smell alcohol on his breath," she said. "He didn't act drunk in the sense that he was staggering and mumbling."

"Describe to us the way that he drove if you would, please."

Colene tipped her head backward, remembering. "He was very cautious . . . he wasn't driving crazy or anything."

"What about the speed limit and stop lights or stop signs, anything like that?"

"Oh, he kept well within the speed limit. He was very aware of it." Colene said, glaring at the defendant.

"During the time that you were driving . . . what did he do with the knife?" Mr. Padilla asked.

"I don't know. I don't know where he put it," she said.

"Did he have it at your throat or chest or anything like that?"

"Not when he was driving . . . no," Colene answered.

"In the residential area? How did he drive?"

Colene twisted her mouth. "Like he knew," she said, "like we were going somewhere. I didn't know where we were because the streets are like a maze. He drove around . . . I guess, like he'd been there before."

"Where exactly did he emerge from the area?" Padilla asked.

"It was right before Highland High School."

Ray Padilla shifted his feet. "What was the conversation at that point in time, if any?"

"Well, I think he said he was from New York, and I said, 'Oh well, how long have you been here?' And he says, 'Well, I've just been here three weeks.' We talked about his car. He said he liked to do body work on cars. I asked him if he'd done any body work on his car and he said no, that he had just bought it."

Colene said that she kept urging him to turn around. She told him that it was time to head back and if he wanted to talk there was a nearby Sambos where they might have some coffee and talk. He told her that was a bad idea because someone might see the three of them there together.

"What was the tone of his voice and his mannerisms?" Mr. Padilla asked.

"He acted rather nervous," Colene said.

Ray Padilla narrowed his eyes and tapping his pen to his pad of paper, asked, "Going out Central . . . did you eventually end up getting on the freeway?"

"Yes, we did," Colene replied sadly.

"What was the conversation while you're going on Central and onto the freeway there?"

"As we got on the freeway, he said—he asked us if we believed in God. And we said yes. And he said that God was really . . . truly his only friend . . . and as we were . . . and this is on the on-ramp . . . and as we're on the freeway, he said that . . . that God's love was like the freeway . . . it was never ending . . . it never stopped . . . and that he just wanted to get on the freeway and drive."

Colene explained how Guzman drove on I-40 East until he got to the Carnuel exit. At that point he got off, started to head back to town but then abruptly turned around and resumed heading east.

Mr. Padilla paused, looked at the jury for a moment and then turned back to Colene. "Where did you go from there?"

"East. Three or four miles."

"Was there any conversation going on in this three or four mile drive?"

"Yes, there was," Colene said.

"Tell us what it was all about."

"I was asking him where he was from . . . again! He said that his parents lived in El Paso, Again, I was asking him about the body work that he did on the cars . . . and what he liked to do." Colene paused. "That's all I can remember now."

Ray Padilla looked at his watch. "What about his attitude? Everything during that portion of the drive? Was it any different than his attitude during the first part?"

"Sometimes I'd ask him questions . . . it would almost catch him off guard and he would get mad at me."

"When he got mad what would he do or say?" asked Padilla.

"He would tell me to shut up. Or just never mind . . . just . . . he would really get almost . . . hatred at me."

"What kind of voice would he use?"

"It was an angry voice," Colene replied.

"How often did that type of thing happen? Did he get mad at you?"

"Four or five times."

She told Mr. Padilla that the defendant was afraid that they were being followed. She said that he stopped, turned off the engine and lights and waited for the purported pursuing car to pass by. Mr. Padilla asked what happened next.

"Then he began backing up very fast," Colene said.

"He backed down the road very fast . . . and he was going towards the edge . . . there's a steep drop off . . . and he was starting to go over there and both Julie and I said, 'Hey, slow down,' you know . . . 'you're gonna go over the edge' and he told us to shut up. He said 'shut up and leave me alone' very angrily. He slammed the car back in gear . . . and then he went down this little road going down the embankment."

"And when you went down this little road . . . what type of an area did you go into?"

"It was the bottom of an arroyo."

Ray Padilla massaged his forehead and then asked, "What did he do? Once you were going down this little road?"

"As he went down the road . . . he swung the car back around . . . in like a little graded off area . . . stopped the car and turned it off . . .and said to us . . . 'Okay ladies, the fun's over now.'"

Colene looked over at the defendant. The entire courtroom looked over at the defendant. Then all eyes returned to Colene.

"Then what did he do?" Ray Padilla asked.

Colene took a deep breath. "He told us to take off our clothes," she said, glassy-eyed.

"Tell us the exact words that he used and exactly what happened at that point in time."

Colene, regaining her confidence, continued. "He told Julie first, he says, 'You take your clothes off '. . . and he said 'if you don't do it, your friend's gonna get hurt really *bad*.'"

"Where did he have the knife?"

"He had the knife at my chest. Right here." Colene pointed to the right side of her chest.

"What was Julie's reaction to his demand?"

"She did everything he said," Colene replied dolefully.

"Did you or Julie say anything to him during this point in time?"

"Yes. Um . . . I said something to the effect . . . 'I thought that you believed in God?' And he told me to shut up . . . that he had a gun and if I didn't watch out he was gonna shoot me. I said, 'Well, can I see your gun?' and he pressed the knife in deeper and he said 'Just shut up and do as I say . . . or I'm gonna hurt you really bad.'"

"What was Julie doing?"

"Julie took her clothes off. He told her to throw her clothes in the back . . . the back seat . . . which she did."

"Okay, what about you?"

"He told me to take my clothes off."

"And what was your response to that?"

"I questioned him. I said, 'Why should I?' He told me to do it or else. I said, 'Okay.'

Very slowly, I took mine off."

"What did you do with your clothing?"

"I threw 'em in the back seat also," she said.

"Was there any conversation going on at this time?"

"Just me asking him 'why?'"

"Did he respond to your questions?"

"No."

Colene told the court that after she took her clothes off, Guzman pulled her out of the car at knife-point, and told her to get in the trunk of the car.

"He said, 'Get in there' . . . and I said, 'I can't get in there.' He goes, 'You know, I don't like you because you're a smart ass.' I said, 'I can't fit in there. There's not enough room.' He said, 'Just get in there.' And he pushed me in there . . . and I grabbed a box . . . thinking that when he slammed the trunk down I could . . . press it in between the lid of the . . . the trunk . . . and the body of the car . . . hoping that it wouldn't lock. But I was on my hands and knees and when he pushed the trunk down . . . it hit my back and I just barely got in in time. He locked the trunk and left."

Ray Padilla walked over to the prosecution table and grabbed another pile of notes. After studying them for a moment, he asked her what she did inside the trunk and she said that she tried to stay quiet and feel around the inside of the trunk.

"Could you hear anything from inside that trunk?"

"I heard noises, like someone scooting across the seat."

She said that once she realized she was alone, she punched through the canvas at the back of the trunk and crawled out through into the backseat of the car.

"And I got through," Colene said, "and I grabbed my pants and I put my pants on . . . and I was gonna put my shoes on . . . and I had just gotten one shoe on and I looked around the corner and I saw a lit cigarette . . . and it was him coming back over this hill. And then . . .

"You say you saw a lit cigarette?" Mr. Padilla interrupted, "And it was him. Could you make out his form or . . . ? Could you recognize him or . . . ?"

"It was just a dark shadow. Or black. It was dark out . . . it was very dark. And what I saw was the lit cigarette which is very bright."

"What did you do when you saw this lit cigarette?"

"I crawled over the back of the front seat . . . and began running. I ran around the side of the car." Colene's said.

"And where did you run to?"

"I was running east."

"What if anything did he do?"

"He saw me running. And he yelled something to me . . . I don't know what he said. And there was a bunch of rocks . . . and I was barefoot . . . and I tripped over these rocks and landed on my chest right about the same time as he got to me. He stabbed me in the back."

"What happened then?"

"I got up. I got away from him. The knife was still in my back. And I ran quite a ways away from him. Until he finally caught up with me . . . and he tripped me and he knocked me down. He was trying to get the knife out of my back. But I kept moving from him and he had a hard time getting the knife out. When he finally got it out, he started to stab me again and I'm sure he got me . . . from then on it was instances of him stabbing me and me trying to get away from him."

"What were you doing in your efforts to get away?"

"I was just trying to run . . . trying to ward off his stabs . . . just trying to get away."

"Was there any communication or any yelling going on . . . or what was going on at that point?"

"He got me up here in the neck." Colene's breathing quickened as she pointed to a spot on the lower part of her neck. "And . . . he hit a main artery or vein . . . I don't know . . . I began bleeding really bad. Worse than the stab wounds that I had received in my back and my chest . . . and I grabbed my throat . . . and I asked him . . . 'I said what is it you want from me?' . . . and he said, "You know what I want from you." And he came at me again . . . and, I would try, I would try to get away . . . I kept trying to ward it off . . . and at one point he said . . . a little bit later he said . . . 'All my problems are because of you Anglos,'" Colene's hands were clasped together, her face colored and her voice angry.

"Did he say that in connection with any specific wounds that you received?" Ray Padilla asked.

"It's when I was down on the ground. I asked if him I could die, 'just leave me alone . . . let me die in peace.'"

"What was his reaction to that?"

"There wasn't any reaction," Colene said disgustedly.

"What happened then?"

"He left me alone for a minute or two . . . and just watched me crawl across the side of the road. I was laying there . . . and he left . . . for a few minutes . . . and then he came back. I was laying on my back . . . and he came over to me and he started stabbing me in the chest . . . he started slitting my neck . . . I kept trying to get away from him . . . after a while he left."

"I tried to get up and move but I kept falling. I was just laying there again in another spot. I was laying on my back. He came back again. And I thought he was going to come back and stab me some more so I laid there. I tried to play dead. I was just kind of curled up. He came back and he looked at me . . . and he turned around and he walked off and he took off real fast in his car."

"After he left, did there come a time when you were able to get up to Old Route 66?"

"Yes, after he left . . . I laid there for a while and . . . decided I didn't want to die in the bottom of an arroyo . . . I began crawling . . ."

Ray Padilla cut Colene off. Judge Cole had previously ruled that such testimony would inflame the jury and create irrelevant sympathy for the victims. Mr. Padilla steered Colene towards describing what happened after climbing to the top of the embankment.

"When you got up on Old Route 66 . . . did you see any vehicular traffic or anything like that on Route 66?" the assistant district attorney asked.

"On 66, I almost got . . . I was almost to the top of where 66 is. I saw a car coming . . . and I thought it was him coming back again . . . the car lights . . . so I . . . there was a guard rail . . . I tried to curl up to the guard rail . . . hoping I would camouflage into maybe the guard rail if this was him . . . maybe he wouldn't see me. And after the car passed, I crawled across 66 or the frontage road and started to go up the second embankment."

"Did there come a time when you then were able to get up to I-40? The highway which goes east and west?"

"Yes."

"And once you got up to I-40 . . . what did you do?"

"Well, I had to get over the guard rail." Colene said. "I was laying on the side of the road . . . I was waving at cars . . . trying to get them to stop . . . and cars passed me . . . and I didn't think anyone had seen me . . . so I moved closer to the white line . . . and finally there was a car that finally stopped . . . and a man got out. That's all I can clearly remember."

"Later on, did there come a point when you relayed this information to police officers?"

"Yes, I did."

Mr. Padilla then asked Colene to identify various photos of her injuries and to describe her injuries to the jury.

"Miss Bush how many total stab wounds did you receive?" Mr. Padilla asked.

"Between 32 and 33."

"Do theses photographs essentially depict all or at least the vast majority of the stab wounds that you received?"

"Yes, they do."

"Anything else that you can think of just right off hand that's not depicted there?"

"Um . . . there was . . . I had bruises," Colene said.

"Describe the bruises . . . just briefly."

"Bruises from being kicked. They were on my legs . . . I had bruises on my legs . . . I had them on my body . . . upper and lower body – my back . . . and like I said in my legs."

"I'll pass the witness, Your Honor."

Michael Guzman's defense attorney, Joe Fine, walked to the podium and spoke into the microphone.

"Miss Bush, do you know for how long a period Mr. Guzman was driving in that residential area?"

"Just a few minutes. Five to ten plus."

"Okay. And do you recall the conversation while you were in this area. Any conversation?" Mr. Padilla asked.

"Yes, I do."

"What was the conversation in that area?"

"This again, pertained to him being lonely and not having any friends."

"Did he ever offer to take you back to your apartment? You or Julie Jackson?"

"No."

"When he pulled over to the side . . . was it your impression that he pulled over as a response to a car following him? He thought a car was following him?"

"That's what he said."

"Was there a car in back of you at that point?"

"Yes, there was."

"Did you have the impression that he probably would have kept going . . . if he wasn't paranoid with respect to that car following him?" Joe Fine asked.

"I don't know," Colene answered.

***

NORMAN JACKSON

"The State calls Norman Jackson, father of Julie Jackson."

Mr. Jackson's testimony was limited by the court to identifying his daughter as the person murdered and to her various achievements. He was asked to give a few highlights of his daughter's life.

"She attended Farmington High School," Mr. Jackson said. "She was an excellent student, member of the National Honor Society, and in her junior year she was selected to be on the gifted program for outstanding students. She was on the Student Council for two years and was a class officer for one year and she graduated with honors. She received several scholarships to the University of New Mexico.

"Her interests lie in mathematics and biology and chemistry," her father said. "She was very strong in those subjects. She was heading for a medical career, hopefully to be a doctor."

***

DR. CARL BARR

Dr. Carl Barr, the forensic pathologist from the Office of the Medical Investigator, was called to testify next. He had performed Julie Jackson's autopsy and explained that when he examined her, he discovered that she had received one stab wound to the heart and was covered with a large amount of dirt, sand and gravel on the front part of the body. During his examination, he discovered several other lesser wounds.

"How many wounds did you locate on the body?" Ray Padilla asked.

"If you're asking about wounds or traumatic injury in general, there were a number," Dr. Barr answered. "Areas of skin abrasion, scrapes if you will . . . bruising, that type of thing in addition to the fatal stab wound."

"Doctor, tell us . . . what happens medically to a person that has received this type of stab wound?" Mr. Padilla asked.

"There is a cavity that the heart rests inside," replied Dr. Barr. "If for some reason there is a massive bleed into that particular cavity, the pressure that it exerts will decrease the pumping ability of the heart so that it can no longer function to pump blood to the remainder of the body, which will cause death."

"Doctor, were there any other symptoms which may have contributed to the death that occurred here?"

"Yes, sir," Dr. Barr said. "As you recall, I mentioned the fact that when the body was first seen there was a large amount of sand, dirt and gravel that I found covering the face and the chest. In doing the examination, I was able to determine that, through probably one or several, very forceful inhalings of air, this material was drawn down into the passageways that conduct air down into the lungs and in fact was so extensive and so massive that it actually had plugged many of the smaller airways and thereby probably to a great degree excluding oxygen from those passageways. And in a sense, when you exclude oxygen from these passageways a type of suffocation can occur."

"Doctor, would you tell us please what your conclusion is as to cause of death in this particular case?"

"The cause of death is . . . what we term insanguination, which is bleeding into the body rather than out of the body, and is what we call a cardiac tamponade, which is a fatal condition . . . a very rapid fatal condition, because pressures build up quite quickly in this closed space around the heart."

"What effect does the foreign matter in the mouth and the lungs have as far as cause of death?" Ray Padilla asked.

"I believe that that secondary condition was important in Julie Jackson's final demise, by eliminating oxygen that could be taken in through the lungs."

"Doctor, can you tell us whether or not the amount of foreign matter that you found in the trachea, the mouth, whatever . . . is that consistent with the head of Julie Jackson being forcefully held into the ground?"

"Yes, sir."

Dr. Barr explained that he found evidence of intact sperm on the body of Julie Jackson, which indicated she was also raped. Even though Defendant Guzman admitted to murder, he never admitted to rape.

***

RICHARD FISHER

Kathy Wright, assistant district attorney for the State and co-counsel with Ray Padilla, called Paramedic Richard Fisher to the stand. "On April 6, 1981, were you dispatched to the canyon, the Tijeras Canyon area, in reference to a female victim?" Ms. Wright asked.

"Yes, I was," Richard Fisher replied.

"What did you find when you got to the canyon?"

"When we arrived in the canyon, it was late; it was very dark, completely dark. The only light in the canyon was from headlights of the vehicles that were there. As we arrived on the scene, I found Colene Bush lying on the inside lane of eastbound I-40. She had been wrapped in a green sleeping bag."

"Mr. Fisher, what was your assessment of Colene, when you arrived at the scene, in reference to her injuries?" Prosecutor Wright asked.

"Initially, my primary assessment showed, as we uncovered her, multiple stab wounds about the chest and the neck."

"Did you try to make verbal contact with her?"

"Yes."

"What was your success?"

"On my very first attempt, there was some moaning . . . her eyes were open . . . I could tell that she was conscious . . . at least barely conscious," Richard Fisher said.

"Did you touch her to determine her body temperature?"

"Yes, I did."

"What did you find?"

"She was extremely cold. The temperature in the canyon that night was, I would imagine, about 35 degrees."

Kathy Wright looked at her notes. "Did you take blood pressure and pulse?"

"Yes, I did . . . or I attempted to. There was no pulse . . . palpable . . . that is, you cannot feel a pulse . . . and so in turn there was no palpable blood pressure."

"Did you start IVs?"

"Yes, I did," Richard Fisher said. "I started two IV lines of lactated ringers, which is a volume expander or replacement for the loss of blood and that type of thing. I started one in each arm."

"Did you bandage any wound because of air escaping?"

"Yes, I did. The upper left chest had multiple wounds and every time she would take a breath both air and blood would escape from these wounds."

"Do you know how long it was, Mr. Fisher, from the time you were dispatched, to the time you returned to Presbyterian Hospital with Colene?"

"The total time that had elapsed from the time that we were dispatched from our station, which is right across the street from Presbyterian Hospital, we arrived in the canyon, got Colene, treated her and by our return to Presbyterian, a total of 31 minutes had elapsed."

"Thank you, Mr. Fisher."

***

DR. RICHARD PHILLIPS

"I call Dr. Richard Phillips to the stand," Kathy Wright said.

Dr. Phillips, the emergency room cardio-thoracic surgeon who treated Colene, was to testify regarding the extent of her initial injuries.

"Dr. Phillips, were you present at Presbyterian Hospital, on April 6, 1981, when Colene Bush was brought in?" Ms. Wright asked.

"Yes, I was," Dr. Phillips answered.

"What were her vital signs when she first came into the emergency room?"

"She was pulseless at that time . . . that is, she had no palpable blood pressure when she came in. She was ashen and in shock."

"Was she hypothermic?"

"Yes . . . she was very cold."

"How does a person get that way?"

Dr. Phillips rubbed his chin. "In this particular case, it was probably related to prolonged exposure to being outdoors and in addition to having lost a fair amount of blood."

"What was the treatment in the emergency room?"

"The initial treatment was to stop all of the obvious bleeding and to treat her shock which was quite profound."

"How did you do that?

Dr. Phillips replied that intravenous lines were inserted into her veins and special catheters were inserted into the major vessels in her heart. He said they did everything they could to get more blood into her. He also explained how they dealt with the many stab wounds to her chest.

"She had multiple stab wounds in her chest," Dr. Phillips said. "What we call a sucking injury. Every time she breathed . . . air would move in and out . . . so there were sizable wounds there and for that reason, chest tubes were inserted into the chest cavity to evacuate all the blood and to allow the lungs to expand."

"How many surgeons, beside you, were involved?"

"At least six."

"How long did this surgery take?"

Dr. Phillips putting one finger to the side of his mouth, thought for a moment. "I believe the surgery started close to 3:30 AM in the operating room and finished around 1 o'clock the following afternoon. So it would be 9 1/2 ... 10 hours."

"Was there any particular reason that you had to insert the chest tube during surgery?" Ms. Wright asked.

"Yes," replied Dr. Phillips. "We had worked, I think, a long time, well over an hour, and we still couldn't get her out of shock . . . so we felt that we had some bleeding at that time that was not well detected. We made the decision to put in another chest tube and when we did . . . there was some blood that was in the left chest and that led us to go ahead and open up her left chest and terminate the bleeding there."

"What did you find when you opened up the left chest?"

"She had multiple stab wounds and into the chest cavity. There were five wounds into the lung substance itself . . . and she had heavy and profuse bleeding from there. We evacuated at least five units of blood from the chest cavity . . . these are normally the kind of wounds which might stop bleeding if a person weren't so hypothermic, weren't so cold, and didn't have problems with coagulation related to that. Because she had lost so much blood she had lost her ability to coagulate the blood and so we had to terminate the bleeding at the time of surgery. We did that with sutures to stop the bleeding," Dr. Phillips explained.

"So the stab wounds went into the lung itself? Is that what you are saying?" Kathy Wright asked.

"Yes, I believe that there were five wounds into the lung substance itself . . . one of which would have been a "through and through" wound . . . which had gone in and then penetrated out. The others just had an entrance point."

"Did you take her temperature?"

"Yes, during the surgery we did record her temperature. The thermometer we used only goes down to 28 degrees Celsius, and she was below that."

"Could you describe for us, in general," Ms. Wright asked, "the number and location of the wounds that you treated?

"Well, there were multiple stab wounds and slash wounds. The worst wounds she had were in the neck region. She had multiple slashes across the trachea area, and they had gone deep enough to make bare and denude the trachea, the windpipe, so that it was visible. The wounds had extended across the external jugular vein, which is the big vein that you can see here. The bleeding was quite extensive and I would say that there were maybe four or five wounds, like slash wounds, that had just gone back and forth."

Kathy Wright leaned in to confer with Mr. Padilla, and then asked; "Now you say it exposed her trachea?"

"Yes."

"Just briefly, what is the trachea?"

"That's the windpipe and it takes quite a little bit to get down to show that. There were, in addition, some stab wounds which had gone into the pharynx, that is into the oral cavity. She had bleeding which was on the inside of the mouth and the inside of the pharynx. Those were created by stab wounds which had actually penetrated the outer skin and muscles."

"To expose the trachea itself, can you give us an opinion as to what type of pressure that would take?"

"It takes a *lot* of pressure to expose these kinds of tissues," Dr. Phillips exclaimed. "Even with a sharp surgical knife it's unusual with a kind of pressure that you apply in attempting to do it . . . to do it in fewer than two or three swipes of a real sharp blade. So it was sizable pressure."

"Are surgical knives pretty sharp?"

"They are when they are new. They are as sharp as any razor you would buy," Dr. Phillips said.

"What other injuries did she have?" Ms. Wright questioned.

Dr. Phillips answered that she had a number of stab wounds to both chests. Four on each side. She also had stab wounds to the abdomen and many slashing wounds to the extremities.

"The stab wounds in the chest area, were they near any major organs of the body?" Kathy Wright asked.

"Well, they were into the lung substance and into the major arteries leading from the heart and came very close to the heart."

"Can you estimate how much blood she lost?"

"She had lost a minimum of 30% of her blood volume and probably half of it."

"What is the blood volume of somebody of Colene's size?"

"It would be like ten pints of blood," Dr. Phillips said.

"Now, of the wounds Colene received, which wounds bled the most and why would those wounds bleed the most?"

"The wounds which bled the most initially were the neck wounds and that was because the major veins were just cut right across . . . so I would guess that was one of the major contributors and in addition into the chest cavity."

"During the surgery was the acid content of the blood checked?" Ms. Wright asked.

"Yes, it was."

"Can you explain what that is and why that's important?"

"Well, the acid content of the blood is important," Dr. Phillips said, "because it is what the metabolic aspect is, how her body is functioning at that time. Normally the body operates in a fairly restricted range of acid based balance. We use the pH to monitor that and the normal pH run between 7.35 and 7.45. It is a monitor of shock and it tells us if the body is doing its job. When it was recorded during surgery, and this was shortly after she had come to the operating room, but after we had gotten most of the bleeding stopped . . . and after a point when we had given her some bicarbonate - that's an alkaline substance which helps to correct the kind of acid which she had built up and after we had given that, her pH was recorded at I believe 6.65. It is generally regarded that if your pH is below 6.8 you can*not* survive. It is almost incompatible with life. She was extremely acidotic," Dr. Phillips said.

"Doctor, were there any particular factors that led to Colene's survival?"

"She obviously had to have been in tremendous physical condition to have tolerated the insult to her body . . . just the amount of shock, the amount of . . . of acid base imbalance . . . all of these factors, not just the injuries to her . . . normally, I would say that would have led to her demise. You know, I think if she were in lesser physical condition, she would not have made it."

"Doctor, do you have an opinion as to whether or not there was a pattern to the stab wounds that Colene received?"

"Not sure I can say there was a pattern. Certainly the wounds that were inflicted, any small number of them were sufficient to have killed her. The number of wounds she had were all of a nature, I think were morbid wounds, she easily could have died and I would think all of the wounds were with the intent that she would die. It was certainly, in my opinion, and based on prior experience I have had in seeing a lot of trauma patients, it was the most savage attack on a human being I've ever seen."

"Was it your opinion, that the wounds that were inflicted on Colene were inflicted in a random manner?"

"Certainly, I would have to say they were scattered throughout her body but I don't think that's the same thing as random. They were into vital areas of the body. And, you know, I mean, it wasn't as if they were all into the arm or into a leg . . . something that wouldn't have killed her. The wounds were placed into places in the body that could have very easily have killed her."

When it was his turn for cross examination, Joe Fine asked Dr. Phillips if *all* of the wounds were to vital areas and he said they were not. Mr. Fine clarified that Dr. Phillips wasn't testifying as to the defendant's sanity, but only whether or not Guzman was aiming for vital areas.

***

JUAN CHAVEZ

New Mexico State Police Officer, Juan Chavez, the first law enforcement on the scene, testified that victim Colene Bush was found on the highway median. He said blood crossed three eastbound lanes of I-40.

"Information that I got from the witnesses was that she was sitting in the median and they thought maybe she was involved in an accident and they stopped by to see what they could do when they discovered her all full of blood," Juan Chavez said.

Chavez said that his next step was to determine how Colene ended up on I-40.

"So, I went ahead and followed the trail of blood across the three lanes of I-40 to the guard rail and noticed that there was more blood going down, so I went ahead and went down to Old 66 and found some more blood on the bottom there."

The officer, told how he slid down one of the embankments, and found that the blood continued further than the eye could see.

"I then proceeded to go down to the bottom there and when I got to the bottom of the dirt road, the gas line road, I saw what looked like more blood and I didn't want to mess up the blood, the blood in the area. I notified Albuquerque what I had and then I went into the Presbyterian Hospital and met Agent Manny Aragon."

Ray Padilla asked the officer to describe the general conditions of the evening.

"I-40 at that time of the night," Juan Chavez said, "is mostly very, very light semi-truck traffic. Old 66 you don't have hardly any traffic. There's a house, approximately half a mile east of the scene and there's a stream down to the bottom there and it's hard to find, to locate that area . . . there's no lights . . . a person would have to know the area to get to it. Due to the degree of darkness, I was using my spotlight to get around."

Officer Chavez, often referring to his reports, stated that he was unable to obtain any information from the victim at the hospital so he went back to the scene to protect it. When additional Santa Fe personnel arrived the next morning, he returned to the task of following the trail of blood to its conclusion, which ended approximately 350 yards straight down, at the bottom of the arroyo. He said that morning; the police discovered multiple car tracks, evidence of some sort of violent struggle and much more blood.

"We got measurements to where the car was parked and further on east, took measurements of where the victim had struggled . . . where the blood was located . . . full of blood . . . where she had fell down . . . measurements to where she started crawling' on all fours . . . to the point where she started crawling up to Old 66 from the bottom."

Officer Chavez told the jury that as the police searched for evidence relating to Colene Bush, the second victim, Julie Jackson, was found.

"At approximately 8:45 PM, Agent Manny Aragon discovered the nude body of a second female lying face down. Agent Aragon immediately walked back to the police vehicle and phoned that in to Santa Fe. The men then began charting exactly what happened where and diagrammed a general view of the scene."

Prosecutor Ray Padilla asked Officer Chavez, in his 14 years of experience, if he was able to discover much in the way of evidence at this crime scene, compared to other crime scenes that he had investigated.

"No. We didn't find any clothes. Other crime scenes or searches I've done in the past, usually we found evidence at the scene like clothes or pieces of evidence like knives left at the scene by the assailant. This one here . . . we couldn't find nothing."

***

TOM ENGLISH

Tom English, New Mexico State Police lead detective, testifying for the prosecution, told the court that once the description of the suspect went out to law enforcement and to the media, he was swamped with tips. After receiving a tip, he would check each one's viability and then take the next appropriate step.

"Anytime that I felt that there was a good possibility that a suspect might have been in the area, might have been able to perpetrate this offense . . . I tried to obtain a photograph of this individual and present it to the surviving victim in a photographic lineup. I believe I showed her five different photographic lineups."

After sifting through the deluge of potential perpetrators, twenty-three promising suspects remained, with a good many of those having the first name Raymond. Agent English focused on the name Raymond because that was the name given to the victims on the night of the crime. Eventually, this clue led him to Raymond Guzman, which led him to his brother, the defendant, Michael Guzman. Michael, however, was not considered a suspect until the moment he turned himself in to police.

Agent English testified that, "The defendant had told me that his brother had told him, they have your picture, I don't want to be blamed for what you've done . . . you better turn yourself in."

After Guzman turned himself in and confessed, Agent English still had to verify that they had the right man. Prosecutor Kathy Wright asked him how he assured himself that the defendant was truly the right suspect in this case.

"I asked two specific questions of the defendant that evening. The first question was how the victim Julie Jackson was stabbed, to which he stated that he stabbed her in the chest which was reversant information, which I had released to the news media and to other sources of information to the public. The information that I released was that she had been stabbed in the back."

"Why did you do that?" Ms. Wright asked.

"I did this to protect the investigation from anybody who might want to falsely confess to the crime. The second question I asked was about the first stabbing of the victim Colene Bush - to which he stated that the knife stuck in her back which also was not released to the news media on purpose and he answered the question properly."

Agent English testified that Guzman showed him where he threw the knife. The police were able to find part of the blade at the location he had indicated that he had thrown it. Guzman also told him that he hid out in El Paso, Texas during the two and half weeks between the crime and his confessions. Agent English said that Guzman told him that he was terrified of being recognized during that time period.

"The defendant stated to me that anytime he saw a police officer while he was in Texas in the City of El Paso, that he would hide his face hoping not to be recognized from the drawings that had been circulated."

"Now outside any formal statement you may have taken from the defendant, did he give you any other information about what he did with the physical evidence in this case?" Prosecutor Wright asked.

"Yes, ma'am," answered Agent English. "During the whole time that he was in my vehicle and while we were proceeding to different locations, he explained the disposition of the evidence . . . such as cutting up driver licenses, flushing them down toilets . . . to cutting up clothing, throwing them out the window of his vehicle while he drove between Albuquerque and Bernalillo New Mexico . . . and also the destruction of his own clothing . . . which was saturated with blood, on his way to El Paso."

"Did the defendant indicate to you at any time whether he did anything to change the appearance of his car?"

"He stated that the tire marks at the crime scene should indicate that there was one different tire from the other three tires mounted on the vehicle . . . that he had rotated those tires after the incident."

Before the first of the defendant's three confessions was played for the jury, Judge Cole excused Michael Guzman from the courtroom because he had communicated through his attorney that hearing himself confess would be upsetting.

Despite the courts many efforts to keep Guzman calm, the jury saw the defendant either sitting in his seat catatonic-like, or shaking or agitated. Tom English told prosecutor Kathy Wright that Guzman had not behaved this way before the trial. He told her of a conversation that he had with Guzman after the taped confessions.

"Mr. Guzman indicated again that he had wanted to cooperate, that he wanted to do his time. I believe that he stated that he felt he should do about two years and then be able to go on and live with his family."

"Did you respond to him in any way?"

"Yes ma'am, I did. I advised Mr. Guzman of the possible penalties that he was facing - being possibly a death sentence or life imprisonment."

"Did he have a response to that?"

"No ma'am, he didn't say anything else from that point on."

"Did he have a physical response to that?"

"Yes, ma'am. He had a facial expression that he was shocked," Agent English replied.

"Pass the witness."

Defense attorney Fine asked Agent English about Guzman's expectations at the time he turned himself in.

"Did Mr. Guzman ever question you regarding the law of insanity?" asked Joe Fine. "Whether he could be acquitted in this case because he was insane?"

"No, sir, he did not."

"It appeared to you that he met with you expecting to be punished, not to get off on insanity? Is this correct?"

"Yes, sir, I would say that's correct."

"That's all the questions I have. Thank you, Officer."

***

JAMES TUTTLE

James Tuttle, the 22 year old fiancé of Julie Jackson, told the court that he had known Julie Jackson for three or four years and that she was the person he had expected to marry.

"When was the last time you saw Julie alive?" asked Kathy Wright.

"I went to a concert with my brother," James answered. "She had come back from the University, from the library, where she was studying for finals. I saw her around 6:30 in the evening."

"What time did you get home that night . . . on the 5th of April?"

"I got home around 11 o'clock and she said she was going to be there before I got back from the concert . . . and she wasn't home."

"Did that concern you?

"Yes."

"Why is that?"

"Well, normally when she says she is going to do something, she does it. She doesn't normally say she is going to do something and not show up. So I called Colene's house and there was no answer."

"What did you do then?"

"I called the police . . . and I informed them that she wasn't there. That I was reporting her as a missing person and they told me that they could do nothing until 24 hours had passed and I called everyone I could think of to call. I walked around looking for her and I found nothing."

"Did you eventually go to bed?"

"Yeah, I went to sleep around 3 or 4 and I got up around 6 and called the police again when Julie wasn't home." Joe Fine objected to this line of questioning, said it was irrelevant. Judge Cole sustained the objection.

Kathy Wright then asked James when the last time he had consensual intercourse with Julie was and he told her on Saturday afternoon. Ms. Wright inquired how often Julie showered and James replied that she showered every day.

On cross-examination, Joe Fine asked James if he knew for a fact that Julie showered Sunday morning. Did he hear the water running or anything like that?

James replied, "Yes, I did hear the water running."

***

ARTHUR CRAIG

Arthur Craig, a crime lab analyst for the New Mexico State Police, testified that he was an expert in trace evidence. He had been to the crime scene in Tijeras Canyon on April 6, 1981, and had taken photos and collected physical evidence.

At the crime lab in Santa Fe, he tested trace evidence from Julie Jackson's body for the presence of acid phosphatase.

"Could you define please, sir, what acid phosphatase is?" Kathy Wright asked her witness.

"Acid phosphatase is an enzyme which is primarily reproduced in the male reproductive system. It's found in its highest concentration in the seminal fluid." Mr. Craig detailed how acid phosphatase corresponding to Guzman's sperm was found on Julie Jackson's body. Forensic use of DNA did not exist in 1981.

***

MONICA JUAREZ

Despite the fact that it was late in the day, Kathy Wright called Monica Juarez, the defendant's girlfriend, to the stand. Ms. Juarez said that Guzman was late coming home from work that night and that when he did come home, he was "full of blood". Ms. Wright asked Monica about Guzman's knife.

"He held it real tight," Monica said in a halting, husky voice, "He even got a little cut from holding it real tight and he had told me to help him wash his hands in the sink. So we went to the restroom and he let it drop into the sink. Then after, he set it on the Bible."

"Where was the Bible?"

"In the hallway upstairs."

"Was there any blood on the Bible?" Kathy Wright asked.

"Well, I didn't really notice. I don't think so."

Monica testified that Guzman told her what happened in the mountains and then informed her that he needed to go back to the canyon.

"You say he wanted to go back. Go back where?"

"To the . . . ah . . . scene of the crime."

"Did he tell you why?"

"Well, he needed his cigarettes and they weren't in his brown t-shirt and I didn't have no money and neither did he . . . to buy cigarettes and he needed 'em real bad and so . . .uh . . . he wanted to go back for his cigarettes."

"What if anything did you see when you got there?"

"As we were going down the dirt road, I saw a little puddle of blood . . . and that's when I decided to close my eyes and I like got down . . ."

"Did you keep your eyes closed the rest of the time?"

"Yes," Ms. Juarez replied.

"Did he say anything to you while you were down in that area?"

"Well, I think he had said, I want to see if they're okay . . . and then I just told him - to hurry up, let's go - so he grabbed his cigarettes and got in the car."

"How did he drive away?"

"He was going real, real fast and like swerving . . . on lanes."

Monica gave testimony that when she and Guzman got back to the apartment; he went through the contents of the bag with the girls' clothes. Kathy Wright asked her what was found in the bag.

"Well, he found two black pills in a blue jacket and um . . . and like some ID and, you know, clothes."

"Do you know what type of ID it was?"

"It was a . . . a U-UNM ID and driver's license."

"Did you ever look at them to see whose name was on them?"

Monica Juarez paused and looked around the room. "I looked at . . . yes, uh, huh."

"Do you recall the name on them?"

"One was . . . it said Julie Ann Jackson on one of 'em."

"Was there any beer either in the house or the car that night?"

"Yes, uh-huh."

"Where was it?"

"Well, there was two-six packs and he had taken 'em inside the house," Monica said.

"Did he do anything with them, once he got them in the house?"

"Yes, he emptied about three or four cans and took the rest to his mom."

"What did you do after all this?" Ms. Wright asked.

"We went to bed," Monica answered.

"And did both of you sleep?"

"Well, I didn't but . . . he was like . . . I don't know if he was asleep or . . . he was like breathing real hard . . . I couldn't tell if he was asleep or not."

Monica then told of the two of them leaving town to live in El Paso, how Guzman rented a U-Haul and that they left the state to start a new life in Texas.

"When we got to El Paso," Monica said, "we rented a motel, and then the next day we went to his sister-in-law's and we stayed over there . . . and we really didn't do nothing . . . that day . . . well, no . . . that's when Michael started looking for an apartment . . . that day . . . and a job . . . most of the day."

Monica testified that she had to return to Albuquerque pretty quickly relating to unforeseen maternity costs.

"The hospital wanted a thousand down . . . almost a thousand down right away, you know, so I could get registered, to have my baby there . . . Michael didn't have that much with him . . . so he asked if we could have them in payments and they had said no. So we were having a hard time, so I just told him, you know, I got really tired, and I told him just to bring me back."

Kathy Wright asked Monica when the next time she talked to Michael was. Monica said that he called her the next day after the baby was born and said, 'I just wanna see my son grow up in the future,' he told me if he ever did have a future and I told him, what does he mean by that . . . and he told me that he was talking to Jim Gutierrez, some uh, officer . . . and uh, then Linda-Linda got on the phone and told me that he . . . he turned himself in."

***

MORE STATE WITNESSES

The State presented its last witnesses. The first two were the restaurant owners where Guzman worked as a dishwasher. The last two were county investigators, Jim Gutierrez and Santos Baca. The restaurant owners testified that Guzman did *not* act out of the ordinary while at work on April 5, 1981 and that he certainly did not act crazy.

"Can you describe to us, if you would, his demeanor that day?" Ray Padilla asked Tom Brennan, one of the owners of the Comme Chez Vous restaurant. "Was there anything abnormal? Did he act normal?"

"He acted normal to me from other days that I worked with him," Mr. Brennan replied.

Mr. Troussaint, the second owner, answered in a heavy French accent. "It (his behavior) was thoroughly fine to me."

Next up on direct testimony was Jim Gutierrez, 13th Judicial District investigator. He had known the defendant since he was eleven years old. It had been Jim Gutierrez that Michael Guzman called when he decided to turn himself in.

"Michael got on the phone and he told me, 'Jim, I've done something horrible . . . I've killed somebody.' He said, 'I want you to come to my house and talk to me. Don't bring the police with you. Promise me you won't bring anybody with you.' And I did, I went by myself. When I first got to the house, I walked in and I advised Michael of his constitutional rights from Miranda. I asked if he would give me a tape recorded statement. He stated that he would. I went back out to the car; I got my tape recorder and a tape."

While Mr. Gutierrez was on the stand, another one of Michael Guzman's recorded confessions was played. Guzman again left the room while the jury listened.

Finally, Santos Baca, chief investigator with the district attorney's office, 2nd Judicial District, was called. He was present when Guzman's third and fourth confessions were given. Because the third confession did not record properly, Guzman gave a fourth confession.

Prosecutor Wright asked Investigator Baca if he made any promises to Guzman in exchange for his confessions.

"Yes," Baca replied. "He requested two items, I believe. One was that I would not have any news media in the area, and two, that I would not handcuff him when he comes into my office. I agreed on that."

With the accused out of the room, the final taped confession was played for the jury.

The State rested its case.

DEFENSE WITNESSES

CHARLES MITCHELL

The defense called Charles Mitchell to the stand. Mr. Mitchell met the defendant in May of 1979 as Mr. Mitchell sat near a bridge on the Rio Grande.

"I turned around and I looked over my shoulder and Michael had took his belt off and hung himself on that cable," Charles Mitchell said. "He said he heard voices that were telling him to hang himself . . . to kill himself."

Mr. Mitchell told the court that he spent a lot of time talking to the defendant that day and that Michael seemed like a disturbed young man.

Under cross-examination, Mr. Mitchell admitted that Guzman told him that he made this suicide attempt not because he heard voices but because he couldn't get along with his mother and didn't like the fact that he had no money.

***

MONICA JUAREZ - RECALL

"I recall Monica Juarez," Joe Fine said.

Mr. Fine asked Ms. Juarez about the incident involving the Anglo girls and an old lady, which took place at a party about a month before the murder. Monica said it was a party full of cowboys and one of them told Michael that he didn't want any dirty Mexicans at the party. She said that a fight ensued between Michael and the cowboy.

"So Michael started fighting," Monica said. "And they had each other pinned down on a green Thunderbird and then they were fighting and then this elderly lady and two younger girls jumped on Michael's back and one had a big brick and was gonna hit Michael in the head with it."

"When we were leaving, the lady jumped on the car and was gonna jump on my back and then Michael turned around and told her not to jump on my back cause I was pregnant. He told her . . . 'Don't do that or else I'll break your neck.'"

Mr. Fine asked her if Michael had been involved in other incidents involving older ladies and she replied that he had. She said that Michael had come home a couple of weeks before the incident involving the UNM girls and told her that he almost killed an elderly lady.

"I thought he was just like joking with me . . . and then he pulled out a paper that said "Gwen" and a phone number on it and then he gave me the paper and then he goes 'If you don't believe me - here's her number - she even gave me her number to talk to her when I need help.' I didn't really believe him . . . so I just got the paper and I just threw it away."

"Did Michael ever mistreat you? Mr. Fine asked.

"Yes," Monica replied.

"What did he do to you?"

"Well, when I was pregnant, he used to hit me a lot . . . and since the day I met him really. He used to hit me a lot and take his anger out on me."

"Were you familiar with Michael's relationship with his mother?" Joe Fine asked.

"Yes, uh huh," Monica answered, shifting in her seat.

"Would you describe that relationship?"

"It was real rough when I met Michael. They were still having it real hot on each other. They wouldn't get along with each other. She would throw beer bottles or plates or big dishes or anything at him . . . just to get him out of the house. She sometimes couldn't stand the sight of him . . . and he would just take off walking."

Finally, Joe Fine asked Monica if Michael had told her that he committed the murder for her.

"Yes," she replied. "He kept repeating and repeating it that night. 'Cause everybody messes with you,' he said, 'and I don't want my baby hurt.' And he goes 'God let me do this.'"

***

WILLIE HILL

Willie Hill, a wiry black man and the live-in boyfriend of Linda Guzman, testified that Michael Guzman came over to his mother's house on the night of April 5, 1981. He brought two six packs of Coors with him, and he seemed agitated.

"He said, "Willie, I bought you and my mother some beer," and I said 'Wassamatter Michael?' Well, he came like a . . . he was shaken up - nervous and he said a . . . he said, 'Willie, I'm tired of people' - scuse my language . . . Should I say what he said?"

"You can say it," Joe Fine advised.

"He said, 'I'm tired a people fuckin' with me.' I said what you mean by that? He said, 'I'm tired Willie, nobody give me credit for what I do for them.' And I said 'Mike, just hang on in there, man.'"

"And was he shaking at that time?"

"Yes, he was. Matter a fact - he was hyper."

When District Attorney, Ray Padilla cross-examined Mr. Hill, he asked him if he had told other people that, if it had been him, if the two girls would have jumped into *his* car, he would have shot them.

"No, I didn't . . . no I didn't," Willie, noticeably angered, shouted. "I did not say that. I said to say that if I was in Michael's shoes . . . if two girls jumped in the back seat . . . I did not say I would shoot 'em like this . . . I said I would whoop 'em with my hands . . . I did not say nothing about no shooting . . . a gun was out of it."

"Matter of fact," Ray Padilla persisted, "You said, 'I would have probably done worse.' Didn't you?"

"I said that. But I did not say no guns and no weapons."

"Thank you, Mr. Hill . . . pass the witness."

***

DR. DON HEDGES

"What is your profession Dr. Hedges?" Joe Fine asked.

"I'm a doctor of osteopathic medicine," Dr. Hedges replied.

With the jury looking at a chart that Mr. Fine had placed on a tripod in front them, Dr. Hedges explained why Michael Guzman had come in to see him on February 16, 1981. He said that Guzman needed to see a doctor regarding back pain he had been experiencing from a car accident a year earlier. Dr. Hedges prescribed Guzman Emperin 3 with codeine on that date.

Dr. Hedges further testified that Guzman came in again on March 16, 1981, complaining of a stomach flu and continued back pain. He also complained of leg pain.

"Was he complaining of anxiety and depression on that day?" Joe Fine asked.

"No, he wasn't," Dr. Hedges answered.

When asked what he prescribed that day, Dr. Hedges replied that he prescribed a quantity of forty Emperin 3 with codeine and a quantity of sixty Limbitrol, an anti-anxiety drug.

Dr. Hedges stated that Guzman came back yet again on March 30, 1981, this time complaining of both back pain and anxiety and depression. On this date, Dr. Hedges prescribed forty more Emperin 3 with codeine and sixty more Limbitrol.

On cross-examination, Ray Padilla questioned Dr. Hedges as to why he prescribed anti-anxiety drugs to someone who came in complaining of physical problems.

"So," Mr. Padilla began. "Even though he may not have said something about being anxious or mentioned specific words, you may have looked at him and concluded he was anxious and depressed, just from the way that he looked?"

"That's correct," said Dr. Hedges.

"By a look in his eyes or from something that indicated to you as a physician that he had that?" Mr. Padilla asked.

Dr. Hedges paused and then replied, "Well . . . yes."

***

DR. SAM ROLL

"I call Dr. Sam Roll," Joe Fine said.

Dr. Roll's qualifications as an expert were presented and they were extensive. Among other things, he was a board certified forensic psychologist, had a PhD from Pennsylvania State University and had studied for his doctorate at Yale. He was also a full professor at the University of New Mexico.

The Office of the Public Defender had initially requested that Dr. Roll evaluate Michael Guzman's psychological condition when he arrived at the jail. To this end, Dr. Roll stated he had read all of the available information regarding Mr. Guzman and also performed a large battery of tests. Mr. Fine asked Dr. Roll if he had an opinion or not on whether or not Michael Guzman had a mental disease at the time of the incident.

"My opinion is that at the time of the incident, Mr. Guzman did indeed have a mental disease."

"Would you put a name on this mental disease, doctor?" Joe Fine asked.

"I wouldn't put a name," Dr. Roll replied. "Names in psychology are just summaries; those kinds of experiences that he's had and has had through his life could be best summarized by the term paranoid schizophrenia."

"Do you have an opinion as to whether or not Michael Guzman as a result of a medical disease could not prevent himself from committing the acts in question which include an alleged rape, kidnapping, murder – picking up the girls and then stabbing both girls?"

"I do, sir."

"What is your opinion, doctor?"

"My opinion," Dr. Roll said as he straightened his tie, "is that because of his disease and his defect of the mind, Mr. Guzman was, in fact, not able to control his impulses that were involved in the alleged acts of the rape and the kidnapping and the murder."

"Was there any significant findings which he revealed to you in interviews?" Mr. Fine asked.

"Yes, he would see his aunt's picture on the wall and then he would begin crying. And then he told about his aunt having put a curse on him. She being a witch or a bruja and she cursed him and she bewitched him. She cursed him because someone in his family, the aunt thinks – the witch thinks – someone snitched to the police about one of her sons . . . got her son in trouble. He interpreted that . . . what was happening to him . . . as being a result of what she was doing."

Dr. Roll went over the entirety of Guzman's childhood, the fact that his mother beat him, his preoccupation with the upcoming baby, the possibility that he might have been on Limbitrol at the time of the murder and agreed with the Forensic Hospital that the defendant had a borderline personality with schizotypal features. Dr. Roll was convinced of Guzman's severe mental disease and was not hesitant to say so.

"Doctor," Joe Fine asked. "Do you have any doubt that Michael Guzman was insane at the time of these incidents?

"No, sir I do not," Dr. Roll replied.

***

DOUGLAS FERRARO

Dr. Douglas Ferraro, a professor of psychology at UNM with a PhD from Columbia University, and a certified psycho-pharmacologist, was called upon to testify as an expert witness. He was considered a controversial witness. Joe Fine wanted Dr. Ferraro to testify as to the effects of drugs taken that were not in evidence. Guzman confided to Dr. Ferraro two days before the trial that he was "messed up on Limbitrol" when he committed the murder and other crimes.

Judge Cole would not allow this information into evidence unless Guzman himself testified. Mr. Fine implied that Guzman just might take the stand. In the meantime, Dr. Ferraro was allowed to testify about the effects of the drug Limbitrol in theoretical terms only.

Joe Fine asked Dr. Ferraro what Limbitrol is used for. Dr. Ferraro replied that it is a combo drug: part Librium to reduce anxiety and part Elavil which is an anti-depressant.

"Would this be an appropriate medication for someone who is psychotic?" asked Mr. Fine.

"Limbitrol would most likely *not* be an appropriate drug for someone who is psychotic," replied Dr. Ferraro. He goes on to say that Limbitrol is not made for psychotics, that it could potentially make that person worse and under certain circumstances might ignite a drug-fueled rage.

***

LINDA GUZMAN

Linda Guzman, the mother of the defendant, took the stand. She told the court that she never liked her son Michael.

"When did you start hitting him?" Joe Fine asked.

"When he was two years old," she replied.

"Why did you start hitting him?"

"It all started when I was trying to potty train Michael. I used to hit him time and time again and it never did work, so what I finally did was . . . ah . . . I set him in the toilet bowl. His whole body in the toilet bowl . . . and flushed the toilet," Linda Guzman said with some embarrassment.

Joe Fine paused and then asked, "What did you do when he was hungry and kept eating a lot?"

"Get upset and hit him," Mrs. Guzman replied matter-of-factly.

"How would you hit him?"

"With my hands."

"Did you ever use anything else?" Mr. Fine asked.

"At one time I used a stick on him," Mrs. Guzman answered.

"And where would you hit him?"

"On the back and on his head."

Mrs. Guzman said that even if she got mad at her other kids she would hit Michael instead. She said that she hated him from the moment that he was born because he looked like his father, whom she also hated. She would often hit Michael to get back at his father. She said that in order to try to please her, Michael would give her as much money as he could.

"When Michael was only eight years old," Mrs. Guzman said, "he was doing yard work . . . and the money he used to make, he would give it to me . . . he was trying to please me . . . for me to, you know, treat him better, cause I beat him so much."

"Did he give you money on other instances?"

"Yes, all the time. As a matter a fact, if he could . . . if it would please me, he would give me his whole check," Mrs. Guzman said with a cat-like smile.

She detailed the many other times that she beat her son and the multitude of implements that she used to beat him. These included electrical cords, bricks, sticks and the butt of a rifle. She also berated him for attempting suicide in her home.

"Once when he was 16, he tried to choke himself with a belt . . . his own belt and my other little boy came downstairs and told me about it and so . . . I ran up the stairway to his room and I told him that if he wanted to hang himself to go do it somewhere else. Not in my house," Mrs. Guzman said.

Despite all of this, Linda Guzman said that prior to the murder; she did not think that her son had any particular problems.

On cross examination, Ray Padilla asked, "Isn't it true that you have told others that you didn't really realize that Michael had any problems, and when this happened . . . then you realized he had a problem?"

"Yes."

"And now you think it's all your fault?"

"Not all of it. It goes both ways, you know. It's my ex-husband's and my fault," Linda Guzman said.

"But it's not Michael's fault?"

"No."

***

DR. IGNACIO MARTINEZ

Dr. Martinez, an expert witness for the defense, was a psychiatrist at the Forensic Hospital in Las Vegas, New Mexico. He stated that he went to medical school in Mexico City and had completed his residency at UNM Hospital in Albuquerque.

Joe Fine asked Dr. Martinez if he had an opinion as to whether the defendant had psychotic episodes in the past.

"Yes," Dr. Martinez replied with a heavy Spanish accent. "I believe that he has had psychotic episodes throughout his life. It would be very hard to determine when and how these episodes have resolved. But there is enough evidence in my mind to believe that he, in fact, has suffered from auditory hallucinations and other psychotic manifestations."

"When the girls got into the car," Mr. Fine asked, "can you tell us whether Michael was able to control himself as a result of a mental disease or defect?"

Dr. Martinez pushed out his lower lip and thought for a moment. "I believe he was able to control himself because he was able to drive the car and to talk coherently and obviously he was able to socialize with these women. I believe at that very point he must have been able to control himself."

"I'd like to bring you to another point, Dr. Martinez," Mr. Fine said. "We are in Tijeras canyon and Michael gets out of the car. Do you have an opinion as to whether at that time Michael Guzman as a result of a mental disease or defect was able to control himself?"

"I think that once this violent outflow, this instinctual drive started, he wasn't able to stop it anymore," Dr. Martinez replied, gesturing extensively with his hands. "Of course, I don't have a way to know at what very second this instinctual storm started. But what I know is that once that massive violence discharge of instinctual drive, in fact, started, I believe he wasn't able to put a stop to it."

"Are you familiar with the drug Limbitrol?" Mr. Fine asked.

"Yes, I am."

"Do you feel this is an appropriate drug to be given to someone like Michael Guzman?"

"I believe it's inappropriate medication for him," Dr. Martinez replied.

Ray Padilla on cross examination asked, "Doctor . . . isn't it a fact, that you have diagnosed Michael Guzman as having been sane at the time of the commission of these crimes?"

"Yes, it is a fact."

"Well, tell us what the legal definition of sanity is . . . your understanding."

"I hope you don't put me in a position to be tested," Dr. Martinez said with a slight smile, "but I think basically that it is that the person is limited in being in full contact with reality, to be in touch with reality, to know the nature of his actions and able to control his actions too and also that the person wouldn't suffer from distorting kind of phenomenon like delusions and hallucinations."

"Using that definition doctor, is it not your opinion that Michael Guzman was sane at the time of the commission of these crimes?"

"He was sane in the sense that he was in touch with reality," Dr. Martinez said, "but yet he was suffering from a major kind of anxiety and some of his controls were diminished too, but I think he was legally sane."

"Thank you, doctor."

The Defense rested its case.

CHAPTER 18

DR. RICHARD FINK

The State is allowed a rebuttal session.

Ray Padilla called Dr. Fink, a psychologist at the Forensic Hospital in Las Vegas, NM. Dr. Fink administered multiple psychological tests on Guzman during his stay at the Forensic Hospital. He gave Guzman an IQ test resulting in a borderline intelligence diagnosis. Dr. Fink also administered the Luria-Nebraska Neuropsychological Test to Guzman, on which he did poorly, because he said he couldn't read or write, which Dr. Fink later discovered to be untrue.

"I found out that he did indeed know how to read and write," Dr. Fink said, "and was actually helping some of the less literate patients at the hospital by writing letters for them."

Dr. Fink testified that while at the Forensic Hospital, Guzman spent much of his therapy time trying to gain sympathy for himself, going into elaborate detail about his unhappy home life.

"He seemed to be kind of manipulative," Dr. Fink said. "Or trying to present himself in a way to get sympathy. He was willing to talk to people but he only wanted to talk about certain things about his life and what an unfortunate childhood he had. He mentioned things about the different kinds of abuse he got at home from his family . . . from his mother."

Ray Padilla asked Dr. Fink if he ultimately came up with a diagnosis for Guzman.

"Yes, we did," Dr. Fink replied. "We came up with a diagnosis of borderline personality disorder with some schizotypal features and a possible learning disability." Dr. Fink testified that a borderline personality disorder is a condition that features rage and depression. The schizotypal part involves a sort of magical thinking, e.g. seeing witches or talking to God. "But it is a personality disorder and not a psychosis," Dr. Fink said.

Prosecutor Ray Padilla asked Dr. Fink if the defendant was legally insane.

"He is not legally insane," Dr. Fink replied. "He does not have a disease of the mind sufficient to make him legally insane."

"What, if anything, is your opinion doctor, as to Mr. Guzman's ability to know right from wrong on the night in question?" Mr. Padilla asked.

"It is my opinion, based on his statements to me, his statements to the police and those of the victim's, that he *did* know the difference between right and wrong at that time. He tried to avoid detection and dispose of evidence. He knew what he was doing was wrong."

***

DR. VERONICA THOMAS

Dr. Veronica Thomas, a clinical psychologist with a specialty in personality disorders at the Las Vegas Forensic Hospital, agreed with Dr. Fink's diagnosis that the defendant was sane. Prosecutor Kathy Wright asked her if the defendant could premeditate a murder such at the one in question and Dr. Thomas said "Yes." Ms. Wright then asked her the basis of this opinion.

"My basis of that opinion," Dr. Thomas replied, "is largely on the fact that he got a knife from work . . . and he said he didn't know what he was going to do with it . . . but that he had to have it."

Dr. Thomas was then asked why the defendant denied the kidnapping and rape charge but admitted to murdering Julie Jackson.

"My opinion is that Michael cannot admit that he does have a hatred for women."

***

DR. NED SEGAL

The next witness, Ned Segal, a private practice clinical psychologist, stated that he received his PhD from North Texas State University and had previously worked at the State Forensic Hospital.

Dr. Segal testified that he administered many tests to Mr. Guzman while the defendant was at the Forensic Hospital. Ray Padilla asked him what conclusions he had reached regarding the Rorschach test and Dr. Segal explained that there are some very particular ways in which people respond to the Rorschach.

"Mr. Guzman only looks at a small part of the picture," Dr. Segal testified. "He was under a tremendous amount of stress, as would be expected. He looks to be a very impulsive person. He did not appear, at that time, to have much control over his emotions. He was an explosive person. But overall, he did not have signs that were consistent with schizophrenia or any other formal thought disorder."

"This was not the Rorschach of a psychotic individual but it was the Rorschach of a person who was under a tremendous amount of stress, who is faced with a situation that was not at all to his liking . . . which was being caught and being in jail," Dr. Segal said.

Dr. Segal testified for the better part of the day on April 26, 1982, and spent the bulk of that time going over pieces of information that the defendant had told him, such as his version of the crime and Dr. Segal's interpretations of those things. Towards the end of his direct testimony, Ray Padilla asked Dr. Segal his opinion on Guzman's sanity, whether he knew right from wrong and could he appreciate the quality of his actions.

Guzman did know right from wrong and did appreciate the quality of his actions, Dr. Segal testified. "He did not claim to be under any type of delusion. He did not tell me anything about acting on the basis of a voice . . . or the fact that someone else wanted him to pick out these girls and sacrifice them or anything like that. He knew what he was doing," Dr. Segal said. He further testified that no one in the Guzman family noticed a change in his personality after the crime was committed. Dr. Segal said if someone was around him and he was psychotic, people would have noticed because psychotic people are very different from regular people. "At no time was his behavior really typical of that of someone who is out of touch with reality."

"Could he have premeditated the murder?" Ray Padilla asked

"Certainly he could have," Dr. Segal answered. "He had a plan and he followed through with the plan."

Ray Padilla asked Dr. Segal if the defendant was legally insane at the time of the crime.

"This is a man who has certainly had a difficult childhood. He looks at problems like an immature, angry person and he does not really put the reins on his temper as he should, but none of that makes him insane," Dr. Segal said.

On cross-examination, Mr. Fine asked him if he thought that Guzman had frontal brain damage.

"The best we can say is that there is a problem in that area . . . we'd have to say that it's at least a mild problem."

Mr. Fine wanted to know from Dr. Segal if he felt that the defendant had a borderline or schizotypal personality.

"I wouldn't call him schizotypal, no. I would suggest that if we are going to make a diagnosis that we could go as far as a borderline personality."

***

GWEN BAREFOOT

Gwen Barefoot was a woman who, two weeks before the crimes in question, was attacked by Michael Guzman in a fashion similar to the UNM coed attack. Only through luck and her own resourcefulness was she able to survive his assault.

"Mrs. Barefoot," Ray Padilla began, "I would like to direct your attention to the date of March the 17th of 1981. On that date, did something very unusual happen to you?"

"Yes, sir. I came home from work," Gwen Barefoot answered. "I worked at the Sundowner at the time and I came out on Central Avenue and turned left and about the time I reached the Volkswagen place, I noticed a car following me very close . . . I didn't think too much about it. So I turned and went to my apartment and by the time I had reached my apartment this other car had pulled in and parked. I sat in my car about three minutes and then I got out and this young man stepped out from behind the bushes and he grabbed me from behind with a screwdriver and threatened me. He said, 'Get into the car, don't make a sound or I'll kill you.'"

Mrs. Barefoot told the jury that this man pulled her by the hair into his car and only stopped when she told him her son was a police officer. She allowed him into her house and talked to him for a few minutes about his problems.

"He kept saying then, that he was sorry that he had tried to hurt me, which I'm sure he was at the time. I said if you need to talk to me later, I'll be happy to help you. So he said, could I call you back and talk to you later? That's when I gave him my name and my phone number."

After Ms. Barefoot testified, both the State and the Defense rested.

CHAPTER 19

CLOSING STATEMENT – STATE

Finally, after six days of testimony, all of the evidence had been presented. Only the closing arguments remained. Kathy Wright, the ADA for the State, reviewed the points in question for the jury.

"Ladies and gentlemen, there are several issues you have to decide in this trial. The defendant admitted that he killed Julie Jackson and that he stabbed Colene Bush but you have to decide both the degree and the type of murder of Julie Jackson. Was it a first degree deliberate killing? Or was it a first degree felony murder? Or was it a second degree murder? And in reference to Colene, you have to decide whether or not he stabbed her with the deliberate intent to kill her. The defendant never admitted rape and kidnapping. Those are crimes charged in this case. You will have to decide if in fact those crimes occurred.

The first jury instruction dealt with intent and forethought. The jury was told that the amount of forethought spent before committing a crime didn't have to be a lot of time . . . it could happen in a few minutes.

"The defendant had a deliberate intent to kill Julie Ann Jackson when he stabbed her," the prosecutor said.

Ms. Wright told the jury that the defendant stole a sharp knife, put the girls in his car and then drove in a virtual straight line to a secluded, pitch dark location - to an arroyo in Tijeras Canyon.

"Then he took Julie Jackson out of the car because he intended to kill her. He already decided that when he left his car. He didn't kill her in the car. He didn't want blood in his car."

"He stabbed her just once . . . took the knife right out of his pocket and he stabbed her just once and it penetrated her heart. She screamed once and she fell to the ground."

She said that the Office of the Medical Examiner had confirmed that her face was most likely pushed into the dirt by the defendant and held down, causing her to inhale dirt and suffocate.

"He did both things . . . because he wanted to be sure. He wanted to be sure he had completed his task of killing her."

Ms. Wright said the motive was explained by the killer himself in his confession.

"'Because I was scared of one of them sayin' something . . . one of them going to the police . . . saying something.'"

"He weighed that decision," Kathy Wright said. "He thought about it, and he decided that he didn't want any witnesses. It showed the deliberate intent to kill Julie Jackson."

Then she analyzed his attack on Colene Bush.

"What about Colene? Did he just stab her randomly or was he stabbing her with the intent to kill her? That's what you have to decide, ladies and gentlemen."

"When the defendant gave his confession, one of the things he said, quote, 'I wanted to do the same thing to the other girl.'"

Kathy Wright told the jurors that the defendant felt he had to kill Colene so he didn't leave any witnesses.

"At one point she says to him, 'Please let me die in peace,' and what does he do? He stops, maybe 30 seconds and then he stabbed her in the chest again and slashed her throat . . . and then he walked away . . . then he came back . . . so she played dead . . . tried not to move and he just sort of studied her and then he left - got in his car and left the scene."

"Those are not the actions of a man out of control . . . of a man that doesn't have a purpose. He clearly had a purpose in what he was doing that night."

The prosecutor said that the fact that Colene lived had nothing to do with the defendant's actions. "It had a lot to do with Colene's actions after he finally left. He did his best to be sure she was dead when he left. The only reason that's she's here is because of what she did afterwards."

Ms. Wright noted that the autopsy report said that a rape had been committed and even though Guzman never admitted rape he was being charged with criminal sexual penetration. "The medical examiner found intact sperm on the vaginal swab from the thigh swab of Julie Jackson." Prosecutor Wright said and then wheeled around and pointed. "It could have only have come from that man right there . . . Michael Guzman."

She discussed the issue of sanity and told the jury that the State had the burden of proving beyond a reasonable doubt that he was sane at the time of the crimes. Ms. Wright said that, "In fact, he *was* sane at the time that each and every one of these crimes were committed."

"His activities that night show that he had a plan, and he followed through with that plan. He may have made that plan up one step at a time, but he did form a plan as the night progressed . . . and he did follow through with it."

"And what about Colene? He could, and did, stop when asked to, and then stabbed her again . . . again, showing he thought about it . . . he didn't want to leave a witness. The doctor told you that those wounds were intended to kill."

"Look at that crime scene! Officer Chavez told you it was one of the cleanest crime scenes he's seen in 15 years of police work," Wright continued.

"He had really covered his tracks well. Agent English told you that he had eliminated 23 suspects in this case. And not a single one of them was Michael Guzman."

"He destroyed evidence, and when he destroyed it, it was after dark, when he was throwing it all out the windows between here and Bernalillo. This is not a man that doesn't know what's going on."

Ms. Wright said that despite the many discussions about beer, the defendant was not drunk and there was no evidence of anyone witnessing him ingesting drugs either.

"I submit that Michael Guzman did know what he was doing. He knew exactly what he was doing and he did it."

"Ladies and gentlemen, when you consider all of the evidence . . . I'm sure that you will find him guilty . . . of each and every crime . . . as charged. First degree murder, attempted first degree murder, rape, kidnapping - two counts - and tampering with evidence. And you will certainly find that he was sane. That he *could* control his behavior that night. Thank you."

***

CLOSING ARGUMENTS - DEFENSE – JOE FINE

"I'd like to thank you for sitting through this case, I know it hasn't been pleasant . . . it hasn't been a pleasant case for anyone. Next, I'd like to clear the air again, with respect to Colene Bush and Julie Jackson," Joe Fine said.

"I am not contending this thing is the girls' fault. I have nothing but sympathy for them and their families. When Mr. Jackson got up on the stand, that was my toughest moment in the trial. What he said wasn't that relevant, but how he said it was. He didn't exude hate or the desire to see Michael Guzman hanged or anything of the sort by his testimony. He really seemed like a very gentle person and I think that's probably what his daughter was like."

"With respect to Colene Bush, there's some suggestions that she brought about what happened. Other suggestions that the girls could have gotten away. That's not my position in this case. It's my position that Colene Bush took an approach and the approach didn't work. I think it was an intelligent approach and I think it's very difficult when you're dealing with someone like Michael Guzman. I have nothing but admiration for Colene Bush for surviving. I don't think too many of us could have survived," Joe Fine said.

"With respect to the exhibits in this case, I would ask you to look at them. They are a little irrelevant. I would ask you to disregard most of them . . . they are really not terribly relevant. The knife isn't that relevant, most of these charts aren't that relevant . . . there's one issue in this case and I've said that from the beginning. The issue is . . . INSANITY!"

"Now, I think that the state has disproved the first two tests of the insanity plea, however, with respect to the third test, they have the burden of proof and I don't feel they have met it."

"I should point out at the outset, there is no instructions saying that Mr. Guzman had to be psychotic or schizophrenic."

Mr. Fine reviewed Guzman's years of child abuse and pointed out that one of the social workers said that the Guzman family was the most dysfunctional family that she had seen in her 16 years on the job. Joe Fine theorized that Guzman's unstable family life could have contributed to his impulse control problems.

Mr. Fine also reviewed the testimony of the expert witnesses and said that most of them agreed that Michael Guzman did have some mental problems and that Dr. Roll testified he had a thought disorder.

"Life isn't black and white," Joe Fine told the jury. "And Michael Guzman certainly did a horrible thing . . . which he's going to regret the rest of his life. However, I would ask you to view the evidence as you take it here and not be prejudiced towards Michael Guzman."

Michael Guzman had a strange way of relating to people, Mr. Fine told the jury. He told them that he did it in the Barefoot incident and again with the girls. "His goal as he told it . . . was to have someone to talk to . . . and he does it in a very peculiar, crazy way. He runs up to people with a sharp object."

The baby was also listed as a stress factor for Guzman. "This baby comes up again and again. It meant so much to him. And you could see why it meant a lot to him. It was gonna be his thing . . . a love object."

The fact that Guzman had been prescribed Limbitrol was discussed. "This drug Limbitrol had the potential to cause Michael to go into a psychotic episode more easily or to get into a more severe psychotic episode. It could have had an effect on him."

"I would ask you to look at this case and not be emotionally aroused by it. It's hard not to be, I admit that. It's a horrible, horrible tragedy, yet I would ask you to fulfill your obligation as jurors and follow the judge's instructions that you're not to be guided by sympathy or prejudice in this case. Really, my only request to you is to go into the jury room, take a look at some of that evidence, the sympathetic stuff, see what its relevancy is and get rid of it. Because it can only serve to inflame you after that."

"My case is very narrow, that Michael Guzman was not able to control himself. And my only request to you is to read the instructions, review the really significant evidence and come back here and tell us whether a reasonable doubt exists regarding insanity. Thank you."

***

RAY PADILLA – STATE'S SECOND CLOSING

Assistant District Attorney Ray Padilla, was allowed a second closing.

"Ladies and Gentlemen, all of the evidence in this case supports a deliberately planned and intended murder . . . ALL OF IT!" Mr. Padilla shouted.

"Look at the route that was taken. The defendant would have you believe that he didn't know where he was going."

"He knew the area. He knew where he was going. He drove in a straight line . . . a straight line to rape . . . a straight line to the attempted murder of Colene Bush . . . and a straight line to the murder of Julie Ann Jackson. He knew exactly what he was doing."

"He made up his mind to kill them. He killed one and tried to kill another. The defendant says, 'After I did it, I went for the other one. I was going towards the trunk, when I seen her putting her clothes on . . . and she started running . . . and I stabbed her in the back.' Just those statements alone clearly show . . . planning and deliberation on the part of the defendant. He knew what he was doing."

"When you retire to the jury room . . . take your time with this case. It is an important case. Review all of the evidence carefully . . . weigh it all very carefully. Once you do that, ladies and gentlemen, I would submit to you . . . that you will have no choice when you return your verdict, absolutely no choice but to return verdicts of guilty on all counts. Guilty of the highest degree of each and every count charged. And the state is confident, ladies and gentlemen, that is exactly what you are going to do. Thank you."

***

JUDGE COLE AND THE JURORS

Judge Cole read the jurors the jury instructions for all of the counts and the jurors retired to the jury room. Seven hours later Judge Cole reconvened his court.

"Ladies and gentleman . . . counsel," Judge Cole said, "I'm informed that the jury has a verdict. I want to caution you that when the verdict is read, I want no outburst from the audience nor the participants. Once the verdict is read . . . I will excuse the jury. And I would ask that no one leave the court room until five minutes after the jury has departed. Sargent, I would ask that you have a couple of your bailiffs accompany the jurors down to the parking structure. Bring in our jury."

In a quiet, packed courtroom, the jury filed in, in their assigned order, and soberly settled themselves. Judge Cole turned to the jury foreman and said, "Would you give the verdict to my bailiff?" The sober-faced foreman handed the bailiff the folder who in turn handed it to Judge Cole. As the judge rustled through the papers, the people in the courtroom collectively held their breath in anticipation. They did not have to wait long. Judge Cole, his almost aviator-style glasses at the very tip of his nose, read the verdicts.

"We find the defendant, Michael Anthony Guzman, guilty in the first degree by deliberate killing as charged in count one."

"We find the defendant, Michael Anthony Guzman, guilty of felony murder as charged in the alternate to count one."

"We find the defendant, Michael Anthony Guzman, guilty attempt to commit a felony to wit, first degree murder as charged in count two."

"We find the defendant, Michael Anthony Guzman, guilty of criminal sexual penetration in the 2nd degree as charged in count three."

"We find the defendant, Michael Anthony Guzman, guilty of kidnapping as charged in count four."

"We find the defendant, Michael Anthony Guzman, guilty of kidnapping as charged in count five."

"We find the defendant, Michael Anthony Guzman, guilty of tampering with evidence as charged in count six."

"Mr. Foreman, is this the unanimous verdict of your jury?" Judge Cole asked.

"Yes, Your Honor"

"Ladies and gentlemen," Judge Cole announced. "At this time, I'm going to excuse you and recess. As you know there is a second phase of this trial which is a sentencing trial. I will begin that tomorrow at 1:30 tomorrow afternoon. I would ask that you be reassembled in my jury room here about 1:15 tomorrow afternoon." The jury was then escorted to the parking lot.

CHAPTER 20

THE SENTENCING PHASE

On the tenth day of the trial, the jurors listened to testimony regarding whether convicted murder and rapist Michael Guzman should be given life in prison or the death penalty. The sentencing phase of the trial focused on the issue of mitigating and aggravating circumstances.

Ray Padilla spelled out the aggravating circumstances for the jury.

"The state is alleging three aggravating circumstances in this case," Mr. Padilla said. "The state is alleging that the death of Julie Ann Jackson occurred during the commission of a kidnapping. That the death of Julie Ann Jackson occurred during the commission of a rape. And that the death of Julie Ann Jackson occurred because she was a witness to a crime or likely to become a witness to a crime."

Defense attorney Joe Fine agreed that all of those aggravating factors were present but he told the jury that there were several mitigating factors regarding Michael Guzman that they needed to look at as well. He asked the jury to consider the fact that the defendant was very young, that he had little other criminal history, that he would likely be receptive to rehabilitation and that he showed remorse for what he had done.

Many of the same witnesses called in the "guilt" phase were again called to testify in the "sentencing" phase. The psychologists, the psychiatrist and the counselors testified again. A minister and a Reverend also testified. Some of the witnesses stated that defendant showed remorse and that he could be rehabilitated. By contrast, other witnesses said the only remorse he showed was for himself and he could never be rehabilitated.

On the morning of April 30, 1982, the jury was handed the Uniform Jury Instructions on death penalty cases and sent off to deliberate. After the jury left the room, Joe Fine made a motion for a mistrial, which Judge Cole denied. Joe Fine then asked the judge for a directed verdict of life imprisonment for the defendant which Judge Cole denied. Judge Cole said that sentencing was a jury issue.

The jury returned to court at 4:09 PM the same day.

Colene, her family and Julie Jackson's family, sat in the front row of a packed courtroom. Security was tight, the room ringed with uniformed bailiffs,

"As all of your realize," Judge Cole said, "this is a very serious time in this criminal case and one of the more serious times that you'll ever see in any type of criminal case. I want to admonish you that I want *no* reaction from the audience nor the participants when I read the verdict. After I have read the verdict, I will excuse the jury and let them exit. I will ask that no one leave the court room until five minutes after the jury has left. Bailiff, will you bring in our jury?"

The jury reseated themselves in the jury box and multiple bailiffs ringed the room. The jury foreman handed the verdict to the main bailiff who then handed it to Judge Cole. Judge Cole read the verdict.

"We unanimously find beyond a reasonable doubt, the aggravating circumstance of murder of a witness as charged. We unanimously find beyond a reasonable doubt, the aggravating circumstance of murder during criminal sexual penetration as charged. We unanimously find beyond a reasonable doubt the aggravating circumstances of kidnapping as charged. We unanimously agree that the defendant, Michael Anthony Guzman, should be sentenced to death in a manner provided by law."

After the verdict, convicted killer and rapist Guzman showed no emotion, merely bending his expressionless face downward, perhaps visualizing his ultimate destination. On the other hand, despite Judge Cole's admonishment to the contrary, Colene, her family and the Jackson family openly showed their relief with silent tears.

The jury was polled by Judge Cole and the sentence was confirmed. The judge thanked the jury and dismissed them as the defendant was led away in handcuffs. The victim's families hugged friends and strangers alike in the hallway as they departed the courthouse, without comment.

PART IV

THE AFTERMATH

CHAPTER 21

GYMNASIUM, UNM   MAY 20, 1982

Colene's reaction to the verdict was unreadable. If someone asked her how she felt, she replied that she was happy that "justice" had prevailed - that the criminal had been convicted and sentenced to death. She wanted to go on with her life now. No more hiding out, no more talking to lawyers and no more dwelling on the past.

It was time to "get over it," as she had been told by those that cared about her. Catch up with her studies. Do all of the things that she used to do, before the "unfortunate incident".

One of her first acts of normalcy was to return to her UNM inter-mural basketball team. Of course, the team was happy to see her. After warming up, the squad ran wind sprints followed by layups, but something didn't feel quite right. When Colene tried to push off and leap high in the air like before, she got maybe a couple of inches off the ground. In high school, she had a 21 ½ inch vertical jump. *Just rusty*, she thought, *just rusty*.

"Tweee-et." The whistle blew. "Two lines, ladies," the coach said. "Alternate bounce passes and chest passes to your partner. Tweee-et."

Stacy snapped a hard bounce pass to Colene. The ball swooshed through her hands. *Hmmm?* Colene thought, frowning. *That's not right*.

"You're good. You're good. Don't worry about it." Stacy called out to her.

Colene tried to zip it back to Stacy, but the pass had no zip. It was an old lady pass.

Stacy pushed another pass, a chest pass, to Colene. Slower this time. Colene couldn't catch that one either. Her hands wouldn't do what she told them to do. She expected them to work right. Like they used to.

Everything was complicated now. The opposite of before. Before everything came easy. School, sports, socializing - everything. Now she had to think about even the simplest tasks. She had to concentrate to zip the zipper on her jacket or write her name. Even taking tests at school required more time. And meeting people, that got harder too. She discovered that crime victims are stigmatized . . . like *they* did something wrong. Not to mention having to explain the scars all over her body. It turned out that for every new person Colene met, from the moment she and Julie decided to have that cup of coffee on April 5, 1981, she had to decide whether or not she would reveal this traumatic part of her past. Life had gotten very, very complicated.

Despite all that, she still expected to be able to play basketball. She expected her athletic prowess to come back. It had already been over a year, for goodness sake. However, the severed tendons and nerves in her hands had taken their toll.

She finished practice that day, but never went back. Turned out, it would take decades for her hands (and the rest of her person) to work anything close to normal.

***

HARTSFIELD-JACKSON INTERNATIONAL AIRPORT, ATLANTA, GEORGIA   JUNE 15, 1982

She called him dad until she was four years old, but since then Ray had scant contact with Colene as she grew up. There had been a reunion of sorts when she was 18, but their kinship was more blood than bond. Even so, when Ray finally found out about Colene's abduction more than a year later, the odds that it was random were low.

Ray, an airline pilot for Eastern Airlines, had a layover in Atlanta. The only plan he had that morning was getting some well-deserved shut-eye. He exited the terminal and jumped on the courtesy shuttle to his hotel. Throwing his suitcase in the back of the shuttle, he noticed a couple of bags tagged "Albuquerque", but didn't think too much about it.

Once inside, Ray started up a conversation with a couple of attractive young women, a blonde and a redhead, seated in the back. He asked them where they were from and they told him that they lived in Albuquerque.

"Albuquerque!" he said. "I have family in Albuquerque." He asked them if either one of them knew his daughter, Colene Bush.

"Yes," the blonde women said. She did know Colene. The woman told Ray that she worked as a dental hygienist and Colene was a patient of hers.

"But that was so terrible what happened to her," the young woman said.

"What happened to her?" Ray cried out, his eyebrows pushed together.

"You don't know?"

"Know what?" Ray asked.

The woman, realizing she was blurting out potentially devastating news, stopped talking.

Ray almost frantic, touched the woman's arm, "What are you talking about? What happened to my daughter?"

"Well, I don't know how to say it but, but . . . about a year ago . . . she was stabbed and horribly hurt . . . and her friend was killed," the woman stammered.

Ray sat back in shocked silence. It was true he hadn't heard from his daughter for a while, but why hadn't anyone told him? He phoned Colene the moment he got to his hotel room and she explained to him what had happened. He was on a plane to Albuquerque within days.

**

12TH STREET, NW ALBUQUERQUE APRIL 25, 1984

Monica was getting a little bit anxious, a little bit fearful for her life. During the previous few months, she had received threatening phone calls and letters from her ex-boyfriend Michael Guzman and she didn't know what to do. According to the letters, Michael had a list of grievances against her. He said that he didn't like the fact that Monica had married someone else, he was mad at her for snitching on him at his murder trial and he wanted her to bring their son to visit him in prison.

While rolling out bread dough at the bakery where she worked, Monica's heart quickened when told she had a phone call on line two.

"Hey, babe," she heard a familiar voice say.

"Michael?" she said.

"I want you to bring my son to see me."

"You're on death row, Michael. I don't want to bring him there."

"Your punk-ass husband's scared, isn't he? Your so-called man is fucking afraid of me."

Licking her lips, Monica said nothing

"Hey. I asked you a question bitch . . . or should I say snitch? It's your fucking fault I'm in here. You're the one that got me convicted. You brought things up in court that never shoulda been said. You're gonna pay for that, Monica."

"I-I can't talk Michael. I gotta work," Monica said in a barely audible voice.

"You need to talk to me bitch or I'm gonna get you took care of. That's what I'm gonna do . . . you lying little snitchin' bitch. My girlfriend'll get you. She's gonna shoot you."

"I gotta go, Michael."

"Yeah, your high ass is too good to talk to me. I know. You know what Monica? I don't want to talk to you neither. I'm too much of a man for you. You run back to your sorry-ass husband and see if he stands up for you like I did. You're not good enough for me. I don't need you no more, Monica. LEAVE ME THE FUCK ALONE," he screamed and hung up.

***

SOUTHEAST HEIGHTS, ALBUQUERQUE MAY 15, 1984

If determination were a grade, she would have been gotten an A+. If determination was a trophy, it would have been a big one. If determination translated into money, as some people said that it did, she would have been a fucking millionaire. But it was none of those things. Not today anyway. Today, determination was as subtle as Colene receiving a piece of paper in the mail. Sure, she was grateful, but it didn't happen how she had planned.

It should have happened a year earlier and she should have been wearing a cherry colored cap and gown, shaking the UNM president's hand on stage at the Pit, maybe even receiving a class ring. Julie Jackson should have been there, too. But none of that transpired. Instead Colene was graduating from college alone - in the quiet of her small apartment.

Back in the spring semester of '81, she had to drop out of college, because even after getting out of the hospital, there were the months of convalescing. Persistent physical problems continued to plague her. Despite the fact that it had been three years, she couldn't take a full breath or run any significant distances. Her hands caused her unending grief. She called them seal hands. They didn't work well, not like before anyway. They stayed curled up, in one position, looked funny and weren't very flexible. She still struggled, whether it was getting dressed or writing.

Colene had received no counseling, either, on how to handle the vague fears that crept into her thoughts or guidance on stifling the bad dreams that stole her sleep nightly. She was always on alert - heard everything . . . saw everything. Years later, she would be diagnosed with PTSD, Post Traumatic Stress Disorder, but knowing that didn't help much and it even came to pass that others used it against her.

Despite these handicaps, she had pushed herself to graduate from UNM. Sadly, she didn't have the money to attend the ceremony.

"Congratulations," nobody said.

***

MAIN POST OFFICE, DOWNTOWN ALBUQUERQUE MARCH 31, 1985

Three and a half years earlier James began working for the U.S. Post Office. It was a career move that others congratulated him on. In those days, the post office paid a lot of money and demanded very little in the way of thinking. Only problem was, the Post Office management had a 19th century mindset regarding their employees. They didn't have "sitting" stools; they had "leaning" stools. You were not allowed to stop working for any reason while you were on your shift. If you cut yourself, you were to raise your hand and someone would deliver a bandage. Stuff like that.

James had no problem working hard, but on his first day of work, he wanted to make an impression. He wanted to make a statement. The statement was, "Leave me alone." His method for accomplishing this was done partly with attire and partly with attitude. On Halloween, 1981, James' first day of work, he arrived at the post office with his newly shortened hair (a buzz cut) dyed a shiny metallic silver with a one inch wide black stripe painted down the middle of his head. He hoped that his appearance would cause others to shun him. They did. This was also the first day of his later-to-be-famous "Painted Boots Project". His ankle-high work boots were painted a day glow yellow. His goal was to appear too weird to talk to. He succeeded.

Despite the fact that some time had gone by since the murder of his fiancée Julie Jackson, James was still a very unhappy man. He wanted others to hate him as much as he hated the world.

In the years that he worked at the post office, James was able to make many a supervisor despise him. This pleased him greatly. He wore a different pair of painted boots to work every day. There were the black and white checkered NASCAR boots, the red, white and blue Stars and Stripes boots, the blue Smurf boots, the red and yellow magma boots, the American Red Cross with a white cross on the toe boots and on and on. He sprayed one layer on top of the other, day after day. His supervisors shook their heads in dismay and wrote everything into his permanent record.

After about a year on the job, James got a hold of an official employee handbook and used it as a guide for pushing the envelope, as a bar he kept on raising, in his never-ending quest to be a thorn in the side of management. He was elated to find out there were no rules against dressing oddly. One day he dressed as Colonel Sanders and according to the employee handbook, there was no rule against that. Another day he came to work as a black man . . . there was no rule against that. On another occasion, he wore a three piece suit backwards, it was very uncomfortable but there was no rule against it. On Mother's Day, he came in dressed as a woman and there was no rule against that. Dressing as a woman back in the 80s, however, was a little risky. His co-workers immediately assumed he was a homosexual which caused other problems.

While suspended from work for taking too many days off, James was advised by his mom that maybe the Post Office wasn't the right job for him. She offered him a tent in her backyard to live for free while he figured out what he really wanted to do. He accepted her offer. On his very last day at the post office, he dressed as a Bernalillo County Sheriff, and he didn't care if there was a rule against it. James was copping out.

***

DEATH ROW, CELL #61, SANTA FE PENITENTIARY NOVEMBER 5, 1985

1985 turned out to be a year of ups and downs for Inmate Guzman. All of his appeals, including the New Mexico State Supreme Court, had been exhausted. His death sentence had been upheld every step of the way. That was a "down". And that pesky Deputy District Attorney Kathy Wright kept trying to get his execution date set and that was another "down". But Governor Anaya had announced to the press that no one would be executed on his watch, so that was an "up".

Then, a really great thing happened. The biggest "up" of them all. He got married. State Penitentiary officials didn't even know about it for weeks. Of course, when they found out about it they were mad. Didn't matter, though, turned out to be legal and also turned out there was nothing they could do about it. And he didn't get married to that snitchy bitch Monica either. It was to a real woman. One he met while he was in prison.

Yep, old Mike still had it when it came to being smarter than everyone else. He got a minister, a couple of witnesses and his dearly betrothed to all visit him at the same time and when no one was looking, boom, he got himself married. Easy as pie. Apparently, no other death-row inmate had ever done this before, but of course, no other death-row inmate had ever been as sharp as old Mike.

***

SANTA FE, NEW MEXICO NOVEMBER 25, 1986

The man wore only a thin white shirt with no tie and faded blue jeans. Perspiration beaded up on his pasty brown skin and the thin white shirt stuck to his back. His body twitched. He was alone and on his knees inside Cathedral Basilica of St. Francis of Assisi, one of the oldest Roman Catholic churches in North America.

"Tell me what to do, Almighty." the man asked.

"It's now or never, Lord. Tell me what the right thing is."

The rays of the morning sun streamed through the stained glass window of the Twelve Apostles. Dust particles moved lazily toward the light.

"I know the Bible says an eye for an eye, and even a tooth for a tooth, but doesn't it also say, turn the other cheek? Is it right to kill the killers, Lord? I promised the victims' families that I would not commute these death sentences during my term. What should I do?" The massive Corinthian columns and classic Roman arches dwarfed the little man kneeling in front of the large crucifix. He drew a handkerchief from his left breast pocket and wiped his brow as he waited for an answer.

The man, who today called himself Toney, wanted guidance regarding retribution . . . or was it forgiveness. He wasn't sure.

"I've been advised that now is the time to forgive these men on behalf of the State of New Mexico. I know I need to do what I think is right . . . what you tell me is right . . . but I'm running out of time, Lord . . . my term is almost up." Toney cocked his ear so that if a response was forthcoming he could better hear it. But with his hands clasped tightly together and his eyes gazing upward, his cocked-ear heard nothing. A stream of sweat ran down his short neck and a slimy sheen coated his unhappy face.

At last, the man stood up and said, "Thank you for speaking to me, Lord. Thank you for helping me with this great decision. I will tell all that ask, that it is your will."

And so, just like Michael Guzman before him, Toney Anaya got his needed guidance directly from God. With the Lord's blessing stashed securely in his back pocket, the Governor left St. Francis Cathedral, climbed into his waiting limo and sped off for an early breakfast.

***

SANTA FE, NEW MEXICO   NOVEMBER 27, 1986

Toney Anaya, the soon to be gone, but not soon to be forgotten, governor of New Mexico, readied himself to deliver the speech that would define his political career. The speech was televised and the majority of New Mexico watched. He wore a black jacket, a black tie and a thin white shirt. He sat in a gray chair against a gray wall, behind a great desk filled with microphones. Six security guards, three on each side, flanked him, as he had told his staff that he feared for his life. He drank coffee from a white mug while he read his carefully prepared speech. The governor told New Mexico's citizens that after much consultation, soul searching and praying, he now knows the right thing to do.

"I'm against the death penalty," he read, "because it is inhumane, immoral, and anti-God and is incompatible with an enlightened society."

"We as a society, crying out for meaningful, effective law enforcement and meaningful crime prevention measures, are perpetrating a cruel hoax on each other. We cry out in blood curdling unison to kill the killers . . . giving ourselves a false sense of security, a false sense of accomplishment, a hollow empty, costly, temporarily satisfying, vengeful outburst of emotions . . . and when the killers are killed we have accomplished none of our crime fighting goals as an enlightened society . . . rather . . . we have lowered ourselves as an organized social order to the very rabble we seek to rid ourselves of."

At the end of the speech, Governor Anaya was engulfed in a sea of well-wishers. Archbishops, priests, anti-death penalty supporters all proclaimed him a great man, a true humanitarian. He basked in the glow of the moment. Others throughout the state of New Mexico had different reactions.

Even the Chicago Tribune weighed in on the subject and called Toney Anaya "one of the most unpopular politicians in the state's history".

***

DEATH ROW, SANTA FE PENITENTIARY NOVEMBER 28, 1986

The occasion just about demanded that they have champagne and one of the five actually tried to smuggle some in, but it was too short of notice. Bummer. Still, it was a very joyful day.

The Felonious Five's new favorite person and definitely their choice for man of the year, Toney Anaya, had come through for them yet again. This man was a convict's dream. Not only had he knocked down every execution date that had been set while he served as Governor, this time he had gone ahead and erased their death-sentences altogether. Commuted all of them.

"What a fucking stud," one former death-row inmate said.

"A fucking humanitarian, I tell you," said another.

The Felonious Five's criminal history read like a bad novel. Ricky Garcia murdered three fellow inmates and prison guard Louis Jewett, while incarcerated. Joel Lee Compton shot and killed Albuquerque Police Officer Jerry Cline during a traffic stop. Eddie Lee Adams kidnapped, raped and murdered 80-year-old Clovis resident Ola Temple. William Wayne Gilbert murdered four people, including his wife, Carol and model Barbara McMullan, but he was on death row for killing newlyweds, Ken and Noel Johnson. Michael Guzman kidnapped, raped and murdered UNM co-ed Julie Ann Jackson. The inmates were very appreciative of the governor's generosity. As Toney Anaya had noted at his press conference the day before, it was very important to him to save these murderers before he left office.

The former death row inmates could not have been happier. They were brought in separately and interviewed one by one by the media. The inmates' opinions on this subject were considered highly newsworthy and were printed in the newspaper the very next day. They had nothing but praise for lame-duck Governor Anaya.

Inmate Guzman spoke for everyone when he said, "It's like an early Christmas present."

***

SOUTHEAST HEIGHTS   NOVEMBER 28, 1986

"Hi," Valerie said with a smile. "How was work?"

"Okay," Colene replied.

"You look tired. Let me get you a drink." Valerie gave her a lingering hug.

"Thanks," Colene said, following her into the kitchen.

"Is white zinfandel okay?"

"Sure," Colene said. She took the glass from Valerie and told her about her day on the UPS circuit where she worked as a driver.

"Some lady tried to lure me in again," Colene teased. "She was only wearing a towel. I think she wanted me."

Valerie laughed and brought Colene another glass of wine.

"Why are you being so nice today?" Colene asked.

"No reason," Valerie answered. "I like being nice." Valerie's expression became serious as she turned and faced Colene. "Did you see the news today?"

"No," Colene replied.

"It's kind of bad news," Valerie set her wine glass down. "Toney Anaya commuted everyone today. He commuted Michael Guzman. Changed his death sentence to life." Valerie held her breath while she waited for Colene's reaction.

Colene said nothing at first, but Valerie saw her jaw set hard and her blue eyes glow with anger.

"That lousy motherfucker," Colene said at last, speaking in measured beats. "I swear to God, if I ever see that goddamn sorrysonofabitch Toney Anaya, he'll be sorry." And without realizing it, she squeezed the wine glass in her hand so hard, that it shattered, cutting her palm and several of her fingers.

***

STATE PRISON, SANTA FE, NM   JUNE 22, 1989

"Hurry up, Dog, they're only not gonna be here for a hour."

"I know, man, I got the shit out . . . good to go."

"Heard you was a good inker."

"You got that right. You drew what you want?"

"Yeah, it's here."

"They're gonna shit a brick about this."

"God wants it. They won't know."

"Kay. Don't tell nobody. I'm not doin' no lockup cause of you."

"You won't. I gotta have it. I'm not tellin'. Just do it."

"Kay, I gotta machine's gonna make it faster, but it's gonna make you wanna scream like a little bitch . . . stay the fuck quiet, Kay? You move, you're gonna fuck it up . . . permanent."

Dog, or Prairie Dog as he was sometimes known, had been in 15 years already. Stubble-faced and completely bald, he was the ink man, the prison tattoo artist. He had killed two people during a motel holdup in Gallup back in '72. A man and his wife. Didn't mean to, but the damn man pulled a shotgun on him when he went behind the cash register to get the money. That wasn't very smart, was it? Dog *had* to pop him - it was self-defense, but that wasn't how the courts saw it. And, who knows, the courts might have been right, too. He probably didn't have to blast them both with a full clip and then reload and do it again. It's just that Dog had an anger management problem, he knew that, and when the man pulled out that gun, it pissed him off. Now he's stuck with two life sentences, but it could have been worse, at least in his mind. He could have let that little pecker at the motel shoot him dead.

Inmate Guzman showed Dog the drawing as they crouched low in a corner of the exercise yard. Guzman had paid a couple guys to be human fences, to screen out the guards so they couldn't see what he and Dog were doing. So far so good.

"That's a big ass ink job, brother."

"Yeah."

"Gonna cost you a couple a decks plus a hundred."

"Got it."

With a Bic pen, a piece of wire and a motor stolen from the warden's Walkman, Dog readied himself to perform his craft. It was a pretty elaborate tat, even for Dog, but he was no stranger to "elaborate". Tattoos covered Dog like a body suit. Curling snakes, naked women, raunchy phrases and hundreds of dogs. He inked most of them himself.

"Kay. Gotta draw it on you, then get ready to cry."

"Do it."

"Cry quiet, though."

Tangles of angels with wings, a giant image of Jesus and both of Guzman's victims' names were drawn and then stained onto the entirety of his large, hairless brown back. Guzman sucked in air to keep from screaming. In the middle of his back, between the names of Julie Ann and Coleen (sic), were the words "God forgave me."

Inmate Guzman knew his new tat would increase his stature among the inmate population. It demonstrated to them that he could commit capital crimes, flaunt them by wearing his victims' names like merit badges, and still have God in his back pocket. Like the shrinks had taught him back at the forensic hospital, it was a win-win situation.

CHAPTER 22

"Let's go Bush. You're falling behind . . . again."

"Sir. Yes, sir."

"Johnny Shitbag's catching up with your fat ass."

"Sir. Yes, sir."

"No one's going to want you for their "82" if you can't stay with the pack."

"Sir. Yes, sir."

"What's wrong with you anyways, Bush?"

"I can't breathe, sir. I can't get enough air in my lungs."

"You're a sorry sack of shit, Bush."

"Sir. Yes, sir."

"Company, Halt! Give me fifty."

"Bush needs rest," the instructor said in a sing-song mocking voice. "She needs air." The class of fifty-five cadets, less Cadet Bush, immediately fell prone onto the filthy, weed infested ditch banks and grunted out fifty pushups. Soaked in sweat and gasping, Cadet Bush stood at attention while her classmates silently cursed her mother for bearing her . . . and then the run began again.

So it went, every Monday through Thursday, the days the Albuquerque Police Department cadets ran the North Valley ditch banks. Each and every time, the group would start off together, and then, eventually Bush and a few of the others would fall behind, but Cadet Bush was always last. She had been fast enough to get into the Academy, of course. That was no problem. The entry requirements were leveled for age and gender. Even though she was 48 years old at the time, the oldest in the class, she believed that she had what it took to be an excellent police officer. Besides, APD must have really wanted her or why would they have accepted her into the Academy?

But despite the fact that she had been accepted into the Academy, she was endlessly asked, "Why'd you wait so long to join?" and her answer was always," I don't know." But what she meant was, "Everybody always told me all my life I was ruined and I didn't think they'd take me, so why even try." And so she never tried, until one day, on a whim, she filled out an APD "information card" and everything mysteriously just fell into place. She passed one test after another until the moment came at the Chief's Selection Board, when her one-time acquaintance, Deputy Chief Mike Castro, said, "Congratulations, you made it into the 104th." She was elated. Briefly.

Shortly after beginning the Police Academy, she was informed that she would now be required to run the mile and a half at the speed of a 20-year-old male: a full four minutes and fifteen seconds faster than she had run the day before. Cadet Bush hoped for the best.

Making in into APD was like a dream come true. It was like the previous 28 fucked up years had now been righted. After a lifetime of sub-par jobs, low expectations and barely getting by, she was finally back on track, back in the pack. Finally getting to do something that she wanted to do, something that mattered.

But then reality set in. During the first week of the Academy, "easy week", the harassment began. Each Academy instructor took turns pointing out the location of the exit gate to Cadet Bush. At first, she laughed it off, took it in stride, expecting a certain amount of hazing, to "toughen her up". Later on, however, the singling out appeared to have a more sinister intent.

"Bush, stand in front of the Chicken Bowl," the instructor screamed inches from her ear. "I know that's where you really want to be."

"Sir. Yes, sir." Cadet Bush said.

While she stood at attention in front of the Chicken Bowl Restaurant on 4th Street, the other cadets were ordered to perform 50 more push-ups on her behalf. Out of the corner of her eye, Cadet Bush could see the hate of her classmates fermenting with each succeeding push up. Different day, different run, same result.

"Why don't you just quit, Bush? You're too mature for this and you know it," the sergeant said.

"Sir. No, sir. This cadet does *not* quit, sir," Cadet Bush said, eyes straight ahead.

Hearing this, the sergeant became highly agitated and yelled even louder. "I'll bet my pension that you don't graduate, Bush."

Cadet Bush said nothing.

"You're dead weight Bush. You and that other fucking loser, Benavidez. Go get DW and carry him."

"Sir. Yes, sir," Cadet Bush said. She and Cadet Benavidez, another older female cadet, fell out of formation and picked up the 180 pound mannequin, the training aid nicknamed "DW" for dead weight. They carried him wherever the class went, for the rest of that day, and many days after.

Every night, Colene would come home after 12-14 hours at the Academy a little more depressed, a little more certain she was being targeted because of her age. Every morning, she would psych herself up to endure one more day, to stick it out no matter what they said or did.

"Johnny Shitbag's right behind you, Bush. He's gaining on you," the sergeant shouted as Colene ran the ditch banks the next morning.

"Sir. Yes, sir."

The sergeant then moved closer to Cadet Bush, grabbed her around the neck and whispered in her ear, "and he's got a knife." Startled, Cadet Bush turned and looked at him. He smirked and let go. She realized immediately that he had read her file and was using yet another tactic to get her to quit. Snickering to himself, he dropped back and let her run off.

Despite the fact that she did well academically and passed the other physical requirements, she was told dozens of times a day what a loser she was. As the days wore on, the requests for Cadet Bush to resign accelerated. Her self-esteem which initially had skyrocketed, plummeted. Finally, on November 3rd, less than four weeks into the program, she and Cadet Benavidez were summoned into the Commander's office and were told to call their squad leaders that night and resign. They refused to make the call. The next day they were fired.

***

2ND JUDICIAL COURT HOUSE, DOWNTOWN   NOVEMBER 16, 2010

"Don't worry, Duder won't be here," her friend Stephanie said.

"I know," Colene replied. "I don't like courts. I want to find out what he's up to . . . but . . . coming here makes me edgy."

Colene and Stephanie entered courtroom 714 and they slid into the second row of polished wooden benches, prosecution side. A habeas corpus hearing was being held for Michael Guzman. Today was the 13th such hearing on this particular habeas. His previous but similar habeas was denied back in 1997. A Writ of Habeas Corpus, Stephanie explained, is a judicial order requiring the government to determine whether the court has the right to continue detaining a particular prisoner. Originally the writ was designed to be a constitutional check on unreasonable government power, not as a de facto instrument for endless appeals of convicted felons. The funny part is that habeas corpus suits are civil suits, usually filed by the felon against the warden and the felon is provided, at government expense, a public defender attorney to assist him with his case.

Today, a long-haired defense attorney and a shaven-haired state attorney sat at their respective manila folder-covered tables chatting and laughing across the aisle, waiting for the hearing to begin.

"You're not nervous are you?" Stephanie asked Colene.

"Kinda," she replied.

Eying the two lawyers, Colene turned to her friend. "Why are they laughing? This isn't funny. Do they think this is some kind of joke?"

"That's just how they do it here," Stephanie replied. "They're not making jokes about you. They are only pretending to like each other."

"I don't like it," Colene said, frowning.

"All rise," the bailiff said.

The robed judge entered the room and sat down. "Be seated," he said. Thumbing through a stack of papers, the judge looked up. "Guzman?" Both lawyers approached the bench.

The pony-tailed public defender spoke first. "My client has brought up a lot of issues," he said. "He's produced a stack of paperwork about a foot high. I think he has a lot of really good points; however, we need more time to prepare. Your Honor, we request a status conference next month to provide you with an update?"

"Okay. Let's check our calendars," the judge said.

***

"THE WAR ZONE" ALBUQUERQUE NOVEMBER 18, 2010

After the police academy fiasco, Colene fought against despair and enrolled in an EMT- Basic class. She loved it, did well and became a licensed EMT-B in New Mexico within a few months. She liked it so much that she applied for and was accepted into a local paramedic program.

Maybe everything was going to be alright after all. She had wanted very badly to become a cop but was now hopeful that she would be able to help people in a different way.

The day after Guzman's habeas corpus hearing, Colene was still bummed out. Why was this guy continuing to challenge his verdict after 30 years? Why was this allowed?

Colene didn't go to paramedic class that day. No big deal, she hadn't missed before. She called in and explained the situation.

The next day, she did go to school, but something bizarre happened shortly after she got there. While on a break with her classmates, she was pulled aside by the Director.

"You seem out of it," the Director said. "You need to go with us."

"What?" Colene asked. "Go where?"

"You seem out of it," he repeated. "Get in the car. We're trying to help."

She was motioned into a waiting car and against her better judgment, she complied. She didn't want to anger the Director but she didn't understand why she was being taken against her will.

She was driven to the UNM psych ward and soon after arrival all of her possessions were taken from her, including her shoes. Colene asked if she could keep her book so she might study. She was told no. Humiliated and alone, she waited in a small room with no windows. While she waited, occasional medical staff would peek in but say nothing. Eventually a nurse entered and asked Colene questions. "Do you often feel sad?" What medications are you taking?" "Have you ever been arrested?" Colene was stunned. She did not understand what she did wrong.

As the nurse got up to leave, Colene again asked for her text book. The nurse frowned but retrieved the book, searching through it page by page to insure that no danger lurked within. Colene didn't understand how the situation had gone from "something bad happened to me," to "I'm bad because something happened to me."

Colene explained to the doctor that she was okay. More humiliating questions were asked. Finally, Colene was told that she could leave. She was driven back to the Academy in silence and the incident was never spoken of again.

***

FARMINGTON, NM   FEBRUARY 8, 2011

It took her about ten minutes to find him on Facebook and another ten seconds to click the "Add Friend Request." It took another couple days for him to get back to her because he was working weird hours. Six 24's, then two off. He had some kind of oil industry job blowing things up.

They hugged each other on the sidewalk in front of the Three Rivers Bar. The hug lasted a good five minutes but could have easily gone on for ten times that. After all, it had been almost thirty years. When they finally pulled apart, she gave him a once over and it all came flooding back. It was a comfort seeing this six foot plus, goofball again.

Inside the dark bar, the old friends shared a dark drink and talked about lost time. He had bounced around, been married for fourteen years, lived in Las Vegas, Nevada, divorced and bounced around some more. He'd been a postal worker, a school band instrument repair guy and a member of countless bands. He said everything was more complicated now. He told her that he heard everything, saw everything and had a hard time sleeping. She told him a similar story.

The two of them, Colene and James, shared a bond that few could understand. They laughed while shooting the breeze about the old days but there was sadness, too. It was in their eyes. The pain was there, just below the surface, akin to having a sharp blade lodged inside your body. You learn to live with it but still it hurts most of the time.

***

CORRALES, NM   MARCH 13, 2011

Albuquerque Journal reporter Leslie Linthicum arrived promptly at 11, backing her blue Corolla into the driveway by the second garage. Colene greeted her at the front door and led her to a round glass table in a room filled with windows. The Sandia Mountains towered in the distance and the sun slanted in.

"Would you like some coffee?" Colene asked.

"Sure," answered the reporter.

Reporter Linthicum had given up a relaxing Sunday morning in response to an email she received from Colene earlier in the week. Colene wrote with the news that Michael Guzman would be up for parole in a couple of weeks.

This reporter knew the case personally as she had sat through the entire trial some 30 years back. Colene had never before talked to the media but she was ready to talk now.

"You wanted it black, right?" Colene said as she sat down with two cups of coffee.

The reporter smiled and turned on her tape recorder. The interview lasted about an hour or so, and seemed harmless enough.

***

"THE WAR ZONE" ALBUQUERQUE   MARCH 23, 2011

A man dressed in black leaned into the doorway of the classroom.

"Colene, I need you to come with me," the man said.

Mystified, Colene got up and followed him to another room. As she entered, a posse of serious faces encircled her like a street gang in a deserted alley. The Director was there.

Wetting her lips, she sat down.

"We saw the articles in the Journal," the Director said darkly.

Colene nodded. From the response she had gotten so far, it seemed like everyone in the world had seen the articles in the paper. The feedback had been supportive. She didn't understand though, why she was being pulled out of class to discuss the articles.

"The newspaper mentioned that you don't have medical insurance," the Director said. "You know you're required to have insurance to be in this program, don't you?"

Stunned, she replied, "I do have insurance."

"Let's see it," the Director said flatly. She showed him the same card that she had shown when applying for the program.

"We have concerns about your progress, Colleen," he continued. Colene's head spun. *What? I've been passing the tests, getting good feedback. What's going on?*

"We're putting you on probation," the Director said in a commanding voice. "Also, you might want to seek career counseling."

The posse, eyes narrow and evasive, said nothing.

***

SANTA FE PENITENTIARY   APRIL 4, 2011

The hearing was held in the Old Main. Built in 1956, it now housed prison offices and conference rooms, and sometimes served as a movie set. But today was serious business. Michael Guzman, age 48, sentenced to death in 1982, commuted to life in 1986, was up for parole.

Colene, her brother Michael, and one of Julie Jackson's sisters were at the hearing. The mood was sociable but somber, like a funeral. Two parole board members served as moderators.

The criminal was there too, via video. A semi-circle of chairs faced the screen as Guzman was led in by three, maybe four armed guards. His hands were shackled and he wore a white jumpsuit.

"I am not a monster," the monster said. He talked of a bombshell that would soon be revealed at an upcoming habeas corpus hearing . . . how he would be vindicated. Whether it was by intent or not, he stirred a cauldron of ire among those in attendance. Colene's nostrils flared and her fingers drummed the table as she watched the inmate on the screen.

As a result of the recent Albuquerque Journal articles, the parole board had received many letters from the public asking that Guzman's parole be denied. Victims' statements written by the victim and the victims' families were read out loud during the parole hearing. Guzman stared downward, showing no emotion as the letters were read, reminiscent of his district court trial.

Colene wrote the following statement:

Dear Parole Board Members

Please do not grant Michael Guzman parole. He is and always will be a danger to society. He raped and killed my friend, Julie Jackson, and when he left the scene of the crime that night, he thought that he had killed me, too.

It's true; I have suffered great and lasting pain as a result of that vicious attack by Guzman. My physical scars are daily reminders of what happened. But honestly, my greatest pain is from the loss of my friend and the fact that I was unable to save her.

Julie Jackson was only 19 years old when she was killed. She had the world at her fingertips and was a loving, giving person. She was on track to become a doctor, a wife and a mother. But she never got the chance. Guzman did not know Julie Jackson, but he chose to end her life and erase her future. I still miss her sweet personality and her beautiful smile.

In 1982, the jury listened to 11 days of testimony and pronounced Guzman guilty on all charges. Among other things, he was convicted of first degree murder and given the death sentence. A man, Toney Anaya, that did not listen to even one moment of the trial, cavalierly overturned the death sentence which had been duly rendered by those 12 jurors. In overturning the death sentence, he made a mockery of the sentencing process and the jurors' time.

From the time Guzman was convicted, he has been asking for favors. First, he begged for mercy from Governor Anaya to delay his death sentence - which was granted. Then he begged Governor Anaya for mercy again to commute his death sentence to a life sentence - which was granted. He is now begging the parole board for mercy to grant him parole which he neither deserves nor was it the jury's intention. This is the same man that gave Julie Jackson no mercy whatsoever. Please deny him parole.

Sincerely,

Colene Bush

The victim's services coordinator later informed Colene that after the articles in the paper appeared, other victims felt empowered to speak up regarding their cases as well.

***

"THE WAR ZONE" ALBUQUERQUE JUNE 21, 2011

It was hot. Sweaty hot.

"Wait outside," the Director said.

Colene waited outside in the heat, while the Disciplinary Committee discussed her fate. One of the administrators had shot Colene an email a couple of days earlier, alerting her that the committee was convening to discuss their options.

The "crime", for which the tribunal met, failing an assessment test by one percentage point. Because of her disability, Colene had asked for extra time to take the test as other students in her class had been given, but the request was ignored.

At last, the Committee summoned her in. Ten committee members, squeezed into a too small, oven-like conference room, eyed her. Clad in black polo's and ill-fitting business apparel, their down-turned mouths said it all. Colene hadn't seen this many grim faces since the time she had flat-lined in the ER over thirty years ago. And back then, the hospital staff had thought she was dead. *Maybe they think I'm dead,* Colene thought. And as it turned out, they did.

"We haven't made up our minds yet," lied a middle-aged faculty member with no lips. "First, we'd like to ask you a couple of questions, if you don't mind."

"Why do you want to be a paramedic?" an overweight woman with discolorations under her arms asked.

I answered those kinds of questions when I was admitted, Colene thought, but she gamely played along. "Because I want to help people. Because I want to give back," she said and looked around the room for a positive reaction. All ten people stared at her as if they had just spotted a spider in the bathtub. *Wrong answer,* she thought.

"You've had your share of troubles in paramedic school, haven't you, Colene?" The skinny guy with the crummy complexion asked.

"Not really," Colene replied, "I've stumbled a little bit here and there . . . like everybody else, but I keep coming back, keep hitting it hard. I really want to be a paramedic."

Silence was the deafening response, their eyes filled with fear and loathing. A few more inane questions and finally she was informed that her session was over. The Director escorted her out and cheerfully told her that the decision would be emailed to her shortly. "Have a nice day, Colleen," the Director said.

Two days later, the administrator, who had recently received an award for her outstanding contributions, shot Colene another email. Even though it was a page-long letter, Colene only saw the first sentence.

Dear Ms. Bush:

This letter constitutes official notice of your dismissal from the Paramedic Program, effective immediately.

***

CLAYTON, NEW MEXICO NOVEMBER 8, 2011

Things hadn't been going so great at the Guadalupe County Correctional Facility in Santa Rosa. He kept getting into messes, making people mad. He had no friends, no one to talk to. Naturally, he was mystified, because he had been as charming as ever. He even had to go into lockup a couple of times and that didn't seem fair. Through the prison grapevine, he had heard about a few threats leveled against him. No one took the threats seriously - except him. He asked the warden for a transfer. Santa Rosa didn't seem like a safe place to be anymore. It took a few months, but he finally got the green light to move on. He was sent to Santa Fe while officials looked for a safer, more permanent home for him. In early November, he got the word that he would be moving to the privately run, medium security prison in Clayton, New Mexico.

Alone in his small cell, his "house", he packed a few personal items and looked at the piece of reflective metal on his wall that passed for a mirror. It had been over 30 years since the jury had sentenced him. In the very early days, he was on death row and everything was a little uncertain. But that was a long time ago, now he was an old man. His hair was gone, his eyebrows bushy and his stature shriveled.

But life wasn't all bad. He had been in two different movies, one while on death-row and one after. Naturally, he played himself. He was also occasionally in the news, which wasn't always complimentary, but like they say . . . there's no such thing as bad publicity. And, he had a wife who loved him and four adoring children. In fact, he had managed to acquire multiple wives while behind bars, mate with them, "father" kids that he would never know and have the state pay for the whole thing. He could take quite a bit of satisfaction for making the best of available opportunities.

Dressed in a yellow jumpsuit, he boarded a bus with a few other inmates and was driven to his new home in Clayton. It looked about the same from the outside as all the other prisons he'd been in: razor wire, watch towers, guards with guns. He hoped the security would be better here. It was getting so a convicted killer wasn't safe to walk around by himself anymore.

As soon as he arrived, he was processed in, new photo taken (each prison picture looking a little bit worse than the last) and told he had to attend an orientation class in the orientation pod. *Whatever*, he thought. He took his seat, listened to the prison administer lecture about the do's and don'ts of Clayton Prison and then stood off by himself waiting to get transported to his new cell. No big deal. He had relocated to many prisons over the years, he was sure this one would be fine. Change of scenery was always nice. All the sudden, though, things didn't feel quite right.

It wasn't anything he saw, at least not at first. It was just a weird tingle he had. Then he heard the shuffling of the other inmates as they massed toward him. He smelled the metal of their hate. Almost immediately, he was knocked unconscious. Completely out of view of any potential liberators, he was surrounded. Even as he recovered from the initial blow, he realized he couldn't breathe very well. Matter of fact, he couldn't breathe at all. There were a lot of guys holding him down, he felt a shot of pain and he couldn't quite figure out what was happening or why. He lost consciousness again. Eventually, the guards broke it up and a medical helicopter flew Inmate Guzman to UNM Hospital.

***

226

"It's depressing here today," Colene said via text. "Everyone here is distant. I ask myself, did I really think 30 years ago, I'd be here doing this? Oh, well."

On the anniversary of the day that wrecked her life, while at work at her retail job, Colene remembered. She remembered what happened 31 years ago, just like she did every day, but this day, April 5th, hit harder. In her mind, she saw a terrified young woman, full of blood, crawling up an embankment trying to find a way out, trying to save herself.

Even after all these years, she did not understand why the man killed Julie and tried to kill her. Julie did nothing wrong. She did nothing wrong. They didn't deserve it.

"I dread this day every year," she said later with tears in her eyes. "It doesn't matter how many years have gone by. People don't understand. You don't understand. Nobody understands. To me, it hasn't been 30 years. I live in a time warp. To me, it's like it was only yesterday."

After arriving home from work, she eventually opened up her computer to check her email and a timely quotation popped up.

"Success is to be measured not so much by the position that one has reached in life, as by the obstacles which he has overcome," Booker T. Washington said on the quote of the day website. *Hmmm?* Colene thought. But it was time to stop thinking.

It was a beautiful day outside and the dogs desperately wanted to go to the park and run. She closed her computer and grabbed a couple of leashes for her energetic labs.

With the Bee Gees blaring on her car stereo, she drove the short distance to the park and pulled into her regular slot. She crossed over to a woman wearing a black hat standing in the parking lot and squeezed her hand. The two struggled with the crazed dogs as they entered the gated area but once Colene threw the ball, for that moment, all was right in the world. The dogs ran and ran.

THE END

PICTURES

Colene Bush on her horse "Patch" - 1971 - 10 years old

Julie Jackson – Girls State – 1978

Colene Bush – Moriarty H.S. vs. Jal H.S. Basketball Game – 1979

Julie Jackson – High School Senior – 1979

Colene Bush – High School Senior – 1979

Police Crime Scene Sketch - The Arroyo – 1981

Colene Bush's Injuries from Attack – 1981

Police Composite of Killer – 1981

Michael Guzman, Right, Attorney Joseph Fine Hear Death Sentence
Copyright: The Albuquerque Journal, Mountain View Telegraph.
Reprinted with permission. Permission does not imply endorsement.
Photo by Jim Fisher

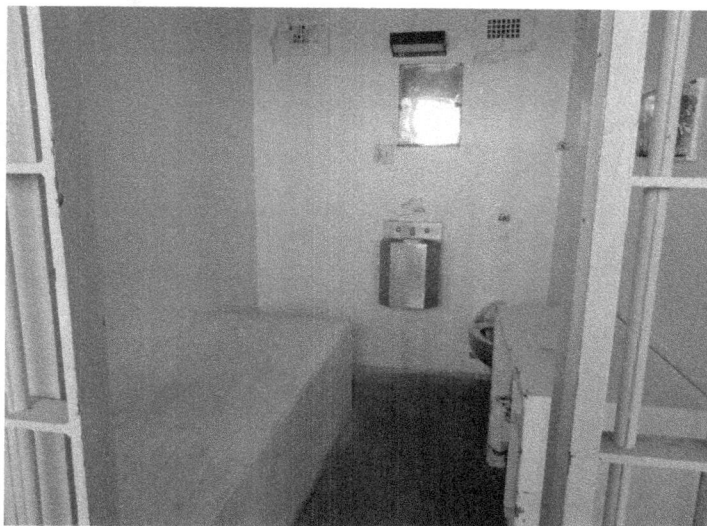

Guzman's Death Row Cell at Santa Fe Prison

James Tuttle and Colene Bush - 2011

ABOUT THE AUTHOR

Joyce Nance

Joyce Nance, award winning documentarian, video editor, Albuquerque Sports News publisher, and paralegal at the Public Defenders Office, has written her first book. Currently, she is pursuing a degree in Criminal Justice and working on her next book.

Originally from Southern California, she now lives in the Albuquerque, New Mexico area.